THE PRINCE OF SCANDAL

GEORGE PRINCE OF WALES

Frontispiece

THE
PRINCE OF SCANDAL

The Story of George the Fourth,
of his Amours and Mistresses

by
GRACE E. THOMPSON

" A noble, nasty course he ran
Superbly filthy and fastidious;
He was the world's first gentleman
And made the appellation hideous."

Harper & Brothers Publishers
New York and London
1 9 3 1

CONTENTS

7

ILLUSTRATIONS

9

'This George, what was he? I look through all his life and recognise but a bow and a grin. I try to take him to pieces, and find silk stockings, padding, stays, a coat with frogs and a fur collar, a star and a blue ribbon, a pocket-handkerchief, prodigiously scented, one of Truefitt's best nutty brown wigs reeking with oil, a set of teeth and a huge black stock, under-waistcoats, more under-waistcoats, and then nothing.'

The Four Georges, W. M. THACKERAY.

THE CHIEF CHARACTERS

THE VILLAIN: GEORGE.

    'The malignant enemy of his unhappy father, the treacherous lover, the perjured friend, a heartless fop, a soulless sot, the most ungentlemanly First Gentleman in Europe, his memory baffles the efforts of the sycophant and paralyses the anger of the satirist.'

              JUSTIN MCCARTHY, *History of Our Own Times.*

THE HEROINE: CAROLINE.

    'What a provoking heroine! for a heroine she is. There is nothing for us but to:
        '"Be to her faults a little blind
        Be to her virtues very kind."'

              Letter from Sir WILLIAM GELL.

THE HERO: THE MOB.

    'The days of chivalry are past. O dull, degenerate Englishmen! If there is a spark of good feeling left it is in the Mob, who give her their acclamations, since no other atonement is made her. The English are a noble nation *en masse*, an odious people individually. Don't you think so?'

              Letter to Lady CHARLOTTE CAMPBELL.

And CHARLOTTE.

    'Scion of chiefs and monarchs, where art thou?
      Fond hope of many nations, art thou dead?
    Could not the grave forget thee and lay low
      Some less majestic, less beloved head?
    Ah! thou, who wert so happy, so ador'd
      Those who weep not for Kings shall weep for thee
    And Freedom's heart, grown heavy, cease to hoard
      Her many griefs for ONE.'

              LORD BYRON.

'CONVERSATION PIECE'

M<small>R</small>. W<small>ALPOLE</small>, in his collection at Strawberry Hill, had several examples of that amusing mode of the eighteenth century, the 'Conversation Piece.' The fashion appealed to him particularly because it reminded him of his own method in another art. With a few deft touches he drew for his correspondents word-pictures of the people on whom his bright, malicious eyes rested. When the plain truth was not artistic, he improved his 'composition.' He rearranged his sitters in groups – family groups, political groups, groups of intimates and groups of enemies. When the conversation fell short of his standard, he varnished it before he exhibited it; when he thought of a *bon mot* he fathered it on George Selwyn, or some other wit. His work, though not perhaps as useful to students of history as that of Macaulay, is more amusing to the student of manners, and, in its way, as valuable. Had Mr. Walpole written biographies of his contemporaries, it is quite certain that he would have recorded conversations and indicated manners with more zest that he would have applied to the investigation of solemn facts, and the result would have been as true in essentials, another facet of that jewel, Truth.

He painted no full-length portrait, but his sketches are most vivid. Consider, for instance, that one of the Princess of Brunswick looking under the sofa for the book,

A Preparation for Death, hidden there by her indomitable mother, and the one of that mother being pursued by hatred to the grave.

Mr. Creevey is almost as fine an artist as Mr. Walpole though in a more robust, less polished, style.

Lord Glenbervie, too, had great talent in the painting of 'Conversation Pieces,' though he inclined towards the photographic, a word, of course, of which he had never heard.

Lady Charlotte Campbell also worked in this genre, but spoilt her word-pictures by using too lavishly the editor's blue pencil, both to add and to take away. By the greatest good fortune she seems to have left the letters of her correspondents almost untouched.

With 'Conversation Pieces' borrowed from these, and others, it is possible, I think, to arrange a gallery of portraits, of George and his friends, of Caroline and Charlotte, of Fox and Duchess Georgiana, of Creevey and 'our Bruffam,' of the King and the People of England during that amazing period which began in 1772 and ended a hundred years ago.

Hampstead, 1930.

BOOK I

THE KEYNOTE

THE little Prince of Wales was ten years old when his grandmother, the Princess Dowager, died. He had feared her and hated her, and was so glad that she was dead that he listened eagerly when the gentlemen of his household spoke of her burial.

The two gentlemen, still in their hats and cloaks, paused by the window and looked out at the dreary February day.

'The funeral should be over,' one of them said.

The other nodded. 'Well, she is gone and no one will miss her. She was a clever, domineering, cruel woman. She kept her household lonely and in gloom, mistrusting all the people who came about her children.'

The little Prince of Wales, hiding in the big chair in the corner, with its back to the room so that no one could see him, had heard the story of his grandmother's tyranny before, and other stories, too – of the wildness of his uncles, Cumberland and Gloucester, as a result of their mother's harshness, of the unhappy marriage of his Aunt Augusta to the Prince of Brunswick, and the marriage of his Aunt Caroline Matilda to the King of Denmark, which had just ended in the most terrible disaster ; Aunt Caroline Matilda had taken a lover; the lover had died, suddenly and mysteriously, and Caroline Matilda was imprisoned in a fortress. The little boy was brilliant and precocious; all the gossip which he overheard conveyed more to his understanding than it should have done.

Of all the Princess Dowager's children only George the King had been docile. Dutifully every evening he and Queen Charlotte had paid a visit to the King's mother at Carlton House. 'George, be a King,' she had urged him, and he, alone of her children, obeyed and, in his way, loved her. The King was good and stupid; the Queen harsh and bigoted. The clever little boy hated his parents as well as his grandmother.

Hate, indeed, seemed to fill the atmosphere about him. No one, though, had been as bitterly hated as the Dowager Princess of Wales, except, perhaps, her friend and counsellor, Lord Bute. Bute was hated with a rage of which England has supplied very few examples. He was the butt for everybody's abuse – for Wilkes in his *North Briton*, for Churchill's cutting satires, for the hooting of the mob that roasted the boot, his emblem, in a thousand bonfires. They called him Lothario and other evil names, but most often they called him 'Mortimer,' and the Princess of Wales 'Isabella,' after they had read Wilkes' *North Briton*, No. 45.

Lord Chatham hated the King's mother no less than the mob did.

'The secret influence more mighty than the throne itself which betrays and clogs every administration,' he thundered.

The pamphleteers caught up the cry. 'Impeach the King's Mother,' was scribbled over every wall at the Court end of the town.

Her influence over the King was, without doubt, disastrous. But what had she done to earn such hatred? Nobody knew.

Now she was dead and, to-day, had been buried. The little boy in the big chair was as pleased as the rest of the world.

At the Queen's House, the usual rigid discipline was relaxed. His governors had gone to the funeral and given the little boy the chance to escape from his own quarters and explore. He had no business in this part of the palace, and when the gentlemen of the household returned he hid in the big chair lest he should be flogged for playing truant.

More of the gentlemen of the household came into the room. The child listened eagerly.

'The mob huzza'd for joy. She was certainly the best-hated woman in England. As the funeral procession moved through the streets from Carlton House to Westminster Abbey the mob went wild with delight. All the black cloth from the platform at the Abbey was torn away before half the procession had passed across.'

'The soldiers on guard, too, lest they should lose their share of the plunder, began to help themselves,' said another. 'She was more hated than anyone in my memory.'

'The day before she died, fifty guineas were offered and refused to insure one hundred pounds on her life. And five offered at the same time and refused to underwrite her for three days.'

'She had courage, I think. She had a cancer in her throat, and must have suffered great pain but never let anyone look in her throat except her German page. The only medicine she was known to try was hemlock and she would not acknowledge her danger to her children. She told the Princess of Brunswick that her illness was only nervous, and that she would go riding in her coach to show the people how well she was.'

'The Princess of Brunswick told one of her ladies that when she came suddenly into the room she found her mother reading, but she hid the book under the couch. The Princess looked at the book afterwards and found it *A Preparation for Death*.'

'Since the news of her daughter's fate came from Denmark she scarce took any nourishment but cordials.'

'Two days before her death she saw Lord Bute.'

'Has she left him anything in her will?'

There was general laughter. 'He had it all during her life. Did you not hear that the King, when he asked about his father's books, said to Lord Bute: "Take care, my lord, that the people do not say you got your riches from the same quarter as you got your books" ? '

'Her income goes to the King.'

'Much use it will be to him. The Queen's House is as dull as the tomb. Have you heard the last lampoon upon the Queen?

> "She hates the manners of the times
> And all our fashionable crimes;
> And fondly wishes to restore
> The golden age and days of yore,
> When silly, simple women thought
> A breach of chastity a fault;

Esteemed those modish things divorces,
The very worst of human curses,
And deemed assemblies, cards, and dice
The springs of every sort of vice.
Romantic notions! All the fair
At such absurdities must stare,
And spite of all their pains, will still
Love routs, adultery, and quadrille."

For my part, I would rather have the late Princess Dowager, though her family was no happier than the Queen's.'

'I have heard the Duke of Cumberland speak bitterly of his childhood. Once the Princess asked him, when he had been long silent, if he were sulky. He replied he was not; he was only thinking. "And pray," said the dowager, "what are you thinking of?" "I was thinking," answered the boy, "what I should feel if I had a son as unhappy as you make me." '

'All her children except the King hated her. And she sowed discord between him and the rest.'

'The Princess of Brunswick has not seen the King alone. The Queen would not permit it.'

'They have never forgiven her for her marriage.'

'Why?'

'The Prince of Brunswick was the idol of the mobile when he came here for his marriage. They cheered him everywhere, and had no greeting for the King. Both he and the Princess would meddle in politics. I heard they went to call on Pitt. *That* would never be forgiven them, but their popularity was worse. The Queen hates the Princess of Brunswick. I have heard that before her marriage the Lady Augusta often mortified the Queen; they all treated her like a child, and when she went to take the sacrament at St. Paul's after her coronation, and would have laid aside her jewels to show humility in accordance to a promise she had made her dead mother, the Princess Augusta laughed, and made the Queen wear all her jewels and so break her promise to her mother. It cost her bitter tears.'

'She has her revenge now. Though her mother had sent for Augusta, the Queen would not let her lodge at Carlton House, but put her in a miserable little house in Pall Mall.'

'To mortify her still further, they would not let her be chief mourner to-day at her mother's funeral.'

'Her fate is on all sides unhappy. She has no money. Her husband slights her, and has many mistresses, and here, where she might have expected kindness, she meets with hate.'

'Hatred seems the keynote of this family,' said a voice which had not spoken before.

The company, startled, dispersed.

The little boy came out of his hiding-place and slipped along the dark corridors to his own rooms.

2

YOUNG LOVE

LIFE at the Queen's House was intolerably dull; life at Kew, if possible, was duller. A wag described the daily round of the King and Queen:

> 'Cæsar the mighty King who sway'd
> The sceptre was a sober blade;
> A leg of mutton and his wife
> Were the chief comforts of his life.
>
> The Queen, composed of different stuff,
> Above all things ador'd her snuff,
> Save gold, which in her great opinion
> Alone could rival snuff's dominion.'

At Kew, the King was able to indulge his harmless passion for agriculture and earn his nickname of 'Farmer George.' The Prince of Wales and his brother Frederick were trained to till their own small plots of land, but they liked it less than the King did.

It very early appeared that the Prince of Wales violently disliked everything which the King enjoyed. All the floggings in the world, and he had many of them, could not alter the Prince's mind. In time he even revolted against the floggings; Bishop Hurd, who took over the thankless task of preceptor from Dr. Markham, once, and once only, emulated his predecessor's reliance on the rod. The Prince tore it from his hand and laid it with goodwill upon the episcopal back. Good Bishop Hurd dispensed in future with thrashings; he found that the easiest way to manage his charges was to shut his eyes and keep them shut.

Their Majesties were shocked and grieved at their rebellious children. The strictest watch was kept upon the Princes; they were forbidden almost all intercourse with the outside world, and spies dogged their steps. Spies, perhaps, could be bribed. Certainly their Majesties' severity was without the desired result, for, as soon as the King went to bed, the Princes slipped out to taste forbidden pleasures.

Such tutelage could not last for ever. The King, reluctantly, gave his heir some degree of liberty at eighteen.

The Prince of Wales came upon the town with a new shoe-buckle and the seduction of a maid of honour. He achieved fame at once; the invention of a new shoe-buckle was an event of immense importance. It was an inch long and five inches broad, reaching almost to the ground on either side of his foot. It was approved by the Bucks, and was an instantaneous success.

No better introduction to the *ton* could have been devised. He followed up his success at the first Court Ball he attended. His coat was of pink silk with white cuffs; his waistcoat of white silk embroidered with various coloured foils and adorned with a profusion of pink paste; his hat was ornamented with two rows of steel beads, five thousand of them, with a button and loop of

the same metal and cocked in a new military style. His
hair was pressed at the sides and very full frizzed, with
two small curls at the bottom. He was at once accepted
by the dandies as one of themselves and, in spite of his
absurdities, charmed sober people, who thought him a
beautiful and elegant young man, a charming change
from Farmer George and his gross Hanoverian predecessors.

The Prince was launched upon the Town by his uncle,
the Duke of Cumberland, and his lively Duchess, who was
not received at Court. The Duke's house was a rendez-
vous of the Opposition, and both Duke and Prince had
no greater desire than to annoy and embarrass the King.

The Prince was still in leading-strings, and resented it.
At the Queen's House and at his little villa at Kew, he
was under the parental eye, and surrounded by servants
nominated by the King. That the attendants did not
serve the King honestly made little difference to his heir's
annoyance.

'It is time I had an establishment of my own,' was his
constant cry.

He sulked, and wept, and lamented, and looked so
pretty a boy that his mother, whose favourite child he
was, relented. The separate establishment was promised,
and his brother and constant companion, Frederick the
Bishop of Osnaburg, sent abroad.

The Prince looked round for amusement and, like any
other healthy young man, fell in love. He fell in love with
a truly royal insolence under his parents' eyes, in the
most public place imaginable, the Royal Box on a gala
night at Drury Lane. All the house saw it happen, and
every letter-writer and keeper of a diary hurried home

to make a note: 'The Prince never took his eyes off Mrs. Robinson. At the end he bowed to her not once, but twice.'

Pretty Mary Robinson, the sweet and artless 'Perdita,' fresh from her triumph in the *Winter's Tale*, found my Lord Malden waiting for her when she left the stage.

'You caught the Prince's eye, Mistress Perdita,' he murmured as he gave her a deep bow. 'I never saw His Royal Highness so charmed before.'

The girl flushed. She was enchanted with her success, and fully aware of the value of such an obvious conquest. Her silly, sentimental heart, too, was all aflutter at the thought of young Prince Charming himself, the beautiful, romantic boy who had set older pulses than hers stirring.

My Lord Malden attended the rising star to supper, sat by her side, and whispered praises of the Prince into her willing ear. 'The Prince,' 'the Prince,' was on every lip – his charm, his grace, his beauty, and the power that would be his. Mr. Fox – Mr. Charles James Fox, the gambler and statesman – was as loud in his praise as any other man. He eyed the fluttering beauty speculatively as he bent over her hand:

'You have stormed the innermost citadel of success, madam. I hear the Queen was enchanted. And the Prince – The whole town observed that he could not take his eyes off you. I felicitate you on the greatest conquest in the world.'

Mrs. Robinson blushed enchantingly. 'Oh, Mr. Fox, you flatter me.'

'Impossible, madam. I will give the company a toast: "The Prince and the beauty and genius he has the wit to admire: the Prince and the fair Perdita."'

MRS ROBINSON

To face page 28

The company drank it with enthusiasm. The pretty Perdita laughed and blushed and stammeringly protested. My Lord Malden grinned sardonically and cast a look at Mr. Fox. But Mr. Fox's swarthy, black-browed face was enigmatic; if he had any deep-laid scheme of his own it did not appear.

My Lord Malden called again when the beauty was alone and Mr. Robinson had been more trying than usual. He hummed and hawed and hesitated, for his errand embarrassed him, not on moral grounds, of course, but because he did not know how she would take it. Gossip was never idle in the theatre, and gossip assured him that the lady was chaste, in spite of many alluring offers. He nervously fingered the letter in his pocket, and at last produced it and laid it in her hand. It was addressed to 'Perdita,' and signed 'Florizel,' and was a love letter of a kind to which her position had long accustomed her. She read it with lifted eyebrows.

'Pray tell me, my lord, from whom this really is,' she begged, curiosity conquering her first impulse to tear it into pieces.

My Lord Malden was relieved. A woman of impregnable virtue would have been indignant, he argued. She was curious. That was the first step won.

'His Royal Highness the Prince of Wales is most anxious to make the acquaintance of the exquisite Perdita,' he said smoothly.

She was incredulous, flattered, excited. She would not yield, yet she must play with the delicious temptation; she could not wholly, instantly, indignantly reject the advance.

My Lord Malden was well pleased with his success.

He returned to the siege again and again. This was the
Prince's first serious essay in love; the coyer the lady the
more his ardour grew. Pretty Perdita made a valiant
effort to resist temptation. She knew something of men,
for she had a brutal husband, and since her first appearance on the stage, had been most persistently besieged by
men of fashion who thought virtue an absurd affecta-
tion in an actress. She urgently, sincerely, wanted to
remain virtuous.

She was too good for the part she was to play on the
stage of the world. Her difficulties were enormous; she
had no friend who could help her and whose advice she
could trust; Mr. Sheridan was the best of them, but Mr.
Sheridan was a friend of the Prince and, more particularly, of Mr. Fox. She was just shrewd enough to see that
they all designed her for a particular rôle, but not shrewd
enough to see the folly of supposing that she could play
the part of a Madame Pompadour. Her beauty was of
the pensive kind which betrayed a sensitiveness which
totally unfitted her for the rôle she was to fill. She was
incurably sentimental; she dreamed of a lifetime's devotion from a prince who would call her 'the wife of his
soul.'

Mr. Sheridan warned her. 'You will lose your place
on the stage and not be able to return to it. You are a
romantic. You have too much sensibility for a king's
mistress.'

She cried out at the horrid word.

My Lord Malden did not use it. He talked persuasively
of Love. She saw herself exercising a virtuous restraining
influence over a young king whose only fault was im-
petuousness. She believed herself capable of inspiring an

enduring passion; she believed she had talents that would enable her to guide and influence him rightly in matters of state. It was a dazzling prospect, and her heart was engaged as much as her vanity or ambition.

My Lord Malden praised the Prince: 'His manners are as exquisite as they are fascinating. He is so handsome, such a leader of the *ton*. He has brains quite out of the common in his family. His courtesy is exquisite. He has a breadth of outlook most unusual and a sensibility that does him infinite credit. The Prince's heart is eager and trusting.'

Her own was. She listened and believed. All the world was talking of the Prince. So far he had won every heart except his father's. The most generous expectations were founded on him. He was about to be set up in an establishment of his own; he would choose his own counsellors.

My Lord Malden murmured tales of the Royal Dukes; both Gloucester and Cumberland had married where their hearts were. Perdita caught her breath with excitement: Mr. Robinson could be disposed of with the greatest ease. The prospect was dazzling. The Prince's messenger put another letter into her hand: 'My fate is in the hands of my Perdita; my life yours to save or ruin. Your Florizel.'

'His Royal Highness is distracted. I left him in a flood of tears.'

She struggled still. My Lord Malden went away to dry his Prince's tears with such comfort as he could.

They saw each other again, at the Oratorio. The Prince's attentions were so marked as to attract the notice of the squib writers. The Queen was angry. Perdita withdrew.

The Prince sent her his miniature with another passionate appeal. '*Je ne change qu'en mourant:* Unalterable to my Perdita through life.'

Mr. Robinson grew more objectionable daily, and spring was in the air. Prince Florizel sent her daily letters. Lord Malden reported floods of tears and agonies of despair; the Prince yearned unspeakably for a meeting. The seduction was poetical; indeed the young man imagined himself most deeply, enduringly, in love. She wept over his letters. The Prince also, in the manner of the day, dropped large splashes on his paper, since fashion decreed that the tear of sensibility should bedew every manly cheek at every emotional crisis. Since sensibility was the mode, whose sensibility so exquisite as that of the Prince?

She capitulated at last in a letter which greatly charmed the impressionable young man.

'Yours is a triumph of chastity,' sighed Lord Malden, his manly eyes also moistened with the ready tears as he took the letter of consent and languished at her with a hint of where his own feelings hovered and would have settled if Prince Florizel had not come between. They dried their eyes in company. 'Now, as to time and place.' My lord grew brisk. 'His Royal Highness is at Kew. Even royal vigilance cannot always be on the alert. I will row you across the Thames by the light of the moon to Kew Gardens. The Prince will do the rest.'

To this she assented, and awaited the evening in alternating moods of joy and alarm. His letters had charmed her – those eloquent letters which breathed his exquisite sensibility in every line of their ardent protestations. And what were letters compared with the beloved's

self? Perdita clasped her hands over her fast-beating
heart: 'The graces of his person, the irresistible sweetness
of his smile, the tenderness of his melodious yet manly
voice, will be remembered by me until every vision of
this changing scene is forgotten.'

She liked the phrases and noted them in her diary for
future use; for, if she shared the Prince's sentimentality,
she had an even greater sense of the dramatic; she was
the heroine of one of the world's great love stories; future
generations must have the details of the wonderful
romance.

The meeting at Kew was truly romantic; it took place
by moonlight and was attended by some risk of discovery
which added to its bliss. Perdita confided to her diary
that 'Heaven could witness how many conflicts her
agitated heart endured' as she waited for the signal from
the opposite bank.

A white handkerchief fluttered in the dusk, and Lord
Malden rowed her over the moonlit river to the waiting
Prince.

The visit was often repeated. Perdita attired herself
discreetly in a dark-coloured habit, but the Duke of York,
who invariably attended the Prince, for some reason
known only to himself, always wore a buff coat, the
colour most likely to show up in the dark.

Mrs. Armstead, Perdita's waiting-woman and herself
something of a mystery, watched the meetings from the
opposite bank, and smiled satirically; in a person anxious
to avoid detection, she found the behaviour of the Prince
as odd as the Duke of York's light coat. Florizel, to show
his happiness, sang aloud to the silent night.

'What exquisite taste,' murmured Perdita to the moonlight. 'Alas, that destiny has placed such a distance between us. How my soul would have idolised such a husband.'

The Prince continued singing, and Perdita coined fine phrases for her journal: 'The tones of his voice breaking on the silence of the night have often appeared to my entranced senses like more than mortal melody.' The Prince, in fact, sang very well.

Malden, the soul of discretion, and the Duke of York, in his buff coat, flitted in and out among the trees.

The Prince ceased singing, and clasped Perdita in his arms.

'Exquisite being! How I wish that you were *mine alone!*'

He set her up in a house in Cork Street, and reality was like her dream. He doted on her. He delighted in her whims, her shy retreats, her sentimentalities which matched his own. He wrote royal verses which she thought wonderful. He seemed to her like a prince out of a fairy tale, without human flaw, so matchless were his courtly graces, so easily did his splendour sit upon him. 'Often have I formed the wish that that being were mine alone to whom partial millions were to look up for protection,' she wrote in her journal.

If a momentary fear oppressed her, she flew to his arms to be consoled with an ardent, 'What alarms the adored of my soul? I know my heart and its tender fidelity. Never fear that my love may change.'

The months went by. Mary Robinson was Queen of the Prince's world. He had his own court, now, at Carlton House, a brilliant Court in which the Duchess of Devonshire, Charles James Fox, and Richard Brinsley

Sheridan were the bright particular stars, but to which almost any man of birth or talent had the *entré*, as long as he was in opposition to the King. All the King's forbodings about his heir, released suddenly and reluctantly from surveillance, were in a fair way to be fulfilled.

The Prince plunged recklessly into pleasure, and there was no wild gaiety in which he did not join; his friends were the wildest and most dissipated men of a wild and dissipated age; they drank, they gamed, they wenched, without concealment or shame. Fox preferred women of the town; Sherry's conscience seldom troubled him as he broke the heart of his lovely Elizabeth Linley, and the Prince, when carried home to his Perdita, was drunk more often than not.

Prince Florizel, as time passed, was less Prince Charming than at first he had seemed. Perdita was his companion in all public places, setting the mode and forming the centre of a bowing court of men. Even Duchess Georgiana followed her lead in fashion, though she looked through her in a crowd. If Perdita had been driven by ambition only, she had reached a dizzy summit, but that sentimental heart of hers, that too-tender conscience, suffered many a pang.

'The daily prints indulged the malice of my enemies by the most scandalous paragraphs respecting the Prince and myself,' she lamented in her journal. 'It was too late to stop the torrent of abuse poured on me from all quarters. Whenever I appeared in public I was overwhelmed by the gazing of the multitude. I was frequently obliged to quit Ranelagh owing to the crowd assembled round my box, and scarcely dared to enter a shop. Many hours have I waited until the waiting crowd dispersed. I cannot suppress a smile at the absurdity of such proceedings.'

If vanity had been her ruling passion she would have been happy enough. But she wanted love, and the Prince tired easily; she wanted to eat her cake and have it, to hold her glittering court and taste domestic happiness at one and the same time. Long before she confessed it, even to her diary, she must have been aware that the Prince's ardour flagged. The observers noted it quite early in their connection: 'She's too sentimental for him, too pensive, cries too easily, is too easily wounded. The Prince wants gaiety and sparkle; she offers him mawkish verses and tearful sighs.'

The Prince grew peevish if there were not a perpetual rattle for him in Cork Street. The Prince was insatiable of amusement. The sensibility which had caught her was only lip-deep; his tears mingled most readily with wine. Sensibility was the keynote of the mode, the ready tear brimmed at any sentimental tale; the Prince wept even more readily than most. Perdita early discovered that that did not mean he had a feeling heart. She wept often and copiously, too, but in time her tears were caused by grief and terror rather than sensibility. The Prince was tiring, and physical exhaustion, due to the whirl in which he insisted on living, made gaiety and sparkle even harder to achieve. Perdita grew more pensive as the Prince grew wilder, more delicate as he grew grosser.

The company he met at Cumberland House made fun of her, called her 'Propriety Prue.' The bonds which bound the Prince to her slackened. He came to Cork Street less often, sought any trivial excuse for a scene. The poor fool wept and uttered reproaches. The Prince

CHARLES J. FOX

To face page 36

flung away in a rage. The Duke and Duchess of Cumberland, using the boy as a weapon to wreak their vengeance on the King, were doing their best to ruin him. Perdita had been a restraining influence; they had a livelier mistress ready for him, Grace Dalrymple Elliott, the notorious Dally the Tall. 'Perdita was a spy in the King's service,' they insinuated. That alarmed and enraged him, and he stormed accusations which she found it difficult to refute; so she retorted with reproaches for his infidelities until she worked herself into hysteria, and lost all control over her tongue.

'Leave me,' she screamed, goaded beyond endurance, when he told her that fidelity was out of his power. 'That is the last insult. You would make me one of a crowd of women as degraded and miserable as myself. Go! Go! I ask nothing from you. I will take nothing.'

The Prince took his hat and vanished, hating the woman he had fondled, and pleased to win his freedom with such ease.

Having wept herself into stupidity, Perdita slept and woke to common sense. She sought a reconciliation. The Prince returned, and swore he had not changed towards her. There were more tears and kisses. Next day he cut her in the Park.

Perdita's emotion was genuine, but the situation also pleased her dramatic sense. The final reconciliation would be as dramatic; Florizel would promise amendment and would seal his bond with impassioned kisses.

He came no more. He sent a letter taking her at her word, and repudiating the money agreement he had made with her.

She was dismissed. He was immovable. Her letters

were returned unopened. She drove to Windsor and was turned from his door. She had his bond for £20,000. He refused to meet it. She had debts amounting to nearly £10,000 incurred largely on his behalf. He declined to pay them.

Perdita, in terror, with the prospect of the debtors' prison before her eyes, appealed to Charles James Fox. He offered her safety on one condition. Because she was weak, because her situation looked hopeless, she accepted the easy way.

The Prince laughed consumedly when he heard that his Perdita had become the mistress of Mr. Fox. Since exchange seemed no robbery he accepted the loan of Mrs. Armstead, who had been the mistress of Mr. Fox.

3

GOOD COMPANY

THE Prince of Wales was, of course, a Whig from infancy, and gave unmistakable proof of it, whether the story of his shouting 'Wilkes and Liberty' outside the door of the King's dressing-room were true or not. He was bound to be a Whig since the King favoured the Tories.

When he made his maiden speech in the Lords, he declared with ardent Whiggery that he existed by the love, the friendship, and benevolence of the people, and he proceeded to vote for the Whigs over the tempestuous India Bill. The King, with his mother's 'George, be a King' still echoing in his ears, was panic-stricken, and his distrust of his heir turned to active hostility.

The Cumberlands were delighted. To corrupt the young man's morals was only to supply a pin-prick; at last they had the chance, for which they had long waited, of avenging themselves adequately upon the Court from which they had been excluded. It was in the Hanoverian tradition for the reigning monarch to be on bad terms with his eldest son; George III should be no more fortunate that his predecessors. The dissipated Duke and his Anne Luttrell, whom Mr. Walpole had described as being 'well made, with the most amorous eyes in the world, and eyelashes a yard long,' took the polite education of the Prince in hand.

Duchess Anne danced divinely and had a good deal of wit of the satiric kind, as well as being a past-mistress of the whole art of coquetry. The Prince of Wales was enchanted with his aunt.

The Duke taught him the mysteries of loo, faro, macao, and hazard. They fanned his taste for wine and amorous dalliance. They had a score of poplollies ready to languish for him, and they had introduced him to that master of all kinds of dissipation, Charles James Fox. Charles had the charm, the wit, the vices, the swarthy heavy features of his ancestor, the second Charles Stuart, and a genius which was all his own. He was the best of good company, but a very bad mentor for inexperienced, headstrong youth.

Mr. Fox took the Prince to Devonshire House, where he made friends of Richard Brinsley Sheridan and the brilliant Georgiana. The Prince loved the Duchess, his 'ever-dearest Duchess,' and Sheridan loved him. Fox, who had a particular use for them all, regarded them with benevolent amusement.

The Duchess was generous in praise of her friends. 'I have always thought that Charles' great merit is his amazing quickness in seizing any subject,' she said. 'He seems to have the particular talent of knowing more about what he is saying and with less pains than anybody else. His conversation is like a brilliant player at billiards – the strokes follow one another, piff-paff.'

Charles lounged past; he who had been the most exquisite of the macaronis had long ago given up his servitude to dress; he wore a shabby and threadbare blue frock-coat with a buff waistcoat, very dirty and slovenly, yet in that brilliant assembly was sure of his welcome.

DUCHESS OF DEVONSHIRE

To face page 40

The Duchess looked after him admiringly. 'He is a man whose idol is popularity,' she said.

Sheridan agreed with her. Despite the difference in their upbringing there was a similarity in the temperaments of the Duchess and Sherry which often brought them to agreements. They were both impetuous and not to be relied on, ready to seek distraction in practical jokes and horseplay, very restless and always in search of new amusements, and extremely sentimental. Profoundly the Duchess admired Sherry's wit and he her charm. As playmates they suited each other admirably.

'Sherry is such a boy;' said the Duchess.

'And you, my dear T. L., are amazingly entertaining,' Sherry replied.

'If you'd leave the drink, Sherry,' Georgiana warned. 'It will destroy the coat of your stomach.'

'Well then, my stomach must just digest in its waistcoat.'

The wit was applauded by the rest of the company – Richard Fitzpatrick, Fish Crawford, Jack Townsend, and the lovely Mrs. Crewe, the 'Amoret' to whom all the world paid tribute.

Sheridan adored her, and had laid his *School for Scandal* at her pretty feet. Of all Sherry's fancies, sweet Elizabeth Sheridan feared Amoret most. Mrs. Crewe was surpassingly beautiful, exceedingly witty, and very intelligent. She was also warm-hearted, impulsive, and indiscreet.

Fox wrote of her: 'Though Brightness may dazzle, 'tis Kindness that warms.'

The Prince of Wales preferred his dearest Duchess.

The Prince's enemies would have stripped him of all

merit and of all gifts but beauty; yet Fox, Sheridan, and Duchess Georgiana, who bestrode their age like three colossi and certainly had more than a fair share of merit and gifts, approved Prince Charming. His manners were exquisite, his taste a little florid but still good; he was well educated and could talk quite brilliantly in good company; he was an excellent judge of music, and had a more than passable voice. He was, in his youth, quick of understanding and not unwilling to learn, and his lively spirits and handsome face were a passport into the affections of most women.

The Prince took to the game of politics like a duck to water. He saw in it a way to annoy his parents and increase his own income; also he liked Fox and disliked North, his father's favourite. The Prince was always emotional rather than principled. He must be dramatic at any cost. When the King heard of his debts and in bitterness of spirit called him an 'ill-advised young man,' he made a striking gesture, closed Carlton House, and sold his carriages and horses by auction to prove the contrary. But he clung to Fox, whom the King would cheerfully have sent to the Tower.

The King wronged Fox; Charles, in fact, had urged the Prince to keep clear of politics; the Prince, emotionally, refused to sacrifice his friend. Fox could have done very well without his help; the Westminster election proved that, however vulnerable the Whigs might be, he, personally, was invincible and could bring up reserves to win any fight.

The Prince of Wales enjoyed that election, but not as much as Georgiana did. She belonged to a family which had long thought that it had the right to meddle in affairs of state. She had chosen her friends from among those who, in the intervals of their pleasures, devoted themselves to the political game. The Duchess longed to be a leader of the Whigs; her chance came when the Coalition collapsed over the India Bill.

'It will be a struggle between George the Third's sceptre and Mr. Fox's tongue,' the great Dr. Johnson had said when the Government fell.

The King loathed Fox. He blamed him for the alienation of his son. The King threw the whole weight of his influence and all his secret funds on the side of the Tories. The Prince of Wales, naturally, sided with the Whigs. The Court party swept the country. Mr. Fox, to his astonishment, found himself likely to lose his Westminster seat to Sir Cecil Wray.

The Duchess of Devonshire and her friends threw themselves into the fray with ardour. They fought for the joy of battle, with a spice of devilry and a disconcerting armoury of tricks.

The Westminster poll opened on April Fools' Day, and for more than six weeks the West end of London was occupied in 'fighting, drumming, screaming, singing, marrow-boning, hooting, hurrahing.'

From Fox's headquarters in St. James' Street came yells of 'Vote for Charles James Fox, the Man of the People.'

King George and the Tories were as energetic and less noisy. The Prince of Wales rode through the streets wearing Fox's colours, buff and true blue, the colour of the American Independents. In the streets the Whig supporters fought the adherents of the Court with staves and poles and cleavers. Heads were broken, special constables enrolled.

Canvassing was not neglected.

'I'll lay you five guineas and stake the money in your hands that you'll not vote for Fox,' cried Charles' election agent to the voters.

'Done,' they shouted, and went to the poll with the guineas in their hands.

Bribery? Of course not; merely the winning of a sporting bet.

Pretty Perdita went canvassing for her protector, but she did Mr. Fox's cause some harm; she rode in a coach and shrank from familiarities.

Mr. Fox himself went supplicating votes.

'Give me your support,' he begged a saddler.

'All I can give you, sir, is a halter,' was the impudent reply.

Mr. Fox was imperturbable. 'Thanks! I have no wish to deprive you of what is doubtless a family relic.' The crowd guffawed, and the saddler stared.

The fight was too closely contested to look safe. Bets were not enough; the Duchess mobilised her pretty friends.

'Votes can be bought with kisses.'

The Duchess kissed with enthusiasm.

'Your eyes are so bright, my lady,' said an Irish labourer, 'I could light my pipe at them.'

The Duchess was enchanted. 'The finest compliment I ever received,' she said, and redoubled her enthusiasm.

'Lord! It's a fine sight to see a grand lady come right smack to us hardworking mortals with a hand held out, and a "Master, how d'ye do?" and a laugh so loud, and talk so kind, and shake us by the hand and say, "Give us your vote, worthy sir, a plumper for the people's friend, our friend, everybody's friend'" the voters told one another. 'And then we hummed and hawed, and the fine ladies asked after our wives and families, and if that didn't do they thought nothing of a kiss. Aye, a dozen of them. Kissing was nothing to them, and it all came natural.'

No man whom the Duchess kissed could do otherwise than vote for Mr. Fox.

The Duchess won the election; Mr. Fox was second on the poll, with Sir Cecil Wray not many votes behind. The mob received the news of the result with frenzied cheering which accompanied Charles all the way to Devonshire House, where the Prince of Wales awaited him at the side of Georgiana and received a share of the cheers.

The Prince gave a fête in the gardens at Carlton House while the indignant King was passing in procession to open his new Parliament.

The King grew petty; he removed his son's birthday from the list of future festivities and expressed his pleasure when the Tory mob hooted outside Carlton House.

Mrs. Crewe gave a brilliant rout at which 'blue and buff' were the universal colours of both sexes. The Prince appeared in the party colours. At supper he toasted his hostess.

'True Blue and Mrs. Crewe.'

Pretty Amoret retorted swiftly: 'True Blue and all of you.'

At the Queen's House, the King stormed at the behaviour of his graceless son, and that corrupter of youth, Mr. Fox.

The Queen excused her son. But she could not win him. The Prince went to call on Lady Sarah Lennox, whom his father had loved long ago, and took care that his mother should hear of it and of the pretty greeting he had given her rival.

Queen Charlotte, perhaps, deserved the stabs which her children gave her, but it was otherwise with the King, who, however mistaken he might be in his treatment of his children, undoubtedly had a heart. More and more did he shrink from strife; more and more did he fear his own excitability; more and more earnestly did he pray that his son might turn from his wildness and learn to do right.

It seemed that his prayers might be answered, though not in the way he would have chosen, for the Prince fell deeply, tempestuously, in love. His emotions were always extravagant, but never before had they been so deep, and never before had his affections fallen on a woman who was virtuous enough to withstand his assaults.

All the town had heard of the rising star, though she did not court publicity. She was a lady of the first fashion, and she created something of a sensation, when, unheralded, she first shone upon the town.

The *Morning Herald* commented: 'A new Constellation has lately made an appearance in the fashionable hemisphere, that engages the attention of those whose hearts are susceptible to the power of beauty. The widow of the late Mr. F–H–T, has in her train half our young nobility: as the lady has not, as yet, discovered a partiality for any of her admirers they are all animated with hopes of success.'

The Prince of Wales had a particularly susceptible heart where beauty was concerned. He had caught a glimpse of her at a water party on the Thames; he saw her again in Lady Sefton's box at the Opera. He fell in love with her at first sight, and did not mind who knew it. He made opportunities of meeting her, he followed her everywhere, he was always at her side, his attentions were so marked that they soon became the most engrossing topic of conversation in the fashionable world. Those who did not know her asked: 'Who is Maria Fitzherbert?' and those who did answered: 'A fascinating Irish widow, well dowered, a Roman Catholic.'

'Phew! Unwelcome at Court if of that Church.'

'She has been presented. The Queen was as gracious as she ever is. Indeed the lady is modest, well spoken of, and undeniably lovely.'

Her hair was of a pale gold and worn unpowdered, her eyes hazel brown, her complexion of the wild rose, un-rouged, her features exquisitely moulded, and her figure full of grace. She was twenty-eight, but looked younger because of her smiling air of sunny candour.

The Prince's passion increased by leaps and bounds; he recognised no limits to the expression of his devotion. Too late she grew alarmed and tried to break off the acquaintance. She besought him with tears and entreaties to leave her in peace. She only added fuel to his ardour.

His parents, a little anxious, made inquiries, remembered Perdita, and were comforted. He had been equally extravagant in his protestations to her; the moth was only fluttering round another flame.

'Besides,' said the virtuous Charlotte, 'this passion might not be sinful. Does he not profess an unseemly devotion to the Duchess of Devonshire, which appears to be innocent, though, God knows, it is fraught with harm.'

Duchess Georgiana and Charles Fox were in the
Prince's confidence. The Duchess's kind heart was
steadier than her head. She would have helped the lovers
regardless of all consequences. Fox took alarm, and,
almost for the first time in his life, counselled prudence.
The situation was peculiarly difficult; not only was the
lady's virtue so unshakeable that the Prince was talking
wildly of marriage – in spite of the folly of such a suggestion in face of the Royal Marriage Act – her faith was as
unassailable as her virtue, and the Prince's marriage with
a Roman Catholic would raise such a storm as the country
had not seen since the Revolution of 1688.

Mr. Fox took the matter more seriously than he had
ever taken anything in his life. The Prince must not for
one moment harbour such a thought in his mind. The
Prince withdrew his confidences. The Duchess listened
to them alone. Since she could not turn him from his
purpose she did the wisest thing in her power, and
extended the hand of friendship to the charming
widow who had captivated the Prince's impressionable
heart.

The Duchess liked Mrs. Fitzherbert without finding her
such a prodigy as the Prince had described. She was
sedate in behaviour as became a well-born, twice-
widowed Catholic gentlewoman of the age of twenty-
eight. She was good-looking without being a miracle of
beauty. Her colouring of skin and hair was perfect, and
the modelling of bust and arms as fine. She was sensible
without being clever, charming rather than seductive.
She had character rather than wit. So the Duchess saw
her. Had she been a Protestant princess rather than a
Catholic commoner no wife could have been better

SHERIDAN

To face page 48

chosen for the excitable, unstable Prince. She was a woman of whom a man would not easily tire.

Duchess Georgiana sighed at love so thwarted, thrilled and trembled at the notion of putting her finger into so dangerous a pie.

'I told him that though I am too inconsiderable a person to become his wife, I am too considerable to become his mistress,' Mrs. Fitz. confided, almost in tears. 'It must be marriage or nothing at all, but since marriage is impossible it would be better for the Prince to forget me.'

'He swears he will abjure crown and kingdom for your sake,' said the Duchess fearfully.

'I must refuse to see him. I will not answer his letters.' Mrs. Fitz. was firm.

The Prince was almost out of his mind with the violence of his passion. He vowed he could not, he would not, live without her. He spent his days and nights in tears and making violent scenes which alarmed all those about him. His intimates hoped the lady would surrender at discretion. They pointed out the madness of his talk of marriage; if there were no Royal Marriage Act he would still risk forfeiting his crown if he married a Roman Catholic, the Act of Settlement made that perfectly clear. The Prince was incapable of hearing reason; the lady's virtue withstood the fiercest siege.

She was worn out with his importunity; since he would not leave her in peace she would go abroad.

The Prince was thrown into such a violent state of agitation that his reason seemed unhinged. He wept and flung himself upon the floor and beat his head.

From someone in his household, now thoroughly alarmed, he caught a whisper: 'Some sort of ceremony which would satisfy the lady and not be binding on the Prince.'

A mock marriage in fact. He caught at the idea. He saw its dramatic possibilities; he saw how he must stage it to win her to play her part. In the privacy of his room he cut himself and smeared his thigh with blood.

'I have fallen on my sword and stabbed myself.' He staggered out into the midst of his terrified servants. 'I shall die. Fetch Keate.'

The surgeon came running, and though he found the wound of no great depth or seriousness he feared for his patient's mind.

'Fetch Mrs. Fitzherbert,' moaned the Prince.

Keate and three of the gentlemen sprang into a coach and hurried to her door.

'The life of the Prince is in imminent danger,' they assured her. 'He stabbed himself and calls constantly for you. Only your presence can save him.'

She suspected a trap. 'I must refuse, gentlemen,' she said agitatedly. 'Not even that will make me pass the doors of Carlton House.' She knew its evil reputation too well to run such risk.

Keate babbled incoherently about the alarming nature of the wound. The lady's resolution was shaken. What if this fantastic story were true?

'I will go,' she faltered. 'If some lady of high character will accompany me.' She hoped that Lady Sefton might perform that service, but the Prince's gentlemen knew a more pliable tool. They took her to the Duchess of Devonshire. Georgiana was enchanted at the thought of so romantic an adventure. Without hesitation she accompanied Mrs. Fitzherbert to Carlton House.

Mrs. Fitzherbert found the Prince pale, with blood flowing from a wound in his side. It was true then; he had done this for her. The tide of sentimentality flowed in her and drowned her common sense. She was so moved that she was deprived almost of consciousness.

The Prince was delighted. In this state of sensibility he could mould her to his will.

'Nothing will induce me to live,' he murmured so low that it seemed he had no strength. 'Unless you promise to become my wife and permit me to put my ring upon your finger.'

In a faint whisper the lady consented, and Duchess Georgiana lent the ring. The Prince surprisingly recovered enough strength to put it on her finger. The Duchess of Devonshire and four of his gentlemen witnessed the ceremony and signed the deposition which was then drawn up. The four gentlemen were jubilant; the Prince was saved and the lady had capitulated; the ceremony, of course, had no value at all.

When she had returned to her home and was able to think calmly, Mrs. Fitzherbert perceived it, too. The gentlemen had conspired unscrupulously to rob her of her honour. The Prince and the Duchess she held quite free from blame. With her own eyes she had seen the bleeding wound.

She realised her danger, and wrote an indignant letter to Lord Southampton, at whose door she laid the blame for the plot.

The next morning she left England.

The Prince gave way to despair. His first thought was to follow her. His friends pointed out that not only was he ignorant of her destination but that the heir-apparent

might not leave England without the permission of the
King. George III, fully aware of his son's infatuation,
refused his consent. Lord Southampton took the Prince,
exhausted with rage and emotion, to the country for
change of air.

He returned to town, a little calmer, but the sympathetic Duchess of Devonshire, Mr. Fox, and that
accommodating lady, Mrs. Armstead, who had now
returned to Mr. Fox, had to listen for hours to the
lamentations of the disconsolate lover. He cried by the
hour, rolled on the floor, struck his forehead, tore his
hair, fell into hysterics.

'I will abandon the crown, sell my jewels and plate,
and scrape together a competence to fly with the object
of my devotion to America,' he swore.

Mrs. Armstead, a woman of notable calmness, must
have listened to these transports with sardonic amusement, but her face betrayed nothing but sympathetic
interest. Fox the fickle, the dissolute, had at last found
the woman who suited him, suited him so well that eleven
years later he married her, and Mrs. Charles James Fox
became a political power.

Foiled in his attempt to follow his love abroad the
Prince set himself to discover her hiding-place. The Duke
of Orleans located her for his friend, and thenceforward
she was shadowed wherever she went, bombarded with
an incessant, heart-rending correspondence – pages and
pages of passionate appeals. He had abandoned the idea
of tricking her with a mock marriage; he offered her a
morganatic marriage according to the laws of Hanover.
Mrs. Fitzherbert declined.

The King dared his son to go abroad without permis-

sion. The Prince sent for Sir James Harris, Minister at
the Hague, and poured out his tale of woe to that astute
diplomatist.

'I see no means of relief but by getting abroad, Harris.'

'I should be very sorry, sir, to see you in Holland otherwise than in a character which would allow me to receive
you in a manner conformable with the respect and
affection I bear your Royal Highness,' Harris said
significantly.

'What am I to do?' the Prince cried passionately. 'Am
I to be refused the right of every individual? Cannot I
travel legally as a private man without the King's consent? I may live unnoticed and unknown.'

Grave Harris permitted himself the ghost of a smile.

'Impossible, sir. The title of the Earl of Chester will be
only a mask which covers the Prince of Wales, and, as
such, your actions will be judged.'

'What can I do, my dear Harris? The King hates me.
He wants to set me at variance with my brother. He
won't even allow Parliament to assist me until I marry.'

'May I suggest, sir, the idea of your marrying? It
would, I should think, be most agreable to the King, and
I am certain, most grateful to the nation.'

'I never will marry,' the Prince protested vehemently.
'My resolution is taken on that subject. I have settled it
with my brother Frederick. No. I will never marry.
Frederick will marry and the Crown will descend to his
children.'

Sir James looked exceedingly grave: 'Till you are
married, Sir, and have children, you have no solid hold
on the affections of the people, even while you are Prince
of Wales; but if you come to the throne a bachelor, and

His Royal Highness the Duke of York is married, and has sons to succeed you, your situation, when King, will be more painful than it is at this moment. Our own history furnishes strong examples of the truth of what I say.'

The Prince was startled. He walked about the room struggling, apparently, with anger.

Harris moved towards the door: 'I perceive, sir, I have said too much. You will allow me to withdraw. I am sure I shall be forgiven an hour hence.'

'You are forgiven now, my dear Harris. I am angry with myself, not with you. Don't question me any more. I will think of what you said. Adieu. God bless you.'

He may have thought of Harris's advice, but he did not take it. Rumour informed him that Mrs. Fitzherbert had become the object of the attentions of the Marquis de Bellois, one of the handsomest scoundrels in Europe. The lady fled from France to avoid him as she had fled from England to avoid the Prince of Wales. She was tired of flight and of resistance. Her heart was traitor to her reason. The Prince was distracted; she began to hesitate, and, hesitating, was lost. Under stress, she promised the Prince, formally and deliberately, that she would never marry any other man. To promise to marry him was but one other step. She took it, on conditions that satisfied her conscience. The Prince had sophistry enough to overcome all her scruples; in a letter of thirty-seven pages he disposed of them all, and added the surprising assurance that 'his father would connive at the union.' Even he, despite his extraordinary powers of self-deception, must have known how completely he lied.

Mrs. Fitzherbert did not believe that one, but she believed the rest of his assurances. She wanted to believe them. Although she was as nearly disinterested as it was possible for a woman to be, her motives varied very little from those which had cheated Perdita. Mrs. Fitzherbert was in love with the handsome, ardent young man; she was romantic and saw herself as the heroine of a touching love story; she was high-principled and saw their love as an ennobling influence which would rescue the Prince from evil courses and protect him from bad friends.

After more than a year of exile she returned to England in December 1785.

Mr. Fox was one of the first to hear of her return to London. He, knowing them both, being fully aware of the Prince's passion, and of the lady's high principles, was exceedingly alarmed. Unless some honourable way out of her difficulty had been found, Mrs. Fitzherbert would not have returned. He was sure of it, and sure of what that way would be.

He sat down to write a letter of protest against the folly he suspected. His letter was fully considered, for he knew the occasion was of immense importance, but even he had no idea how large a part in history that letter of his and the Prince's reply to it were to play. It was a long letter, but its urgency justified its length:

'The Rt. Hon. C. J. Fox, M.P., to H.R.H. the Prince of Wales.

December 10th, 1785.

SIR,

I hope that your Royal Highness does me the justice to believe that it is with the utmost reluctance that I trouble you with my opinion unasked at any time, much more so upon a subject where it may not be agreable to your wishes. I am sure that nothing could ever make me take this liberty, but the condescension which you have honoured me with upon so many occasions and the zealous and grateful attachment that I feel for your Royal Highness and which makes me run the risk even of displeasing you for the purpose of doing you a real service.

I was told just before I left Town yesterday, that Mrs. Fitzherbert was arrived; and if I had heard only this, I should have felt most unfeigned joy at an event which I knew would contribute so much to your Royal Highness' satisfaction; but I was told at the same time, that from a variety of circumstances which had been observed and put together, there was reason to suppose that you were going to take the very desperate step (pardon the expression) of marrying her at this moment. If such an idea be really in your mind, and it be not now too late, for God's sake let me call your attention to some considerations, which my attachment to your Royal Highness and the real concern which I take in whatever relates to your interest, have suggested to me, and which may possibly have the more weight with you when you perceive that Mrs. Fitzherbert is equally interested in most of them with yourself.

In the first place, you are aware that a marriage with a Catholic throws the Prince contracting such a marriage out of the succession of the Crown. Now, what change may have happened in Mrs. Fitzherbert's sentiments upon religious matters I know not; but I do not understand that any public profession of change has been made: and surely, Sir, this is not a matter to be trifled with; and your Royal Highness must excuse the extreme freedom with

which I write. If there should be a doubt about her
previous conversion, consider the circumstances in which
you stand; the King not feeling for you as a father ought,
the Duke of York professedly his favourite, and likely to
be married agreably to the King's wishes; the nation full
of its old prejudices against Catholicks, and justly dread-
ing all disputes about succession. In all these circumstances your enemies might take such advantage as I
shudder to think of; and though your generosity might
think no sacrifice too great to be made to a person whom
you love so entirely, consider what her reflections must be
in such an event, and how impossible it would be for her
ever to forgive herself.

I have stated this danger upon the supposition that the
marriage would be a real one; but your Royal Highness
knows as well as I that according to the present laws of
the country it cannot; and I need not point out to your
good sense what a source of uneasiness it must be to you,
to her, and above all to the nation, to have it a matter of
dispute and discussion, whether the Prince of Wales is,
or is not, married. All speculations on the feelings of the
publick are uncertain; but I doubt much whether an
uncertainty of this kind, by keeping men's minds in
perpetual agitation upon a matter of this moment, might
not cause a greater ferment than any other possible
situation. If there should be children from the marriage,
I need not say how much the uneasiness (as well of your-
selves as of the nation) must be aggravated. If anything
could add to the weight of these considerations, it is the
impossibility of remedying the mischiefs I have alluded
to; for if your Royal Highness should think proper, when
you are twenty-five years old, to notify to Parliament your

intention to marry (by which means alone a legal marriage can be contracted) in what manner can it be notified? If the previous marriage is mentioned or owned, will it not be said that you have set at defiance the laws of your country; and that you now come to Parliament for a sanction for what you have already done in contempt of it? If there are children, will it not be said that we must look for future applications to legitimate them, and consequently be liable to disputes for the succession between the eldest son, and the eldest son *after* the legal marriage? And will not the entire annulling of the whole marriage be suggested as the most secure way of preventing all such disputes? If the marriage is not mentioned to Parliament, but yet is known to have been solemnised, as it certainly will be known, if it takes place, these are the consequences – first, that at all events any child born in the interim is immediately illegitimated; and next, that arguments will be drawn from the circumstances of the concealed marriage against the publick one. It will be said that a woman who has lived with you as your wife without being so, is not fit to be Queen of England; and thus the very thing that is done for the sake of her reputation will be used against it: and what would make this worse would be, the marriage being known (though not officially communicated to Parliament), it would be impossible to deny the assertion; whereas, if *there was no marriage*, I conclude your intercourse would be carried on as it ought, in so private a way as to make it wholly inconsistent with decency or propriety for any one in publick to hazard such a suggestion. If, in consequence of your notification, steps should be taken in Parliament, and an Act passed (which, considering the present state of the power of the King and Ministry is more than probable) to prevent your marriage, you will be reduced to the most difficult of all dilemmas with respect to the footing upon which your marriage is to stand for the future, and your children will be born to pretensions which must make their situation unhappy, if not dangerous. Their situations appear to me of all others the most to be pitied; and the more so, because the more indications persons born in such circumstances give of spirit, talents, or anything that is good, the more will they be suspected and oppressed, and the more will they regret the being deprived of what they must naturally think themselves entitled to.

I could mention other considerations upon this business, if I did not think those I have stated of so much importance, that smaller ones would divert your attention from them rather than add to their weight. That I have written with a freedom which on any other occasion would be unbecoming, I readily confess; and nothing would have induced me to do it, but a deep sense of my duty to a prince who had honoured me with so much of his confidence, and who would have but an ill return for all his favour and goodness to me, if I were to avoid speaking truth to him, however disagreable, at so critical a juncture. The sum of my humble advice, nay, of my most earnest entreaty, is this – that your Royal Highness would not think of marrying till you can marry legally. When that time comes, you must judge for yourself; and no doubt you will take into consideration, both what is due to private honour and your publick station. In the meanwhile, a mock marriage (for it can be no other) is neither honourable for any of the parties, nor, with respect to your Royal Highness, even safe. This appears so clear to me that, if I were Mrs. Fitzherbert's father or brother, I would advise her not by any means to agree to it, and to prefer any other species of connection with you to one leading to so much misery and mischief.

It is high time I should finish this very long and, perhaps your Royal Highness will think, ill-timed letter; but such as it is, it is dictated by pure zeal and attachment to your Royal Highness. With respect to Mrs. Fitzherbert, she is a person with whom I have scarcely the honour of being acquainted, but I hear from everybody that her character is irreproachable, and her manners most amiable. Your Royal Highness knows, too, that I have not in my mind the same objection to intermarriages with princes and subjects which many have. But under the circumstances a marriage at present appears to me to be the most desperate measure for all parties concerned that their worst enemies could have suggested.

I am Your Royal Highness' most devoted servant,

CHARLES JAMES FOX.'

The letter was typical of Fox. It showed his political acumen, his shrewdness and foresight, his worldly wisdom, the low estimation in which he held all women, and the laxity of his moral code. He was quite unable to appreciate the genuineness of Mrs. Fitzherbert's scruples and the strength of her religion. His 'any other species of connection with you' was a phrase which she could never forgive.

If the letter had made any impression on the Prince, her

distress and indignation drove it away. He was quite
determined to have his own way, trusting to circumstances to pull him out of the scrape and lying cheerfully
and fluently in the meantime.

Fox was quite ready to believe the Prince's glib denial,
though no one knew better than he how fluent a liar that
young man was. The Prince did not doubt that he could
silence him and, with him, all the Whigs. He sat down
and pulled pen and paper towards him:

'MY DEAR CHARLES,

Your letter of last night afforded me more satisfaction
than I can find words to express; as it is an additional
proof to me (which I assure you I did not want) of your
having that true regard and affection for me which it is
not only the wish but the ambition of my life to merit.
Make yourself easy, my dear friend. Believe me the world
will soon be convinced that there not only is not, but never
was, any ground for these reports which of late have been
so malevolently circulated.

I have not seen you since Eden seceded from the Whigs,
and joined the Tories. I think this apostasy ought to have
the same effect upon all our friends that it has upon me,
I mean the linking us closer to each other, and I believe
you will easily believe these to be my sentiments; for
you are perfectly well acquainted with my ways of thinking upon these sort of subjects. Where I say my ways of
thinking, I think I had better say my old maxim, which
I ever intend to adhere to, I mean that of swimming or
sinking with my friends. I have not time to add much
more, except just to say that I believe I shall meet you at
dinner at Lord North's at Bushey on Tuesday; and to

desire you to believe me at all times, my dear Charles, most affectionately

Yours,

GEORGE P.

Carlton House,
　Sunday morning, 2 o'clock,
　　December 11th, 1785.'

The Prince knew the risk as well as Fox did, and though his passion had outrun all thoughts of real prudence, he had every intention of throwing dust in the world's eyes.

As she read Mr. Fox's letter, Mrs. Fitzherbert's mouth set in as hard a line as the Prince had yet seen there. He did not show her his reply.

'We will not tell him,' he said soothingly. He sealed the note and called a servant, and sent him with a message to the Reverend Robert Burt.

On 15th December 1785, at dusk, the Reverend Robert Burt married the Prince of Wales to Mrs. Fitzherbert, according to the rites of the Church of England in the drawing-room of her house in Park Street, Park Lane. Mr. Henry Errington, her uncle, and Mr. Jack Smythe, her brother, were the witnesses and signed the certificate of marriage, which the Prince wrote out with his own hand. No other persons were present, but the Prince's friend, Mr. Orlando Bridgeman, kept the door.

Immediately after the ceremony bride and bridegroom set out for her villa at Richmond. It was a bitter winter's night, and the road so blocked with snow that it was almost impassable. The horses broke down, and the travellers supped at an inn at Hammersmith, while fresh horses were sought by the cursing postillions.

In London the air was humming with rumours. Those who knew the secret kept it; but too many had been given hints, and something of the truth was noised abroad. At a rout at Devonshire House, Duchess Georgiana was the centre of an eagerly questioning crowd.

'The town all talks of the Prince of Wales' marriage.'

'I believe it is totally without foundation.'

'He has taken a box for Mrs. Fitzherbert at the Opera, and constantly passes the greater part of the night with her.'

'She is, or is to be, at Carlton House.'

'She was married, I hear, by a Roman Catholic priest, is to have £6000 a year, and is to be created a duchess.'

'No doubt the Marchioness of Buckingham will be first lady of the bedchamber.'

'The noble Marquis himself, perhaps, at the head of the Papistical Court?'

'Does her Grace of Devonshire know the truth?' someone whispered.

The smiling Duchess denied it. 'I know nothing but the buzz of the day, nor can say more of it.'

Mr. Walpole hobbled by, very lame with the gout, but eager to collect the latest news for his correspondents. The Countess of Upper Ossery received one of his most amusing letters:

'Oh, but the hubbub you are to hear and talk of when you come to town – and you are to hear and talk of nothing else, for they tell me the passengers in the streets of all ranks talk of it, – is a subject to which your letters, having already atuned you and on which I alone, for certain reasons, will say nothing, but if you don't guess, madam, I will give you a clue: don't you remember that after Louis Quatorze had married the Maintenon and the Dauphin Mdlle. Chouin, the Duchess of Burgundy said to her husband: *"Si je viens à mourir feriez vous le troisième tome de votre famille?"* You may swear that my mysterious silence is not dated from my privity or knowledge. I do not know a tittle from any good authority, and though a mass of circumstances are cited and put together, they command no credit; whoever believes must believe upon trust.'

4

BRIGHTHELMSTONE

Mʀs. Fɪᴛᴢʜᴇʀʙᴇʀᴛ's discretion was admirable, though the Prince's public chivalry helped her over many a difficult place. They were so deeply in love that they could not hide it.

The fashionable world found itself in a quandary. If the lady had been the Prince's acknowledged mistress, the society leaders would have known what to do; but a possible *sub rosa* marriage made it unwise to offer slights.

Mrs. Fitzherbert was indifferent. Risk is the salt of romance, and the sense of the delicious peril in which they stood provided an enchantment which a conventional marriage could never have supplied. Her conduct in public was irreproachable. She kept her former friends and made new ones, and winnowed some chaff from the wheat of the Prince's intimates.

They heard the rumours at Windsor. The King was frankly incredulous. The Queen eyed the lady suspiciously, and Mrs. Fitzherbert ceased to go to Court.

The mob liked the romance and cared little about the exact terms of it. Caricaturists might be malicious, but the man in the street sang a sentimental ballad:

'On Richmond Hill there lives a lass
More bright than May day morn,
Whose charms all other maids' surpass
O rose without a thorn.

This lass so neat, with smiles so sweet,
Has won my right good will,
I'd crowns resign to call her mine,
Sweet lass of Richmond Hill.'

Happiness steadied the Prince. He made an effort to curb his expenditure and face the mountain of his debts. They were overwhelming. Once again he made a dramatic gesture, and abandoned Carlton House. He had bought a farm-house on the Steine at Brighthelmstone, where he had often gone for the sea bathing. He retired there to economise, and, deprived of London's entertainments, began to build furiously. Soon there arose in the little fishing village one of the most amazing exotic buildings which England ever boasted. 'The Pavilion' at Brighthelmstone became an astonishment and a jest. Marble pillars and a Chinese gallery, a fantastic Oriental dome and stables copied from the Paris Corn-market swallowed money faster than Carlton House had ever done.

The caricaturists seized their pencils and posted down to Brighthelmstone by the greatly improved service of stage coaches. The Whigs flocked down to bathe and sun themselves upon the Steine in the Prince's company. The traffic on the Brighton road became a byword. All the whips endeavoured to break the record, and drove recklessly without regard to pedestrians or their own

MRS FITZHERBERT

To face page 66

limbs. Since Carlton House was closed and the Prince
had no town house, the Duchess of Cumberland,
delighted to annoy the Court again, entertained for them.
The season of 1786 was particularly brilliant.

The Prince was enjoying himself. Mrs. Fitzherbert was
less happy. Social gossip did not trouble her, but they
were concerning themselves overmuch with her in the
House of Commons in connection with the Prince's debts.
The Prince lightheartedly rallied her on her low spirits,
but presently caught some of her alarm and drowned his
doubts in uproarious gaiety. He reeled into Lady Portar-
lington's ball almost stupefied, pale as ashes, and with
glazed eyes. The Duchess of Cumberland caught his arm
and made him sit by her, and kept him tolerably peaceable
till they went down to supper, when he was most gloriously
drunk and riotous indeed. He posted himself in the
doorway, flung his arms round the Duchess of Ancaster's
neck, and kissed her with a great smack, threatened to
pull Lord Galloway's wig off, and knock out his false
teeth. Behaved, indeed, in a most gentlemanly fashion,
until some of his companions called his carriage and put
him into it despite his protests.

Mrs. Fitzherbert's heart sank. Was this reckless,
rollicking boy the only rock on which she could depend?
She pleaded with him, and, bitterly repentant, with the
tears which flowed so easily rolling down his cheeks, he
promised good behaviour and a devotion such as no
woman yet had known.

'Why, if it will please you, dearest Maria, I'll make a
clean breast of it, and tell my father, and let the Crown
go hang.'

Her tears flowed as fast as his. 'And how could I ever

forgive myself if I cost you such a sacrifice as that? No, beloved, insults and pointed jests are powerless to hurt me, as long as I am sure of your protection and your love.'

'Till Death, my soul. I never have nor ever shall love anyone but you.' The little cloud vanished in tempestuous kisses.

In the House, Mr. Pitt whispered mysterious, pointed hints, but Mr. Rolle, the member for Devonshire, was tiresomely outspoken. It was obvious that the Tories had wind of the ceremony. Still, as long as the witnesses kept silent, there could be no more than guesses. Sheridan gallantly came to the rescue and dealt with Mr. Pitt. Mr. Rolle, however, was persistent, and Fox, with the Prince's letter in his pocket, was determined that the denial of the rumoured marriage should be emphatic and complete. His popularity had suffered on account of the rumours; he had been accused of conniving at the Prince's marriage with a Roman Catholic. The caricatures of Gillray, which were printed and sold by thousands and were a never-ending source of talk and laughter, showed Fox present at the marriage ceremony, giving away the bride, while Burke, in cassock and biretta as a Jesuit priest, conducted the service. Fox resented the cartoon, both as a private person and as a leader of the Whig party, which it was designed to injure. It could not be made too plain that the Whigs were not cognisant of the marriage; that he, the Prince's intimate, did not believe it had taken place.

He rose to speak in a crowded House: 'With respect to the allusion to something "full of danger to the Church and State" made by the honourable gentleman, one of the members for the county of Devon; till that gentleman thought proper to explain himself it was impossible to say with any certainty to what that allusion referred, but he supposed it must be meant in reference to that miserable calumny, that low malicious falsehood, which had been propagated without doors, and made the wanton sport of the vulgar. In that House, where it was known how frequent and common the falsehoods of the time were, he hoped a tale only fit to impose upon the lowest order of persons in the streets would not have gained the smallest portion of credit; but when it appeared that an invention so monstrous, a report of a fact which had not the smallest degree of foundation, a report of a fact actually impossible to have happened, had been circulated with so much industry as to have made an impression on the minds of members of that House, it proved at once the uncommon pains taken by the enemies of His Royal Highness to propagate the grossest and most malignant falsehoods with a view to depreciate his character and injure him in the opinion of his country. When he (Mr. Fox) considered that His Royal Highness was the first subject in the kingdom, and the immediate heir to the throne, he was at a loss to imagine what species of party it was which could have fabricated so base and scandalous a calumny. Had there existed in the kingdom such a faction as an anti-Brunswick faction he should have certainly imputed the invention of so malicious a falsehood to it – for he knew not what other description of men could feel an interest in first forming, and then circulating with more than ordinary assiduity, a tale in every particular so unfounded, and for which there was not the shadow of anything like reality.

'This being the fact, and as the occasion had made it necessary for him to declare as much, he hoped it would have this good effect upon the House and upon the country, that it would teach both the one and the other to distrust the reports circulated to the prejudice of the Prince, and lessen any opinion that they might in consequence take up injurious to the character of His Royal Highness, who might be said to be a person in whose fair fame that House and the country were deeply interested. The whole of the debt the Prince was ready to submit to the investigation of the House; and he was equally ready to submit the other circumstance to which he had alluded to their consideration, provided the consideration of a House of Parliament could, with consistency, with propriety and decency, be applied to such a subject. Nay, His Royal Highness had authorised him to declare that, as a peer of Parliament, he was ready in the other House to submit to any, the most pointed, questions, which could be put to him respecting it, or to afford His Majesty or His Majesty's Ministers the fullest assurances of the utter falsehood of the fact in question, which never had, and common sense must see, never could have happened.'

The House listened with mingled incredulity and relief. Honest Mr. Rolle was not content. 'The question which would affect both Church and State' had been stated and discussed in newspapers all over the kingdom, and had made an impression upon him and upon almost all ranks of men in the country who venerated and loved the Constitution. The right honourable gentleman said it was impossible to have happened. They all knew that there were certain laws and Acts of Parliament which forbade it; but though it could not be done under the formal sanction of the law there were ways in which it might have taken place, and those laws, in the minds of some persons, might have been satisfactorily evaded, and yet the fact might be equally productive of the most alarming consequences. It ought, therefore, to be cleared up.'

Mr. Fox cleared it up. 'He denied it *in toto*, in point of fact as well as law. The fact not only never could have happened legally, but never did happen in any way whatsoever, and had from the beginning been a base and malicious falsehood.'

Mr. Rolle asked: 'Whether in what had fallen from the right honourable gentleman he had spoken from direct authority?'

Mr. Fox put his hand to his breast, where the Prince's letter was, and declared solemnly 'that he had spoken from direct authority.'

The House accepted his assurance.

So Mrs. Fitzherbert was publicly denied, and the wrong done her was never publicly righted. The rock on which she leaned was shifting sand. Mr. Fox did not like her; he regarded her, indeed, as his enemy, since she distrusted and hated his intimacy with the Prince; but he did not wilfully calumniate her; he believed what he said. If there had ever been a ceremony of any kind it must have been another mock marriage like that of 1784, more convincing in detail to satisfy the lady, but no more binding in fact. He was sure of it.

When he left the House that evening he strolled to Brook's, feeling very pleased with himself for his service to the party and the Prince. In the Club he met Mr.

Orlando Bridgeman, who hailed him with some agitation and led him aside.

'Mr. Fox, I hear that you have denied in the House the Prince's marriage to Mrs. Fitzherbert.' He looked around cautiously and spoke in a low tone. 'You have been misinformed. I was at the marriage.'

Mr. Fox was not a man to show his feelings.

'You will drink with me, Mr. Bridgeman,' he said politely, and called for a bottle.

During the progress of the debate in the House, messengers kept the Prince constantly informed. When the House rose the Prince broke the news to his wife with assumed gaiety, and, taking both her hands, said: 'Only conceive, Maria, what Fox has done. He went down to the House and denied that you and I were man and wife. Did you ever hear of such a thing?' Silent and pale she listened and waited and hoped. This was the supreme test of the character of the man in whose hands she had placed her happiness and honour. Would he stand by his wife or his friend?

The silence grew unbearable.

'I'll send Grey, Sheridan, to defend you,' he cried at last, avoiding her eyes and hurrying from the room.

The tears welled up slowly and overflowed. In profound agitation she clasped and unclasped her hands. He had, as she had known he would, though she had striven to blind herself, failed her in the most important crisis of their lives. Never in the future would he be able to recede from the position which he now took up. It was the supreme test of character, the parting of the ways between the spoilt, wild boy with splendid possibilities, and the man who would never consider anyone but him-

self. Hadn't she heard once that Dr. Hurd had prophesied that his pupil would become either the most
polished gentleman or the most accomplished blackguard
in Europe? That was an exaggeration, of course; fiercely
she rejected it in its entirety, but hadn't she always
known, herself, that the possibilities for good and evil
were evenly balanced in the man she loved? He must
inevitably grow into greatness or deteriorate. Now, at
this crisis which so nearly concerned her happiness and
his own honesty, he had proved shifty, true neither to
Fox nor to her.

Yet she hated Fox, unjustly, as a woman so essentially
just must have been aware. Fox had not known that he
lied, yet his lie had repudiated her wifehood and shown
her her idol's feet of clay. Nothing would ever be the
same again. Her exquisite dream of happiness was
broken and spoilt. She could not be just to Fox.

'He rolled me in the kennel like a street-walker and he
knew that he lied,' she cried vehemently.

Sherry defended her in the House of Commons in a
speech which might have sparkled in one of his own
comedies, for his eloquence flitted over the crisis and left
the House waiting eagerly for the next scene. 'There was
another person who must be unnamed, on whose conduct
truth could fix no just reproach, and whose character
claimed, and was entitled, to the truest and most general
respect,' he pleaded.

That was all very well, but Fox's statement was not
denied. Sherry covered himself with glory, and London
rocked with amusement. Fox went abroad.

The Prince had lost his friend and most of his friend's
friends. Mrs. Fitzherbert was white and silent. The

Prince, less pleased with himself than he had ever been
in his life, grew moody and plunged into the wildest
dissipation. Fox might not have been the best of companions for a reckless youth, but his greatness seemed to
excuse him; there was no such excuse for those who took
his place. The Prince yearned for more dissolute and
flattering company. He would never again listen to
advice from any man, never again consent to shine as a
secondary star. Soon he was to be found, day and night,
surrounded by such men as the Barrymores – Hellgate
and Cripplegate – George Hanger, the 'Jockey' of Norfolk, 'Jehu' Lade and his wife Letty, Jack Payne and old
Queensberry. John McMahon was installed as his
'confidential adviser,' a post into whose duties the respectable found it wiser not to inquire. 'Pandar' was not
the worst epithet bestowed upon the man who was soon
advanced to the dignity of Private Secretary and Keeper
of the Privy Purse. He was an Irishman of low birth and
obsequious manners, a little man with a red face covered
with pimples, always dressed in a blue and buff uniform
with his hat on one side, copying the air of his master to
whom he was a prodigious foil, ready to execute any
commission, however delicate and complicated. His
origin was, at least, some excuse for his toad-eating:

'Once a boy in ragged dress,
Who would little Mac caress
When in the streets, starved and sad,
I was a common errand lad?'

George Hanger, almost as disreputable in his behaviour,
was of totally different character. A dissolute, jovial

rogue with a coarse tongue and an exuberant sense of humour, Lord Coleraine's son, who sold coals for a living and sat in an applewoman's chair to carry on business for her while she went away for her tea. A man who never forgot a friend, nor ignored one because he had fallen on evil days. Good company for the Prince, but Prinney cooled towards him because he had not a flatterer's tongue.

'Jehu' – Sir John Lade – managed the Prince's racing stable, and fell under suspicion when Sam Chiffney, the Prince's jockey, was warned off the turf. A libel, probably, was this implication of Sir John; for he bore the reputation of being honest, except, of course, in such a trifle as the paying of tradesmen's bills, which no gentlemen, certainly not the Prince of Wales, would have dreamed of doing. It was Sir John who bet Lord Cholmondeley that he would carry him twice round the Steine. Since my lord was a giant and the baronet a dwarf this drew an eager crowd. Lord Cholmondeley asked for what Sir John was waiting. 'Till you strip, my lord,' Jehu cried with a twinkle in his eye. 'I engaged to carry you but not an ounce of clothing; so hurry, my lord, make ready, lest we disappoint the ladies.' The ladies tittered and Lord Cholmondeley stalked away sneering, 'Sharp practice.' Still, he paid, and the crowd laughed.

Sir John had a taste for low life, and it was his constant ambition to be mistaken for a groom, whose dress and language he affected. He liked nothing better than to take the coachman's place and drive the Prince's 'German waggon,' and six bay horses from the Pavilion to Lewes races with a great many oaths and tremendous cracking of the whip. Dr. Johnson had once proposed him as a fitting husband for the authoress of *Evelina*, but John himself took his pleasures in Covent Garden and St. Giles'. He took his wife from a bagnio in St. Giles', and Letty Lade had a lively time as procuress for the Prince. Her gift for bad language was so striking that it became a proverb: 'He swears like Letty Lade.' Lady Lade was as fine a whip as her husband. She offered to drive a coach against another, tooled by a sister-whip, eight miles over Newmarket Heath for five hundred guineas a side, but when it came to the point no one had prowess enough to take up the wager. There were lesser lights among the Prince's friends. There was 'Cripplegate' Barrymore who invented the first 'tiger' and 'Hellgate' his brother, and sister 'Billingsgate,' whose nicknames explained their style. There was 'Skiffy,' whom a caustic friend described as 'an admirable specimen of florid Gothic.' He wrote verses which Lord Byron did not admire, and was an irresistible peg for the caricaturist since he generally chose to appear in a dark blue coat with gilt buttons, a yellow waistcoat with loud inexpressibles, large bunches of white ribbons at the knees, or else in a *vieux rose* satin suit with a wig, rouged cheeks, and blacked eyebrows, so that he looked like a French doll and smelt like a perfume shop.

And last, but by no means least, there was the 'Jockey' of Norfolk, eleventh Duke, whom a wit compared with Charles II in that 'he diffused his Maker's image through the land with great and indiscriminate zeal.' He could 'swill wine like a Silenus and gorge beafsteaks like a Buckhorse.' His devotion to the bottle had one advantage; it enabled his servants to wash him when His Grace had drunk too much to resist. He could not bear the

GEORGE III

To face page 76

sight of water in any form when sober. A man of gross appetites yet with more kindliness than his princely friend, and with a gift for brilliant, cultured conversation which made him welcome in better company.

Brighthelmstone filled to overflowing, not a house nor lodging was to be had by late-comers, and its virtues were extolled to the skies. The Prince amused himself hugely, and the fashionable world followed his lead. Mrs. Fitzherbert made the best of things and had the tact and self-control not to complain. Parliament considered the Prince's debts and would not pay them. The King and Queen were completely estranged from their eldest son.

Rumours reached Brighton that the King's behaviour was really very odd. His conversation, always abrupt, had become more abrupt and rambling than ever. His moods were very changeable, his mind abstracted. It had even been whispered that he had been caught at his old trick of talking to the trees. He went out in the dew one morning and, instead of changing his shoes and stockings, went to town in his wet ones. He returned very feverish and talking wildly. Undoubtedly the King was ill.

Brighton wanted more particulars. More particulars were given. The King complained of sleeplessness and physical weakness. 'His manners,' voices were lowered, 'were really odd in the extreme. One day when Mrs. Siddons was reciting, he handed her a sheet of paper which was blank, except for his signature. His disordered dress and vacant stare at the levee at St. James' had given rise to a great deal of talk. A review had been cancelled. His strength seemed going. His face was altering. 'You see me all at once an old man,' he had cried.

A kinder voice took up the tale. The poor King had been out riding and had remained silent for hours. When he returned to Windsor he had run through the passages terribly agitated, and had flung himself on his knees in his own apartments, bursting into tears and crying out in a pitiful tone: 'I am going to be mad, and I wish to God that I may die.'

The Queen was weeping secretly; the musicians had been sent away. Nobody stirred in the palace; not a step, not a voice was heard.

The Prince of Wales posted from Brighthelmstone. The silence of Windsor was broken, broken horribly. The King, in a frenzy, seized by the throat his rebellious, insolent, dissolute son, who had caused him so much grief, and thrust him against the wall.

The King was mad.

'Farmer George' had been unpopular; the mad King suddenly had the most loyal subjects in the world. The country was shaken: 'The poor King!' But 'His death would bode no good,' quickly followed pity. The people considered the heir with dismay.

The Prince of Wales took possession of Windsor. The Queen, stunned and miserable, lived entirely in her own apartments, seeing only her daughters and a few of her ladies. The physicians reported to the Prince; the Queen was ignored. 'What will become of me; what will become of me?' she wept. Her desolation won for her a compassion which she had never earned before, but it was the King who needed pity. He was not really mad, for he never forgot who he was, nor his circumstances, nor his family; he was, at his worst, only extremely eccentric in his behaviour and the victim of hallucinations; he was not violent except in his anger against his son. But the age had a horror of madness; insanity was far worse than crime. The Prince seized his opportunity. He shook his head and wiped the tears of sensibility from his eyes, and gave orders that the King should be removed to Kew, which he hated, and that the Queen and her daughters should go too, but that she should not be allowed to see the King.

Sir Lucas Pepys, one of the physicians, ventured to deplore the idea of removing the King by force. 'Without a doubt his smallest resistance would call up the whole country to his rescue.'

The Queen's heart misgave her. 'The King's dislike of Kew is terrible to think of, and I cannot foresee where it will end.'

The Prince was brusque, and, the Queen said, heartless. Even with those sentimental tears flowing from his eyes. He had dried his tears to open his father's private cabinet, to help himself to some secret papers and a vast hoard of money and jewels.

'His dissolution is the best thing that can be hoped for,' said the Prince.

Cynical observers noted that he spared no pains to hasten that dissolution. The King was persuaded, with great difficulty, to leave Windsor. Only three of his gentlemen were with him, but the whole population of Windsor assembled to see him off, believing that they looked their last on him. On passing through the gates of the Park he put his hands over his eyes and wept, but hastily recovered himself to remark that he was looking with great pleasure to rejoining his wife and daughters.

At Kew no fires were lighted; the house was in a

miserable condition, the rooms dirty, uncarpeted, and
with ill-fitting windows through whose frames the wind
blew gustily. The King, still docile, allowed himself to
be led to a strange room instead of to his usual quarters.
His equerries, by the Prince's orders, withdrew. The
physician went back to London. The Queen did not
come. The King, alone with his pages, demanded to see
his family according to the promise made him when he
consented to leave Windsor.

The promise was fulfilled. Outside the shut window,
in the winter dusk, the Princesses passed. The King,
delighted, rushed to open the window. It was screwed
down. The doors were locked; the pages were keepers.
If the King had not been insane he would have been
driven to madness. He had a violent paroxysm and so
delivered himself into his gaolers' hands. The physicians
said that cruelty was the shortest method of restoring
reason to the insane. So they enclosed the King's body
in a machine which left him no liberty of action; they
chained him to a staple, beat him, starved him, and
threatened him with violent language. His chief attendant was a German page, named Ernst, who struck him
at his pleasure, insulted him, and thwarted all his desires.
The King raved a little, but was nearly always gentle.
No one tried kindness to restore light to his darkened
brain.

The Prince of Wales found great entertainment in
mimicking his father's gestures and ravings. Mimicry was
one of his gifts and his friends were vastly entertained.

At Brook's they had a cant phrase at the whist table:
'I play the lunatic' when they played the king. They
made bets on the question of a Regency. The Opposi-

tion ardently championed the claims of the Prince of Wales.

Mr. Pitt opposed him and named the Queen.

'Mr. Pitt's chastity will protect the Queen,' sneered the Prince's friend, Jack Payne, and added a whispered ribaldry.

'The Queen is uneasy,' the Prince of Wales laughed. 'The other day when we went to look for the King's money and jewels my mother grew angry as we opened the drawers. York, my brother, is a very fine fellow. He never forsakes me. He said to the Queen: "Madam, I believe you are as much deranged as the King." '

The Duchess of Gordon, very white and stately, cast a contemptuous look at the Prince and turned to Jack Payne: 'You little, insignificant, good-for-nothing up-start, pert; chattering puppy, how dare you name your royal master's royal mother in that style.'

The Prince bowed to her. 'Madam, you are a Pittite evidently.'

The Duchess did not deny it but withdrew from company in which she might meet the Prince or his friends. The ladies of the Opposition wore Regency caps, badges, and ribbons, and talked openly of de-posing the King.

Mr. Fox, recalled from his travels to lead the Whigs, was eloquent in the House. There the battle of the Regency raged fiercely between the Government and the Whigs.

The Prince entertained the Town, gave the great offices of State to his friends, and urged Dr. Warren, one of the King's physicians and the Prince's ardent partisan, to declare his patient incurable. Dr. Warren did so with

enthusiasm. But Mr. Pitt did not relax his hold upon
the reins. The Government sent a fresh physician, the
Reverend Francis Willis, to join the staff at Kew.

The King looked at him quietly: 'Why have you given
up your sacred calling for one which brings you more
worldly profit?'

'Sir,' answered Willis gently, 'our Saviour went about
healing the sick.'

'Yes. But he did not get seven hundred a year for it,'
said the King sagely. Nevertheless he regarded his new
doctor with less abhorrence than the others. Dr. Willis
was kind; the others had been cruel. The King opened
his heart to him.

'The insolence of the pages is intolerable. I am not
allowed to see my wife or daughters. I am not allowed to
use a knife or fork or a razor, in case I should cut my
throat,' he said indignantly.

'Your Majesty is too good a Christian and you have too
much sense of what you owe your people to commit such
an act,' said the doctor, handing him a razor.

The King quietly shaved himself.

Dr. Willis took him for a walk.

'My daughters will not show themselves,' said the King,
wistfully looking up at the windows.

The doctor brought wife and daughters to see him, and
the patient was overjoyed.

'The patient's recovery is only a question of time,' said
Willis firmly to the Commons' Committee.

The Regency Bill passed the Commons and was carried
to the Lords. The same day Dr. Willis sought the Lord
Chancellor and stated that the King was cured.

'I do not believe it,' said the Chancellor.

Willis set his mouth. 'I will publish the King's restoration. Impeachment is an evil fate for a Lord Chancellor.'

Lord Thurlow gave him a sour look, and went to see the King.

There was no doubt about it. Even the Opposition doctors were forced at last to sign a bulletin that 'His Majesty's illness has entirely ceased.'

The Princes visited their father, but the King insisted on seeing them in the Queen's apartments so that 'all parties might have that caution which at the present hour could but be judicious.'

He embraced them, and they all shed many tears.

'Since I have been ill,' said the King, 'I have rubbed up all my Latin and my piquet is much improved. I play much better than Mr. Charles Hawkins.'

'They will magnify that into instances of insanity,' whispered Lord Winchelsea drily.

They tried to. They talked, harshly and wildly. It was useless. The King was sane, and went to the Cathedral to give his thanks to God. Mr. Pitt was relieved. London rejoiced wholeheartedly. The Prince of Wales returned to Brighthelmstone. His bitter hatred of Pitt was the most honest of his emotions.

With the King's recovery the crown seemed further out of his reach than ever. If he might not rule, he might at least enjoy. The years 1789-1793 were the happiest and gayest of his life, for that small spark of conscience which had sometimes troubled him in earlier years had long been quite extinguished.

The Bastille fell, and the baskets under the guillotine filled and overflowed. The fashionable world, with innumerable connections in France, was shocked and excited. The refugee aristocrats poured into Brighthelm-stone and Richmond with tales which made the hearers' blood run cold and brought them back for more. The ceaseless round of gaiety went on, and the refugees whirled as madly as those who had not supped full of horrors.

The Pavilion grew, and Brighton, having shortened its name, expanded. Horse-races at Lewes and Newmarket, cricket-matches at home, casual amours, delighted the Prince. He loved horses and was clever with them; those who despised him granted him that. He had a talent for music, too; parties at the Pavilion were very musical indeed.

Life at Brighton was one long carnival. The presence of the Prince and his friends frightened away a number of old maids from visiting the sea; the children of old-fashioned people came there no more. But Brighton was prospering, and did not care.

Mrs. Fitzherbert's stately presence kept the worst elements in check when she was there. She kept the Prince's affection, though her influence over him waned as the years passed. He grew more reckless and self-indulgent, more deeply involved in debt, more infantile in his amusements, fatter, heavier in mind and body, less and less inclined to curb his vanity and his appetites. McMahon and Letty Lade fed his grosser tastes; George Brummell appeared and turned his taste for dress into an overwhelming passion; Lady Jersey turned the battery of her dark eyes upon him and, without warning, Mrs. Fitzherbert's empire crashed and fell.

Quite unprepared, she received one June morning an unsigned note from Brighton which informed her that the Prince would never enter her doors again.

The beautiful Lady Jersey had him in her toils. Mrs. Fitzherbert made no struggle to keep him, uttered no word of protest, sent no answer to his letter, but with silent dignity withdrew.

Lady Jersey was a friend of Lady Harcourt, the Queen's Lady of the Bedchamber. Queen Charlotte encouraged the new favourite, who knew her wishes with regard to the Prince. She wanted him to marry and, if possible, to marry her niece. Lady Jersey was to forward this plan and keep the Queen's countenance in her equivocal position. The poor, kind King hoped that the separation from Mrs. Fitzherbert meant that the Prince had decided to turn over a new leaf. He, at least, did not believe in that marriage of which the foolish, gossiping Town had talked so much. The total of the Prince's debts appalled him. He was eager for a reconciliation, only desirous that the Prince should marry and settle down with a good, domesticated, German wife, as he had, and bring up as fine, though perhaps less turbulent, sons as he had done himself.

All he wanted, the poor, kind old King, was to rule in peace with the Tories in power, sing hymns when he felt like it, listen to his beloved Handel, pop in and out of his subjects' homes as the benevolent whim seized him, and go early to bed. If the people would not insist on making scenes and upsetting him, his health would be as good as that of anyone else. Nothing soothed him as much as listening to Handel's music; when he felt excited, music brought him calm content. He listened to Handel while the Prince made up his mind about a wife. Only on his marriage should his debts be paid. Parliament and the King were agreed about it.

For the last time the Prince's conscience stirred. He had a wife and had loved her; in his way he loved her still. How could he marry another woman? Wasn't it blasphemous to perjure himself? As well as deucedly unsafe?

The debts piled up and the pressure grew insistent. Which Princess would he choose? The Queen's niece or the King's? The Queen's niece was beautiful, Lady Jersey had heard, and would, perhaps, prove a rival; the other would be best. She whispered in his ear.

'Not the Queen's, certainly,' sneered the Prince. 'One of that family is enough.'

'The King's, then? The Princess Caroline of Brunswick?'

'If my debts are paid, and if I must.'

The die was cast. The Prince drank himself stupid, cursed the unknown cousin who was to be his financial lifebuoy, and sought comfort, not in the arms of the woman whom he loved and was so deeply wronging, but in those of the charmer who had chosen his bride.

BOOK II

CAROLINE

Visitors to the Court of Brunswick were trained in a very formal school.

'A low bow first and then two measured paces forward with one hand on your sword and the other in your breast, then another bow, then more paces and then a third bow,' chanted Monsieur Dupré, the dancing master. 'You will do, sir, when you are presented to the Duke.'

The English boy tossed the hair out of his eyes and took his riding lesson. The riding school was part of the palace and the Duke was liberal in his supply of horses and attendants for it. The mode of riding taught was anything but English; high demi-piqued saddles kept the riders firm in their seats, and rising in the stirrups was not to be considered.

Young John Stanley found the manners of Brunswick very strange, but he was there for his education. Dancing lessons, riding lessons, fencing lessons over, he was allowed to go to the opera for relaxation.

His frank young face with the hair about the ears and his shirt collar open announced his English birth so unmistakably that the English-born Duchess noticed him, and, casting etiquette to the winds, sent for him to come to Court as he was.

'That was not to be thought of,' said his tutor, 'he must

certainly wear Court dress.' So the boy hastily rigged
himself out with a dress-coat and ruffles, a hat and a
sword, but he forgot all the good M. Dupré's instructions.

The Court of Brunswick was *en fête* for the marriage of
the Duke's elder daughter with the Prince of Würtem-
burg. All the ducal family was in attendance, but
fifteen-year-old John Stanley had eyes only for the
Princess Caroline. She looked enchanting in a pale blue
gown of the simplest fashion with fair powdered curls
hanging upon her neck; laughter flickered in her eyes,
and pretty phrases on her lips.

The boy thought and dreamed of her by day and night
all the time he was in Brunswick, and the young girl
undoubtedly thought a good deal of him. She was kept
most strictly in Brunswick, and her mother's tales of
England excited in her the liveliest interest and delight.
She would have John Stanley to talk to her and, very
willingly, he talked to her for three or four hours every
day.

'She is a star out of my reach,' thought the boy, but he
loved her all the same in the idealistic, exquisite way of
extreme youth.

The Duke had lately laid out his gardens according to
English taste in patches of shrubberies with winding walks
between high, hornbeam, clipped hedges. Fountains
tinkled and there were innumerable birds. To John
Stanley it seemed that Brunswick was full of birds; they
flitted overhead, flashing in and out of the trees in the
Duke's garden with excited twitters and ecstatic songs,
and every Brunswicker kept at least one in a cage so that
the streets as well as the gardens seemed full of song. The

English boy bought one to be in the mode, and talked to it comfortingly through the imprisoning bars.

He told the Princess Caroline of his purchase as they walked together in the charming gardens of the Duchess' villa at Little Richmond. He told her that his memory of Brunswick would always be of green and leaves and innumerable birds. To himself he added, 'and of a lovely, lively girl with light and powdered hair hanging in curls about her shoulders and cherry-red lips from which it seemed that only sweet words could flow, with animated looks and charming, simple, modest clothes.' The air of the Court filled him with a vague distaste; it was not that it was more immoral than other courts in Germany, but that the carelessness in morals seemed to touch everybody; not even his exquisite Princess could escape the slanderous tongues.

Sometimes the girl seemed a little *distraite*, and with a jealous pang he remembered the whispers he had heard of her partiality for a soldier employed about the Court. Major von Töbingen, was he? John Stanley did not think much of him. Gossip had plenty to say of the little, innocent, indiscreet notes she sent him, and of how her parents had determined to send her away to the other side of the Duchy for a time to forget this folly, while the too susceptible major was sent back to the army.

John Stanley went back to England, but he did not forget his earliest love.

The Princess Caroline's upbringing, though injudicious, had been of the strictest. She had had for years a governess who would not allow her to look out of the window. She was seldom allowed to dine at table or go downstairs when there were visitors. If she did, she was constantly corrected, and her eyes were full of tears; her mother scolded, and bade her go on crying, for it was only her own naughtiness that made her so passionate.

She escaped from discipline sometimes, climbing out of windows and playing impish practical jokes. Her mother, after all these years in Brunswick, remained completely English, and chafed against the strict etiquette of the petty German Courts. She was a silly woman, but her heart was kind. Her daughter was even more unconventional. Her passionate love of children was a constant embarrassment. She never saw a pretty child unattended in the streets but she must run to it and fondle it and ask it questions. She did not mind how dirty these children were, how diseased; they needed only to be small and helpless. She had a number of little *protégés* all over the Duchy in whom her interest never flagged.

At Court they made a jest of this love of children, and the Princess, thwarted in her desire to attend one of the great balls, used the jest to take an impish revenge.

The ball had only just begun when a messenger came post haste to the Duke and Duchess to tell them their daughter had been taken seriously ill. They rushed to her apartments and found her in bed screaming.

'What is the matter? What is the matter?' the distracted Duchess cried.

'I am in labour,' the girl declared. 'Send for an *accoucheur*, I beg you.'

The silly Duchess, inexpressibly shocked and dismayed, obeyed. When the *accoucheur* arrived, the Princess sprang out of bed, wiping the livid colour off her face as she laughed, 'Now, madam, will you keep me another time from a ball?'

About the Court they whispered the tale. Those who had been eye-witnesses shook their heads over the madness of such an unseemly practical joke; those who had not been present preferred to believe that the story had been true. 'She is mad,' said some. 'What have they done with the child?' whispered others.

Two of her brothers were imbeciles; strange tales of her sister's flightiness had already drifted back from Russia. A naughty girl's wild prank to revenge herself upon her parents was the foundation stone upon which many subsequent scandals were built.

She returned from a long stay in a distant part of the Duchy to find that the man to whom she had given her young heart had been sent away. She hid her grief and, perhaps, recovered, though she never forgot.

She was popular in Brunswick; she was generous, kind-hearted, and there was no doubt of her courage. People quoted admiringly a tale of the schoolroom when her governess had asked, 'Where is the lion found?' And the girl had answered, 'In the heart of a Brunswicker.'

She herself had no fear. Once when they were playing the favourite game of the carousel, the Princess was eager to mount one of the horses.

'We beseech your Highness not to try. The circular motion will make you giddy,' urged her attendants.

Caroline turned on them with laughing contempt: 'A Brunswicker dare do anything. Fear is a word of which we are ignorant.'

She had a brave spirit, a bright wit, and an impish humour, but, alas, no tact. She was lively, indiscreet, and too talkative. Suitors found her an attractive young woman with a marked individuality; too marked for the timid, for those who were not dismissed by her drew back and found brides elsewhere.

'Caroline is born for adversity; nothing would destroy her,' prophesied the Duchess, shaking her head.

The Duke looked at his daughter sombrely; it seemed to him that tragedy stalked the members of his house; two of his sons had been idiots, a third blind; they were dead, and the fourth, who survived, had a melancholy air as if he knew himself fated. The end of Charlotte, his elder daughter, was wrapped in mystery. The radiant bride, whom young John Stanley had seen, had vanished; strange stories were told of her sojourn in Russia, of a secret lover and a jealous Empress and of a sudden death in the cellar of a fortress. His daughter had disappeared, and no member of her family ever saw her again: not all the Duke's inquiries could come at the truth. He set his hopes on Caroline, who was obviously unhappy in the difficult position in which she found herself at Court.

The Duke loved his mistress, Mdlle. de Hertzfeldt, and was indifferent to his wife; he had loved and been proud of his natural son, and bitterly disappointed in his legitimate children. The Duchess complained to her daughter about the Duke's infidelities. Caroline despised her. She loved her father, but was afraid of him. Mdlle. de Hertzfeldt she could have loved, but found herself on very delicate ground. Between their loves and hates and jealousies she found her life unbearable and sought eagerly for a way of escape.

'The Prince of Wales seeks your hand in marriage, Caroline,' her father told her. 'If you wish to marry on the Continent, I never wish to get rid of you or send you away, but if you are determined to marry, this situation

seems sent by Providence for your advantage and you
should not slight it.'

'As a drowning wretch catches at a straw I caught at
this crown and sceptre,' the Princess Caroline told a
friend in later years.

No pressure was put on her to accept the offer; she
accepted it willingly, though with a heavy heart.

'I feel that I shall never be inexpressibly happy,' she
wrote to her friend. 'Estranged from my connections, my
associations, my friends, all that I hold dear and valuable,
I am about entering on a permanent connection. I fear
for the consequences. Yet I esteem and respect my
intended husband and I hope for great kindness and
attention. But, ah me, I say sometimes, I cannot *now*
love him with ardour. I am indifferent to my marriage,
but not averse to it; I think I shall be happy, but I fear
my joy will not be enthusiastic. The man of my choice I
am debarred from possessing, and I resign myself to my
destiny.'

Lord Malmesbury, who, as Sir James Harris, had once
before been called into consultation by the Prince of
Wales, was despatched to Brunswick to make formal
demand for the Princess Caroline's hand.

His instructions were from the King, and were ex-
plicit; he was given no discretionary powers to tender
advice or send information. Bitterly, later, he regretted it.

The Duke received him pleasantly, the Duchess with
enthusiasm. Caroline was much embarrassed on her
first presentation to the envoy. He found her 'pretty face
not expressive of softness, figure not graceful, fine eyes,
good hand, tolerable teeth but going, fair hair, and light
eyebrows, good bust, short, with what the French call

des épaules impertinentes, vastly happy with her future expectations.'

It was the Duchess who was happy; she could talk of nothing else, and she talked incessantly. The envoy found them all very agreable, though the Duke seemed a little odd. At a Court ball Malmesbury danced with Caroline, and played ombre with the Duchess. They supped at round tables, but the Duke did not stay for supper. He was wholly absorbed in military schemes.

The Duchess talked very indiscreetly, Malmesbury thought. She said that Edward, Duke of York, was her favourite brother; the King was very good, but not liable to deep impressions. The Queen she found detestable, an envious and intriguing spirit, who was extremely jealous of the Dowager Princess of Wales and herself and took an opportunity when the Princess of Wales was dying to alter the rank of the ladies of the bedchamber. Never would she, Augusta, forget the horrors of her mother's death and funeral.

Lord Malmesbury must, perforce, listen, but he answered as little as he dared. This was not the talk Caroline should hear of Queen Charlotte. The Duchess then turned to the marriage of her daughter, and acquainted him with all the injunctions and advice she had given her.

'All the young German princesses,' she said, 'have learnt English in the hopes of being Princess of Wales, but I never would give the idea to Caroline, and she never thought it could happen, as the King has often expressed his dislike to the marriage of cousins-germane.'

Lord Malmesbury left the Duchess with some relief, and called on Mdlle. de Hertzfeldt, who was an old

Berlin acquaintance. He found her clever and agreable, but full of lamentations and fears. She was chiefly concerned with the Duke's military ambitions: 'he had been cruelly used,' she said, 'and the King of Prussia was abominable in his behaviour.'

'I always thought him a *bête*, and not a *bon bête*.'

She talked of the state of Europe and of the *Iluminés* and their sects, and of the Duke's griefs and difficulties.

Letters came from England, and the Duke paid a formal call on Lord Malmesbury, who told him his instructions. The Duke nodded abstractedly, and took a paper from his pocket, which he said he wished to read to King George's envoy that he might be more *au fait* with his situation, and might better understand his refusal to take command of the Allied army, and the grounds on which it rested. It amounted to his thinking it impossible to be of use unless there was a renewal of the Convention with Prussia or unless a large body of Prussian troops was assured him.

'My situation is very difficult,' he said. 'Most serious consequences might follow to myself and family if I irritate the King of Prussia. I am afraid of the King of Prussia. I am afraid to take command of the Austrians. The men are good but the officers Jacobinically inclined. I fear that nonsensical sect of the *Iluminés* who were laughed at and treated too lightly in the beginning but have now taken such a root and acquired so many followers that they govern everywhere.'

The Duke was entirely absorbed in thoughts of the war; he seemed to have forgotten that the question of the moment was the marriage of his daughter. The envoy, who knew of his reputation as one of the bravest and most

famous soldiers on the Allied side, was astonished and
concerned at his indecision. England was as interested in
the war, however, as the Duke was, and Malmesbury had
had instructions to sound the Duke. He needed no
sounding, he could talk and think of nothing else. If the
French continued their victorious advance they might,
and probably would, overrun his Duchy; he simply could
not afford to offend the King of Prussia.

Lord Malmesbury was entertained with cards, walks,
dancing, the opera, while he waited for fresh instructions
from England. 'Princess Caroline improves on acquaintance,' he noted, 'is gay and cheerful with good sense.'

Except for the Duchess, all the Court of Brunswick
could talk of little else than the war and happenings in
France. There were letters from Paris with news of the
overthrow of the Jacobins on the 13th of November, and
of the noticeable reappearance of luxury, carriages, and
dress there. The horrors of the Revolution were over.
The Parisian ladies were throwing themselves feverishly
into the urgent question of fashions again; they were
discarding their corsets and petticoats, and waists were
creeping higher and higher; soon, indeed, it would be
the mode to wear nothing at all under one's muslin gown.

Lord Malmesbury, anxiously consulted by the Princess
Caroline, gravely assured her that such extremes of
fashion were never tolerated in England, where good
taste ruled the fashions, and Queen Charlotte set her face
firmly against any extravagance in dress.

Early in December, Major Hislop and a courier arrived
at Brunswick with urgent letters from the Prince of Wales,
who sent his picture and vehemently urged that his bride
should set out at once.

Europe was at war, Malmesbury thought drily, the Prince had evidently forgotten it, and that the bridal party must set out when there was a comparative lull in the hostilities. The moment, in fact, seemed fairly favourable. He requested a formal interview with the Duke, who was embarrassed, and the Duchess, who was in tears. At the betrothal ceremony Caroline was much affected, but replied distinctly and firmly.

Malmesbury played whist with the Duchess, and watched Princess Caroline, who now took the rank of Princess of Wales. There was a great supper at which the Duke appeared wearing the Garter. The Duke was certainly oddly indecisive for so famous a soldier.

'We depend on you, my lord, and you will assuredly do the right thing,' was his constant answer to Malmesbury's remarks.

The Duchess, nervous and agitated, recommended her daughter to his lordship and entreated him to be her adviser.

The Duke took him aside confidentially. 'I fully enter into her future situation. I am perfectly aware of the character of the Prince and of the inconvenience that would result, almost with equal ill effect, either from his liking the Princess too much or too little. There will be difficulty with the Queen, too, and perhaps with the Duchess of York. My daughter n'est pas bête, but she has no judgment. She has been brought up very strictly, and it has been necessary. I beg you, my lord, to recommend to her discretion not to ask questions and above all not to be free in giving opinions of persons and things aloud. The Duchess of Brunswick is, perhaps, apt to forget her audience and talk unreservedly; for my daughter in such different surroundings in England, such unreserve would probably be unwise.'

'Your daughter, sir, seems to me to have good sense.'

'She *will* ask questions. Advise her, my lord, never to show any jealousy of the Prince, and if he has any *goûts*, not to notice them. I have written her all this in German, so that there is no possibility of her misunderstanding, but enforced by you it will have double effect.'

After the Duke had finished, Mdlle. de Hertzfeldt began: 'You must be very strict with the Princess Caroline. She is not clever or ill disposed, but she has a temper easily wrought on, and she has *no tact*. Your advice will be better than the Duke's for, although she loves and respects him, she also fears him, and considers him a severe father. She has *no* respect for her mother, and is inattentive to her where she dares.'

Lord Malmesbury took Princess Caroline in to supper. She was very gay and lively, but turned to him with sudden seriousness: 'I beg you will guide and direct me, my lord.'

Malmesbury, full of misgivings, recommended a perfect silence on *all* subjects for six months after her arrival.

Lady Elizabeth Eden arrived from England, and told him that Lady Jersey was very well with the Queen, and had been appointed one of the Princess' ladies-in-waiting.

Lord Malmesbury was dismayed. 'If this is true it is *most strange*, and *bodes no good*,' he thought. If only he had been given discretionary powers and might have written his opinion to the King. He did not dare, but he gave more advice to Caroline. 'Avoid familiarity. Have no confidants, and avoid giving any opinion. Be perfectly

PRINCESS CAROLINE OF BRUNSWICK

To face page 100

silent on politics and party, very attentive and respectful
to the Queen, and try in all events to be well with her.'

Caroline took it all very well, but was rather tearful,
because she had been saying good-bye to her friends. She
earnestly meant to follow the advice given her. She took
great pains to find out the tastes of the Prince of Wales,
and model her behaviour upon them. She could not, of
course, see that she had undertaken the impossible. Lord
Malmesbury saw it. He found she improved very much
on acquaintance; she was cheerful and loved laughing,
and showed herself exceedingly good-humoured.

She embarrassed him by asking about Lady Jersey,
supposing her to be an *intrigante*, but knowing nothing of
any connection between her and the Prince of Wales.

He replied with an optimism which he was far from
feeling: 'With regard to Lady Jersey, she and all your
other ladies will frame their conduct towards you by
yours towards them. I do humbly advise that this should
not be familiar or too easy. Be affable, but never forget
that you are Princess of Wales. Never listen to them when
they attempt anything like a *commèrage*, and never allow
them to appear to influence your opinion by theirs.'

Caroline said wistfully: 'I should like to be popular.
I am afraid you recommend too much reserve. Probably
you think me too prone *à me livrer?*'

Malmesbury bowed.

'Tell me freely,' Caroline begged.

'To be frank, your Royal Highness, I do. It is an
amiable quality but one which cannot in your high situation be given way to without great risk. As to popularity,
it never was attained by familiarity. It can only belong
to respect. The Queen is a model in this way.'

'I am afraid of the Queen. I am sure she will be jealous of me and do me harm.'

'It is of the last consequence to be attentive towards her, to be always on your guard, never to fail in any exterior mark of respect towards her, or let drop an unconsidered word.'

The prospect appalled Caroline.

'I beg you will continue to be my mentor in England,' she said earnestly. 'I am determined never to be jealous. I know the Prince is *léger*, and am prepared on this point.'

Lord Malmesbury tried to reassure her. 'I do not believe you will have any occasion to use this very wise resolution. If any of the women about you' (he remembered Lady Jersey) 'should, from the love of fishing in troubled waters, endeavour to excite jealousy in your mind, on no account allow it to manifest itself. The surest way of recovering a tottering affection is softness, endurance, and caresses. I know enough of the Prince to be quite sure he could not withstand such a conduct, while a contrary one would probably make him disagreable and peevish, and certainly force him to be false and dissembling.'

Caroline promised docilely to bear it in mind. Her resolution was to spare no pains to make this marriage a success.

Mdlle. de Hertzfeldt, who had a genuine affection for her as well as a deep love for the Duke, repeated her warning to Malmesbury that the Princess needed *strictness*. 'I know you will not compromise me. I speak to you as an old friend. The Princess has never done anything wrong, but her speech is always quicker than her thought. In England they will put meanings into her words which were not there. She speaks wildly without realising what she is saying. I am devoted body and soul to the Duke. I have ruined myself for him. It is only the good of his family that I have at heart. He will be the unhappiest of men if this daughter does not succeed better than her elder sister. You know the story of the Princess Charlotte?' Malmesbury nodded, and she went on: 'I repeat this girl has never done anything wrong, but she has no judgment, and I fear the Queen. The Duchess here passes her time in thinking aloud, or in not thinking at all when she speaks. She does not love the Queen, and she has spoken too much about her to her daughter. As her happiness depends entirely on being well with the Queen, I entreat you, for God's sake repeat your advice to her constantly. She will listen to you. You make more impression on her than her father does. She fears him too much, just as she fears her mother not at all.'

The Duke, Malmesbury found, was always harping on one string, Prussia. When he remembered his daughter, it was to voice his misgivings. Malmesbury grew increasingly depressed. This was no wife for the Prince of Wales.

Caroline persisted that she wanted to be *loved* by the people. Malmesbury, knowing how such a thing would rouse the fury of the Prince, said sententiously: 'The sentiment of being loved by the people is a mistaken one. A great Princess can only be so by making herself respected and *rare*.'

'I shall never learn this,' sighed Caroline. 'I am too open, *trop légère*.'

Malmesbury was too discreet to confide his alarms to a letter, but he wrote in his diary: 'My eternal theme to her is to think before she speaks, to recollect herself. With a *steady* man she would do vastly well, but with one of a different description there are great risks. She takes advice well, but in the long run it must displease.'

Lord Malmesbury had his first difficulty over Mdlle. Rosenzweig, Caroline's *lectrice*, whom she wanted to accompany her to England. Both the King and the Prince were against it; the Prince positively forbade it. A German confidante was wholly undesirable.

Caroline was angry and hurt. The Duke and Duchess both pressed it. Lord Malmesbury produced his positive orders, and they gave way.

The Duke remarked nervously: 'The only reason I wished her to be with the Princess was that my daughter writes very ill, and spells ill, and I was desirous this should not appear. I suppose it is the Queen's doing.'

The Duchess was in tears, Caroline angry, and the Duke stalked away to avoid a scene. They were making the Queen a bogey to frighten the girl; in his heart Malmesbury was afraid they would prove right. The Duchess burst out suddenly: 'I have had an anonymous letter from England abusing the Prince, and warning me against Lady Jersey as the worst and most dangerous of profligate women. My daughter and I are uneasy and distressed.'

Malmesbury was dismayed. 'Madame, it is unwise to pay any attention to anonymous letters and imprudent to publish their contents.'

'The foolish old woman,' he thought, 'to show it to her daughter. It is the work of Mdlle. Rosenzweig in anger at being refused.'

The Duchess kept returning to the subject of the letter.

'Its object is to frighten the Princess with the idea that Lady Jersey would lead her into an affair of gallantry and be ready to be convenient on such an occasion.'

Malmesbury turned to Caroline. 'Lady Jersey would be more cautious than to risk such an audacious measure, and besides it is *death* to presume to approach a Princess of Wales and no man would be daring enough to think of it.'

Caroline opened her eyes: 'Are you in earnest?'

'Such is our law. Anyone who presumed to *love* a Princess of Wales would be guilty of *High Treason*, and punished with *death*, if she was weak enough to listen to him and so would *she*.'

The Princess looked startled, but the Duchess was sceptical. Had she not lived at Carlton House during the reign of Lord Bute?

THE MARRIAGE

They left Brunswick on 29th December, passing through a great crowd; cannon were fired, and loud cheering greeted the Princess. The Duke at the end forgot his preoccupation with military affairs and was deeply affected at parting with his daughter.

'Write to me, Malmesbury. Take care of her. Be her second father.'

Caroline clung to him, the tears raining down her cheeks. In spite of his sternness and her fear of him she adored him; in his way, it appeared, he loved her.

Malmesbury watched the Princess carefully, and noted her faults: 'She is very *gauche* at cards, calls the ladies, strangers to her, *mon cœur, ma chère, ma petite*.' It was not the royal manner, judged by Queen Charlotte's standard, in which *decorum* was the chief necessity. He, meaning well, advised until he bored himself and her. He summed her up sadly: 'Quick parts without a sound understanding, loving to talk and make *missish* friendships which last twenty-four hours. Some natural but no acquired morality and no strong innate notions of its value and necessity, warm feelings and nothing to counterbalance them; great good humour and much good nature. No appearance of caprice. Rather quick and *vive*, but not a grain of *rancour*. From her habits, from the life she was allowed and even compelled to live, forced to dissemble. In short the Princess in the hands of a steady and sensible man would probably turn out well, but when it is likely she will find faults perfectly analogous to her own, she will fail.'

Malmesbury's judgment was right. Caroline's faults and virtues were part of her; she was consistent. Twenty-five years later the verdict on her by those who wished her well was essentially the same.

Lord Malmesbury found the journey trying; the rivers were frozen, the roads were bad. It was bitterly cold, and the Duchess was extremely peevish. The way was full of delays and was dangerous because of the fluctuating fortunes of the war. The Princess was good-humoured, but, released from discipline, was very gay and missish. The unfortunate man had to deliver at least one sermon on decorum every day, chiefly about her lack of caution in conversation, her love of gossip, her too-quick friendships, her insatiable curiosity, her disrespect to her mamma. There were other matters which required more delicacy. Caroline's personal habits filled him with disgust. She had a tooth drawn, and sent it down to him by a page. He had arguments with her about her toilet. She prided herself on dressing quickly and he, mindful of that exquisite dandy, his master, disapproved of this. Caroline was obstinate. She would not take trouble. The harassed man, prevented by delicacy from being quite frank, sent Madame Busch to her to explain that the Prince was very delicate in his tastes and that he expected a long and very careful *toilette de propreté*.

Caroline thought it eccentric. 'Even in France they do not bath,' she remonstrated. 'I have heard there was but one bath-tub in Versailles, and that they grew flowers in it.'

'They think a great deal of washing in England, Madame. The Prince is very particular on that score.'

Caroline laughed, and with her usual good humour washed herself all over in order to oblige the Prince of Wales.

Malmesbury felt called upon to drive the lesson home. He knew she wore coarse petticoats, coarse shifts, and thread stockings, and these were never well washed nor changed often enough. He lectured her on cleanliness, on delicacy, and on the importance of the toilette. She flushed a little, but as usual took it in good part.

'I will listen to advice from *you*,' she said, 'but I do not like it from others.'

Malmesbury, almost against his will, had grown to like her. Never had he found a woman so cheerful, so *accommodante*, so pleasant in uncomfortable circumstances, so devoid of fear and of complaint as his charge.

The long, delayed, and trying journey overland came to an end at last, and they embarked on the *Jupiter*, whose officers declared they would have had more trouble with any London lady than Her Royal Highness gave. The sailors were delighted with her good humour and her enjoyment when they chased some French privateers. She was immensely popular on board.

Mrs. Harcourt, the Queen's friend, who attended her, and who might have been prejudiced against her, declared that the Princess reminded her of Mrs. Fitzherbert when young – the comparison was meant as praise.

'She is all openness of heart, and has not a shadow of pride,' she said.

Lord Malmesbury was doubtful if that were desirable. 'That is one of my fears,' he said thoughtfully. 'She is too free. In her position she *ought* to have some pride.'

'She is so good-humoured, so perfectly void of art or design,' protested the lady.

'Will that please the Prince?' his lordship asked drily. Mrs. Harcourt was silent.

The voyage was an enchantment for the Princess Caroline; she had a passionate love of the sea, and her popularity on board the *Jupiter* delighted her after the small liberty and importance she had had at home.

If she had had only to do with men all might have been well, but at Greenwich Lord Malmesbury stepped into the background and the women began to take chief parts.

The King's coaches had not arrived. My Lady Jersey had delayed them in order to arrive insultingly late. When she appeared, without apology, she began to find fault with the Princess Caroline's attire. She proceeded to dress her victim in a white gown which did not suit her; she would have added an unbecoming turban, but the Princess insisted on wearing her beaver, which looked incongruous with the gown. Lady Jersey succeeded, however, in rouging her cheeks which, with Caroline's naturally fresh colour, made her look florid and coarse.

Mrs. Harcourt protested. Lady Jersey was rude.

My Lady put her hand to her head and protested that she could not possibly ride in the coach with her back to the horses. On Caroline's lips hovered an invitation to sit by her side.

Lord Malmesbury thought it time to intervene: 'It will

give me great pleasure if your ladyship will ride in the coach sent for Claremont and myself. Mrs. Aston and Mrs. Harcourt can accompany Her Royal Highness.'

Lady Jersey gave him a sour look, and took her proper place in the Princess' coach. It was unfortunate that Lord Malmesbury did not insist on the arrangement he had proposed, for the journey, short as it was, proved long enough for Caroline to pave the way to disaster.

Lady Jersey's tactics at Greenwich had made the Princess nervous. Commodore Jack Payne of the *Jupiter* had enlightened her as to her ladyship's relations with the Prince. Caroline remembered her resolve to show no jealousy. She was quick enough to see that her marriage might be made or marred by this lovely, brilliant woman, of whom she had heard such sinister tales, and who obviously regarded her with disdain. The Princess made the initial mistake of trying to conciliate her rival and at the same time trying to impress her with her own wide experience and knowledge of the world. She forgot Lord Malmesbury's counsels, and with incredible folly confided in her rival, telling her a long, exciting, and largely fictitious tale of her own deep love for a young German soldier whom it was, of course, impossible for her to marry. Lady Jersey's malice encouraged her with leading questions. The Princess was all sympathy for a tender passion which must be conducted under the rose. Poor Caroline!

They drove almost unnoticed through the streets of London.

At St. James' there was no one to receive them. Lord Malmesbury sent for the Prince, who came at once. In accordance with etiquette no one else was in the room when Lord Malmesbury presented the Princess to the Prince. Caroline, remembering her instructions, fell upon her knees. The Prince raised her, gracefully enough, and embraced her. Then, to her astonishment, retired to the other end of the room crying out: 'Harris, I am not well, pray get me a glass of brandy.'

Lord Malmesbury was shocked. 'Sir, had you not better have a glass of water?' he ventured.

The Prince swore. 'No! By God! I will go directly to the Queen.' Without looking at the Princess he rushed from the room.

Poor Caroline, amazed and dismayed, turned to Lord Malmesbury. '*Mon Dieu. Est-ce que le Prince est toujours comme cela? Je le trouve très gros et nullement aussi beau que son portrait.*'

'The Prince is overcome by the emotions of a first interview,' Lord Malmesbury lied with more heroism than conviction. 'He will be quite different at dinner when you meet him again.'

Lady Jersey had been with the Queen. The Queen, triumphant, with an air of 'What did I say?' behind her decorum, condoled with the Prince.

At dinner the Prince's manner, if possible, seemed worse. The Princess, too, had had a shock and the result was, as Malmesbury had feared, to drive all his advice out of her head. She was flippant, rattling, affecting raillery and wit, throwing out vulgar hints about Lady Jersey and quizzing the Prince about his fancy. Malmesbury, fully alive to the disaster, was unable to check her. 'No. When I saw my *futur* and her ladyship together I knew how it was, and I took my *partie*,' she said obstinately.

Lady Jersey said nothing, but missed nothing, and with eyes and brows was eloquent indeed.

The Prince made his disgust quite evident. Poor, nervous, tactless Caroline plunged wildly on towards her doom. From dislike and distaste the Prince passed to loathing and hatred under Lady Jersey's bright, malicious eyes; her victory was won without a single battle.

She carried the news of their joint victory to the Queen.

The King liked his niece. He only asked Lord Malmesbury one question: 'Is she good-humoured?'

'In the most trying moments I have never seen her otherwise.'

'I am glad of it.'

He turned back to his politics with relief. The Prince would settle down. Parliament would pay his debts, and his wife would provide him with an heir. The King was satisfied. Indeed, being simple in his own tastes, he liked Caroline's openness.

Lord Malmesbury's part was played. He went home filled with foreboding, and regret. He wished well to both of them; he had done his best; yet after the first meeting he entered in his diary: 'It is impossible to conceive or foresee any comfort from this connection, in which I lament very much having taken any share, purely passive as it was.'

The Queen greeted the Princess with extreme coldness. Her daughters held themselves persistently aloof. Caroline was more excitable than ever. Lady Jersey had slyly put spirits in her drink without her knowledge. The lady-in-waiting whispered that she must try to please the Prince. Caroline had heard that he admired long hair;

her own was beautiful; she shook it down about her shoulders.

'You should have seen the poor man's face,' she said afterwards, between dismay and mirth.

A crowd assembled outside her window. Delighted, she bowed repeatedly. The Prince hastily shut the window and said that she was too fatigued. She designed to steal his popularity, did she? He cast her a vindictive look.

'I do not like your shoes,' he said.

'Make me a better pair and bring them to me,' she retorted.

On the day before the wedding the Prince rode past Mrs. Fitzherbert's house. The windows were shuttered.

The Princess had too much spirit to make a parade of her dismay. If she wept, she wept in secret. She thought, too, that after the wedding he would be different. Too many people were interested in the matter for her to be unaware of the truth. Lady Jersey was the present and most disagreable stumbling-block to her happiness, but in the background was the far more serious question of the Prince's other wife. Caroline heard nothing but good of her and, of course, could obtain no confirmation of the tale of the secret marriage. Those who knew the secret kept their lips tight sealed. In any case she would not have regarded it as a serious impediment to her own marriage with him. She was completely ignorant of the laws of England; such a left-handed marriage was at once legal and no bar to a state marriage in Germany.

Caroline dressed for her wedding gravely but without despair.

All eyes were on her curiously. She talked cheerfully

to the Duke of Clarence as she waited at the altar for
the Prince. He came, so drunk that the Dukes of Rox-
burgh and Bedford had to hold him up. He wept when
the Archbishop asked solemnly if there were any just
impediment. The Primate, ill at ease, repeated twice the
injunction to forsake all other but his wife.

The Princesses squeezed their hoops with great difficulty through the narrow passage left for the procession.
'The Prince looked like Death,' they whispered.

Caroline was the only cheerful person present. She
hoped the marriage ceremony would put everything
right.

A messenger went to Mrs. Fitzherbert with the news
that the wedding had actually taken place. To the end
she had not believed it could. She gazed incredulously at
the messenger, swayed, and fell in a deep swoon.

The bridal supper was like a funeral feast, with Lady
Jersey alone getting some grim amusement out of her
own taste in practical jokes; she had added Epsom salts
to the bride's supper, a jest which would, she hoped,
inevitably seal the unloved bride's fate.

The Prince of Wales reeled drunk to the bridal chamber and fell into the fireplace, where the bride left him
the greater part of the night. In the early morning the
pages in the outer chamber heard loud voices, the door
burst open, and the Prince rushed out wildly. Rumours
spread like wildfire.

Caroline was too frank for the comfort of her ladies, but
she never wholly lifted the veil from the secret of that
bridal night. The Prince carried his tale to pour into the
ears of Beau Brummell. The Beau had the decency to
keep it to himself, but he wrote it in his diary. Years later

a muck-raker sought high and low for that diary. The book was lost. It may be in existence still.

Whispers made a mystery of that night, and drew fantastic stories out of it, and strange theories which cast uneasy doubts on the legitimacy of the heir to the throne.

Caroline herself aided the whisperers. 'I began to be with child, and I did not believe it,' she confided indiscreetly. Why did she not believe it? The whisperers began again and more loudly.

Poor Caroline loved to make a mystery where no mystery was. She did not dare to believe it because it was the thing she desired above all others, and she was so unhappy that she could not believe fortune would be so kind to her. Her love of little children was accounted an absurdity; it was indeed sufficiently excessive to appear absurd. To have a child of her own was her most fervent wish. The hope came into a prospect which was darker than anything she could have imagined. The gay, good-humoured Princess was as miserable as it was possible for her to be. Her courage alone kept her from despair. Her husband refused to act the part of her husband; he flaunted Lady Jersey before her face in every circumstance of insult and humiliation. He brought into her house, where she was attended only by Lady Jersey, a crowd of drunken boon companions who snored on her sofas with their boots on, and treated her with no courtesy at all. He took her jewels from her, and gave them to Lady Jersey in front of her. He set spies on her and mocked in her presence at the tales they brought of her indiscretions and personal habits. He, who frequented the bagnios of Covent Garden, was exceedingly gross because he found her not scrupulously clean.

The Princess faced her situation with dignity and silence. The Queen was unkind and did not visit her; the Princesses were distant; only the King was kind and willing to be her friend, but she would not worry him with her troubles. She confided in no one until a new distress faced her. She hugged her secret joy in the child who was coming until she was told that it would not belong to her. Then she wept a little and wrote to one of the friends of her girlhood:

'I do not know how I shall be able to bear the hours of loneliness, only I trust in the Almighty. The Queen seldom visits me, and my sisters-in-law show me the same sympathy. But I admire the character of the English and nothing can be more flattering than the reception which is given me when I appear in public. . . . I am surrounded by miserable, evil minds, and everything I do is put in a bad light. The Countess is still here. I hate her, and I know she feels the same towards me. My husband is wholly given up to her, and so you can easily guess the rest. . . . The Prince wishes for a son, but I do not mind, for according to the English laws the parents will have little to do with the child in the future. I am so afraid of what is coming. . . .'

The Prince had a fresh grievance against her. He had married her in order to have his debts paid. Parliament refused to pay them, but insisted that he should pay them himself out of the increased allowance; but as the House did not trust him to pay, a proportion of his allowance was deducted at source. He was insulted and aggrieved; he blamed his wife.

To her mother, Caroline threw the best light she could upon her situation, but she was very funny and indiscreet on the subject of the Queen. 'Old Snuffy' was as terrible as even the Duchess of Brunswick had reported, and on that, at least, she need keep nothing back from her mother. She could make the Queen as ridiculous and disagreable as she chose. Even so much frankness was a relief, and she dispatched the letter by a trusted messenger.

The letter, by a series of accidents, came into the hands of Lady Jersey, who promptly carried it to the Queen. 'Old Snuffy' had no hesitation in reading other people's letters and she did not like what she read.

The Princess of Wales was made to feel that she was in complete disgrace.

The position was intolerable; her high spirit would not brook it. She refused to dine with Lady Jersey unless the Prince were present. He stormed and insisted; Caroline at last begged the King to remove her obnoxious lady-in-waiting.

The Prince promptly retired with her to Brighton, where her insolence knew no bounds. The Prince's secretary, Tyrwhitt, remonstrated; the lady fainted from sensibility. Tyrwhitt was obliged to go.

On January 7th, 1796, the Princess Charlotte was born. The Princess of Wales' labour was long and difficult, and the Prince showed some agitation, though his emotion took the uncomfortable form of precipitately hurrying his wife from place to place the week before her confinement, to the fury of the King.

With her child on her arm the Princess bloomed into beauty. For this darling she would willingly go through misery a thousand times worse than anything she had suffered yet.

'My darling, my sweet, my treasure,' she whispered.

The baby was christened. The Princess left her bed and prepared to take up the burden of her life once more.

Lady Cholmondeley, the Chamberlain's wife, came to her in great distress, entrusted with an abominable message which she was at a loss how to deliver. She blurted it out at last in all its brutality: 'The Prince sends a message, madam, that he does not intend ever again to treat you as his wife.'

Wide-eyed, the Princess stared at her: 'I should prefer to have the Prince's message in writing,' she said at last calmly. 'Then I shall be sure I understand it.'

Lady Cholmondeley, shocked and embarrassed, brought the letter which her husband had received from the Prince.

Caroline read it with unmoved face.

'Our inclinations are not in our power,' he wrote, 'nor should either of us be held answerable to the other because nature has not made us suitable to each other. Tranquil and comfortable society is, however, in our power; let our intercourse therefore be restricted to that, and I will distinctly subscribe to the condition which you required through Lady Cholmondeley, that, even in the event of any accident happening to my daughter, which I trust Providence in his mercy will avert, I shall not infringe the terms of the restriction by proposing at any period a connection of a more particular nature. I shall now finally close this disagreable correspondence, trusting that, as we have completely explained ourselves to each other, the rest of our lives will be passed in uninterrupted tranquillity.'

A letter not without dignity; Caroline, judging by his

conduct, thought he could not have composed it himself. Her eyes sparkled.

'I am free,' she said gaily. 'It is a great relief. But I will be safe. The King must hear of this. Help me to write an answer to my husband, Lady Cholmondeley. It must be well expressed.'

'. . . I should have returned no answer to your letter if it had not been conceived in such terms as to make it doubtful whether this arrangement proceeds from you or from me; and you are aware that the credit of it belongs to you alone. The letter which you announce to me as the last obliges me to communicate to the King, as to my Sovereign and my Father, both your avowal and my answer. You will find enclosed the copy of my letter to the King. I apprise you of it that I may not incur the slightest reproach of duplicity from you.'

'Thank God, I am free. I shall go to my villa at Charlton,' said the Princess.

Lord and Lady Cholmondeley were discreet, but Carlton House was full of eavesdroppers and gossips. The town heard the whole story in the course of a day or two; the mob knew it in a week. No one doubted where the blame lay. The Princess had an ovation each time she appeared. When she visited the opera there was a great demonstration.

Caroline, having won her freedom, did not want to widen the breach between her husband and herself. She would have retired. The Duke of Leeds, however, persuaded her to stand up and curtsey. The house rose, and every man and woman in it clapped incessantly.

Lord Malmesbury, had he been present, might have smiled ruefully: the Princess had won the love of the people for which she once had craved, but it was through her griefs, of which, then, she had not dreamed.

The people felt enraged at the treatment she had received.

'It was well *two* other persons, the Prince and Lady Jersey, were not there, as insults were loudly declared to be intended, and on their not appearing, God save the *King* was called for and sung with the same view. Their Majesties were not there, or a third person, the Queen, might have heard something unpleasant, as the town had got a notion of too much favouring Lady Jersey at least,' wrote Horace Walpole, relishing the scandal.

The Prince of Wales was furious. The Princess had rejoiced too soon; she might be free from personal intercourse with her husband, but she was not free from his control. He chose the members of her household, and could, and at the first opportunity did, forbid her to enter his house or to see her child. Caroline loved her little Charlotte passionately, but even while the child was still an infant seldom saw her more than once a week.

The Prince, finding himself so unpopular in London, retired to Brighton. Presently he would be able to persuade himself that he was not unpopular but, in the first moment of the shock, he saw the truth. Henceforward he and the Londoners were enemies.

For once he blamed the next most blameworthy person – he was, of course, incapable of blaming himself. Lady Jersey had over-reached herself. His vindictive temper sought revenge on her. His coldness was obvious. Society cold-shouldered her. The story of her share in the scandal was known to the mob. She was exceedingly unpopular and her carriages and servants were pelted with mud.

'Lady Jersey is now in the Transit of Venus,' said a wit. The *mot* flew round.

The position grew unbearable. The Prince was distant. Lady Jersey handed in her resignation from the household.

The Prince of Wales cut her in a public place and, when she was persistent, sent McMahon with a curt message: 'It is the Prince's desire that you should not speak to him.'

Lady Jersey was dropped. With a shrug of her shoulders she delivered a parting thrust: 'The Prince is a sequence: King, Queen, and Knave.'

Caroline, as well as the Prince's household, knew why Lady Jersey was dismissed. The Princess of Wales' husband was anxious to return to his lawful wife. It was a tribute to Caroline's real greatness of heart as well as an odd comment on her tolerant morality that she had liking and admiration for Mrs. Fitzherbert.

'I hope my husband will not feel me any impediment to the reconciliation he is so desirous for,' she said, not entirely in irony.

He certainly did not, but Mrs. Fitzherbert was not so easily re-won. She had never believed that the marriage with Princess Caroline could take place; when it had, something died in her.

In spite of the Princess' charitable hope, Mrs. Fitzherbert refused to see the Prince. He became dramatic, wept, stormed, threatened to reveal the secret marriage. Mrs. Fitzherbert was exceedingly alarmed. The ad-

mirable woman was not prepared to vindicate herself at
the cost of such incredible embarrassment to the State,
distress to the Royal Family, an intolerable position for
the Princess Caroline and the baby Charlotte. She was
wise enough, too, to see that conditions had changed.
Public sympathy which might once have been enlisted
on the Prince's side, had definitely turned against him
now. Society and the mob, for once, were in accord.

Mrs. Fitzherbert loved him, and was sorry for him; the
very magnitude of his errors and their consequences made
her long to recover her influence over him and lead him
back to the excellent ways he had abandoned when he
had abandoned her.

She could not make up her mind. She sent to Rome
for guidance, and let the decision pass out of her hands.

The Popes had learnt the folly of interference in the
matrimonial affairs of English princes when Henry VIII
showed how *he* could treat an interfering Pope. France
had taught the reigning Bishop of Rome that it was no
time for the spiritual powers to defy the temporal ones.
He was anxious only to recover what he had lost, not to
involve himself in fresh trouble. Mrs. Fitzherbert was
insistent. The Pope told her messenger that her marriage
was lawful, but he wisely kept no written record of his
decision. Nevertheless the *viva voce* statement was accepted
by the English Catholics, who said pretty loudly that
Mrs. Fitzherbert was the Prince's lawful wife, and that
the Princess of Wales was not legally married. The
English law said otherwise, and the Princess of Wales had
no occasion to be alarmed because the unpopular
Catholics cast doubt upon the validity of her marriage.
The Papal decision, however, enabled Mrs. Fitzherbert

to return to *her* husband with a clear conscience. His conscience does not appear to have troubled him at all.

The two women thought of each other often and long. Caroline without envy, since she did not love Mrs. Fitzherbert's husband, yet wistfully because she craved for love more than anything in the world.

Mrs. Fitzherbert thought of the Princess compassionately since she had been so abominably cheated, yet with disapprobation because she took such unroyal ways of seeking distraction. She herself had invariably been dignified; Caroline was not dignified at all.

The two women had nothing in common but a negative quality – a lack of pettiness and malice in a petty and malicious world. Caroline was a disturbing, passionate woman; Mrs. Fitzherbert tranquil and invariably cool. The Princess was a young woman and had virtually had no married life; Mrs. Fitzherbert was over forty and had had three husbands, each of whom had been devoted to her. The balance of gifts was undoubtedly on Mrs. Fitzherbert's side, yet Caroline had Charlotte and Maria had no child of her own.

Mrs. Fitzherbert devoted earnest and troubled consideration to her own conduct and its probable effect upon the unhappy Princess. Nevertheless in January 1800, she gave a public breakfast 'to meet the Prince of Wales' and announce the resumption of their connection. For eight more years she was again a devoted wife to an intermittently devoted husband.

They withdrew from London to Brighthelmstone, which grew from a village to a town. People, other than the Prince's friends, viewed it with mirth and amazement.

'There are great additions to Brighthelmstone since I

was there last,' said Lord Glenbervie after a visit of
inspection in 1801. 'The Prince is now adding two large
bulges or bow window rooms to each end of his house
fronting the Steine, and also throwing out two bows in
the back.'

Grave Mr. Wilberforce delivered himself of a witticism
that made him more popular than any discourse upon
slavery or saints: 'A remarkable building,' he said, eyeing
the Pavilion with lifted eyebrows. 'As though St. Paul's
Cathedral had had a litter of cupolas.'

Mrs. Fitzherbert, though restored to favour, had less
influence than she had had in former years. The fashionable world treated her with some coldness, in which the
Prince, himself, shared to some extent. The truth of the
matter was that he had begun to run to seed. He had
been, when she married him, a bad man with brilliant
qualities; the badness remained, but the brilliance had
faded. Duchess Georgiana and Charles Fox were no
longer his intimates; Sheridan was going downhill even
faster than his Prince. His intimates, nowadays, were of
a different quality. Mrs. Fitzherbert was not happy.

The Prince's life was ruled by caprice and two permanent occupations – an indecent eagerness to snatch
the Crown from his father, and a mean, underground
plotting to rid himself of the Princess of Wales. In the
interval of waiting for success in these hopes he must kill
time.

The fate of Europe hung in the balance while England
and France grappled. The Prince's interest was theatrical;
he was anxious to don military uniform, and to champion
Nelson's Lady Hamilton in the face of a shocked and
angry world. He demanded the right to serve in his own

army; the King, obstinately, yet not unnaturally, refused. Mr. Pitt regarded the Prince as distrustfully as ever, the question of the Regency during the King's recurring attacks of illness was an ever-open sore.

The Prince designed the uniforms which he was not allowed to wear. He had always had a passion for dress; the passion became a mania. The most intimate of his new friends had no other passion.

BOOK III

PRINNEY'S NEW FRIEND

In 1794 the Prince of Wales met Mr. Brummell at Devonshire House, where he was a great favourite. After that he met him on the Terrace at Windsor and then caught sight of him when he paused to see the cows milked at a small cottage, on the Piccadilly side of the Green Park, where the handsome young man was visiting his aunt, whose house it was.

The Prince was charmed with him, and, learning that he was to be a soldier, promised him a commission. He was as good as his word, and George Brummell was presented with a cornetcy in the Tenth Dragoons of which His Royal Highness was colonel-in-chief.

The Tenth Light Dragoons was, of course, the pink of fashion; among its officers were Lord Petersham, who had taught the Prince the art of mixing and sniffing his snuff as well as the necessity of varying his snuff-boxes according to the season, Lord Edward Somerset, Lord Charles Ker, Lord Charles Manners, and Lord Robert Manners, with all of whom George Brummell cemented friendships which were broken only by death.

He had some fame already; they told stories of his Eton days where his fastidiousness both in dress and behaviour had won him the respectful tribute of the nickname of 'Buck' Brummell. There were anecdotes of his school-

days which had preceded him, of his famous toasted
bread and cheese and his prowess at cricket, of the noted
encounter between some Etonians and a bargee, when
the boys, ready to throw their enemy into the river, were
arrested by the Buck's languid 'My good fellows, don't
send him into the river, for the man is evidently in a high
state of perspiration, and it almost amounts to a certainty that he will catch cold,' and released their victim
in a gale of laughter.

His wit had the rare merit of being free from malice.
Despite his humble birth his mess-mates liked him.

It was not arduous soldiering, for the regiment was
nearly always stationed in the neighbourhood of its
royal colonel, either in London or Brighton. The cornet
did not take his military duties very seriously; wags even
protested that he did not know by sight the troop to
which he was attached. He broke his beautiful Roman
nose when thrown from his horse at a Grand Review. If
he was not useful, however, he was ornamental, and his
gifts put him, of course, into the innermost circle of the
Prince's set.

Mr. Brummell accompanied Lord Edward Somerset,
who was in command of the escort sent to bring Princess
Caroline from Greenwich to London, and at the wedding
was in attendance on the Prince. He said Princess
Caroline was 'a handsome and desirable-looking woman'
and his tribute was of value.

In his ear the Prince poured the story of his wedding
night. He was never the Princess' enemy, though he
remained the Prince's friend.

Mr. Brummell found his duties as a soldier, lightly as
he took them, exceedingly irksome. He desired to change

his club to White's; he objected to powdered hair, which was still compulsory in the army. He objected even more to residing in such a spot as Manchester when the regiment was ordered there.

In 1798 he requested his royal master's leave to resign. The Prince, reluctantly, consented.

Buck Brummell was at last free to give the rein to his ambition. He had set his heart on being the arbiter of fashion, the beau of beaux. He chose his point of vantage well; he chose his hour of attack even better. Chesterfield Street still echoed with anecdotes of those distinguished men – Horace Walpole, the king of letter-writers, and George Selwyn, the king of wits. The aspirant king of fashion took a lease of No. 4 in the street to which the latter had given additional fame, and perfected his plans.

One fine morning George Brummell set out quietly from his home and strolled nonchalantly down St. James' Street. Heads turned, eyes started, mouths opened. A new era had begun. Mr. Brummell's cravat was *different*. 'Instead of a bandage round the neck, a towel tied under the chin, a limp loose rag, a covering rather than an ornament, Mr. Brummell's cravat had an exquisite, crisp precision; in a frolicsome wind, beneath innumerable bowings, it remained undisturbed, immaculate, in elaborate, neat folds.'

In St. James' Street, in the clubs, in the fashionable houses, and in a widening circle to the perilous fringes of the modish world there was but one question: 'How is it done? How is the muslin made to retain its place?'

Every one had a suggestion to offer; every one rushed away to experiment in secret; there were tears of mortification and curses of rage as failure after failure attended

frantic efforts to produce a rival cravat. The secret was
well kept. Not until Mr. Brummell's name had been
dinned repeatedly into the ears of every man who was in,
or who aspired to enter, the world of fashion, did that
gentleman whisper into a friend's ear the magic word,
'*Starch*.'

The Prince of Wales had made his bow with a new shoe
buckle. 'Beau' Brummell was launched with a more
world-shattering invention than that.

No. 4 Chesterfield Street became the School for Cravats,
The Beau was modest over his achievement. He acknowledged that he had been practising for months in the
privacy of his dressing-room behind locked doors. His
valet, sworn to secrecy, had carried away armful after
armful of crumpled muslin pieces which he collected
mournfully as 'Our failures.' Even now, sometimes a
finger slipped and perfection was spoiled. But not often.
To the dressing-room of the arbiter of fashion the eager
pupils trooped; not all of them, perhaps, fully alive to
the importance of the occasion. Was there not a satirical
undercurrent in one student's description of the lesson
which found its way into the Press:

'The collar which was always fixed to his shirt was so
large that, before being folded down, it completely hid
his head and face, and the white neckcloth was at least
a foot in height. The first *coup d'archet* was made with the
shirt collar which he folded down to its proper size, and
Brummell, then standing before the glass, with his chin
poked up to the ceiling, by the gentle and gradual
declension of his lower jaw, creased the cravat to reasonable dimensions, the form of each succeeding crease being
perfected with the shirt which he had just discarded.'

That was from one inside the magic circle. Embittered outcasts might be as satirical as they pleased:

'What an apparent superiority does not a starcher give to a man! It gives him a look of *hauteur* and greatness which can scarcely be acquired otherwise. This is produced solely by the austere rigidity of the cravat, which, so far, by any means, from yielding to the natural motions of the head, forms a strong support to the cheeks. It pushes them up and gives a rotundity of appearance to the whole *figure*, thereby unquestionably giving a man the air of being puffed up with pride, vanity, and conceit (very necessary, nay indispensable qualifications for a man of fashion), and appearing as quite towering over the rest of mankind and holding his fellow creatures covered with the deep disgrace of his disgust. I need only appeal to any common observer to prove the veracity of the above assertions. Let any person take a stroll up and down some fashionable street of the Metropolis at the proper time of day, and remark the men who do and who do not wear starchers. What a conscious sense of their own superiority in the former. What a full conviction of their own paltriness and insignificance in the latter.'

The starched cravat was epoch-making.

The Prince of Wales was one of the earliest of Brummell's pupils. The Beau took infinite pains with him, curbing, as far as he could, his pupil's taste for the extravagant and bizarre.

'Sir,' he begged earnestly, 'be simple.'

That was too hard a lesson for the Prince. Witty Luttrell told the Beau that his pupil was so well dressed that people turned to look at him. Brummell sighed. 'Then he was not well dressed,' he murmured.

After that first sensational stroll down St. James' to trumpet the arrival of a new power, it was his proud boast that he never attracted attention in the street, that he could walk from his house to his Club without being noticed.

'If John Bull turns round to look after you, you are not well dressed, but either too stiff, too tight, or too fashionable.'

Since he wished to keep the Prince's friendship, it was perhaps fortunate that his tastes were quiet. George of Wales liked to be noticeable; George Brummell preferred to be inconspicuous. Prinney could admire and copy, with embellishment, and yet not regard his master as a rival. In time, indeed, he had imagined himself into the master's rôle.

George Brummell, from the day of his appearance in a starched cravat, became the despot of fashion. He could, with a look, make or mar the reputation of a would-be dandy, raise a tailor from poverty to wealth.

Mr. Pitt, looking round desperately for a new source of revenue to pay for the war, had put a tax on hair powder; Beau Brummell put the nails into the lid of the coffin of that tax. The Beau did not powder; powder ceased to be worn.

Mr. Brummell looked at other items of the toilet with disapproval; the collar of the shirt was too low; he raised it, and added a frill to the shirt itself.

How many heads had tumbled into the baskets under the guillotine? The fashionable world did not know; but Mr. Brummell did know, with disgust, that the rule of the *sans-culottes* had brought a certain slovenliness of attire in its train, and that that deplorable feature of the Revolution had spread to England. '*Sans-culottes!*' He set about tightening the pantaloon and improving the knee-breeches and silk stockings of evening attire. An afterthought banished knee-breeches; only at Court, at the opera, and at Almack's were knee-breeches and *chapeau bras* correct wear after King Brummell had reigned ten years.

Next he introduced white tops instead of brown tops into the hunting field. Each change he made was well considered, carefully planned as a commander-in-chief might plan a campaign, modified if necessary (though it seldom was necessary), polished, until the perfection of elegant simplicity was attained. Mr. Brummell's religion was simplicity; and all who met him for the first time, having heard of him with awe, were astonished at the plainness, the studied elegance of his simplicity. Others might indulge themselves in the Napoleon, the Mail-coach or Waterfall, the *Trône d'Amour*, the Osbaldeston cravats; might copy his severity, without such happy results, in the Mathematical tie, or fall into absurdity with the Oriental tie, which was so high that the wearer, if he were tall, could not see where he was going, and so rigid that he could not turn his head. Mr. Brummell could gently quiz the absurd one.

Not of him had the satirist written:

'They've made him a dandy,
　A thing you know, whiskered, great-coated, and lac'd
Like an hour-glass, exceedingly small in the waist;
　Quite a new sort of creature, unknown yet to
　　scholars,
With heads so immovably stuck in their collars
　That seats like our music-stools soon must be found
　　them
To twirl when the creatures wish to look round them.'

Brummell read and smiled, and went on polishing his craft with delicate exactitude.

Prinney, admiring, aped but could not equal. He threw himself into the art with his whole soul. Mrs. Fitzherbert had a rival, more dangerous, because less transitory, than another woman. How could love, an old love, compete with this delicious business of setting fashions, of stealing the empire of fashion from blood-soaked France? Prinney tightened his corsets, conferred with Beau Brummell, and put the seal of his approval upon the sartorial rules which Mr. Brummell had laid down:

'In the morning a gentleman of fashion must wear pantaloons with Hessians or top boots, or buckskins with a blue coat and a light or buff-coloured waistcoat; in the evening, blue coat and white waistcoat, black pantaloons made of stockinette, buttoning tight round the ankle, striped silk stockings, and opera hat.' The tricorne was quite dead.

In dowdy circles there was some talk of Napoleon's campaigns and of a young sailor named Nelson who had covered himself with glory. The Prince was engaged with Brummell as to the amount of jewellery permissible with the new attire.

Mrs. Fitzherbert failed to appreciate the enormous importance of this point. The Prince began to think she might, after all, be a little stupid. Lady Hertford, now, fully entered into his feelings in the matter; *there* was a woman who understood him and was both sympathetic and intelligent. Mrs. Fitzherbert, of course, was still useful as a confidante; he wept out the story of his love for Lady Hertford upon her shoulder.

He drowned his woe at the lady's (temporary) rejection of his love by giving parties at the Pavilion. Sherry was still great fun; though fifty-five he was as merry as a boy. First he came to the Pavilion disguised as a police officer to take up Lady Sefton for playing some unlawful game; then, when there was a phantasmagoria and all were shut up in perfect darkness, he sat himself upon the lap of a haughty Russian dame who made hubbub enough for all the town to hear.

Among other people who came to the Pavilion in 1805 were Mr. and Mrs. Hastings. Prinney introduced Sheridan to Warren Hastings, which seemed an odd thing to do, as Sherry's parliamentary fame had been built upon his celebrated speech against Hastings.

Old Thurlow was there, dressed in a full suit of clothes of the old fashion, great cuffs and massy buttons, great wig, long ruffles, with black eyebrows of enormous size and a voice like the roll of thunder, ready to do battle with Sir Philip Francis, whom half the world believed to be that rattlesnake 'Junius.'

Thomas Creevey, that pillar of the Whigs, was there, coining amusing phrases for his letters to his friends.

The Prince, just back from a visit to Weymouth, was very indiscreet in his talk about the King's infirmities.

'He is so blind that he nearly fell into a hole at Lord Dorchester's.'

'Poor man, sir,' said Mr. Creevey pointedly.

The Prince stared, and changed the subject.

The ladies, as usual, found Prinney very agreable.

After supper the Prince led all the party to the table, where the maps lay, to see him shoot with an air-gun at a target placed at the end of the room.

Then the band played a waltz, and he offered to dance with Miss Johnstone, but once round the room made him giddy, and his partner was glad to sit down.

Mrs. Fitzherbert was playing cards as usual. The Prince kept his rooms as hot as an oven, and nearly made her faint, but she put on no airs to be interesting and very soon recovered.

Sherry asked George Hanger: 'How do you feel yourself?'

'Hot. Hot as Hell,' said George.

Sherry nodded sympathetically. 'It is quite right that we should be prepared in this world for that which we know will be our lot in another.'

Harry Grey came in with an account of the death of poor Nelson which affected the Prince extremely. They fell to talking of Lady Hamilton. Mrs. Fitz. said: 'I am all for Lady Nelson and against Lady Hamilton, who, hero as he was, overpowered and took possession of him quite by force. Poor creature! I am sorry for her now, for I suppose she is in grief.'

Prinney went to town and called to breakfast in Chesterfield Street to discuss his tailor, and was so engrossed in the subject that he stayed to dinner. The Prince approved Stulze, who was generally considered at the top of his profession, but the Beau had not the highest opinion of him.

'Stulze aims at making *gentlemen*, not *coats*,' he said. 'There is a degree of aristocratic pretension in his stitches which is vulgar to an appalling degree. There are better tailors. That fellow Weston is an inimitable fellow, a little defective, perhaps, in his linings, but irreproachable for principle and button-holes. He came to London, sir, without a shilling, and he controls more realised thousands than the Crown, if I may say so. He is not only rich, but brave; not only brave, but courteous; not only courteous, but candid. The other day he was coming up from some d – d place on the coast by that thing, the – the stage coach. There were two women in the coach, two deucedly pretty women, and an overdressed fellow, who was of course an ass, and who was so over-civil to the prettier of the two, that the persecuted creature appealed to quiet little Weston for protection. Weston, sir, picked up the fellow, shook him by the seat of his pantaloons, and thrashed him, saying: "It will be a pleasure to you to tell your friends that you have not only been thrashed, but thrashed by a tailor." '

'I will try him,' said the Prince gloomily. 'I hear Pitt is not likely to recover.'

'He never dressed well,' sighed Mr. Brummell.

TWO GREAT MEN DIE

Trafalgar was followed by Austerlitz, and on that red tide the life of William Pitt went out. If ever a man died of a broken heart he did, for his lifetime's dream of England's glory seemed at an end.

The Prince of Wales was compelled to turn his attention from cravats and Hessians and the respective merits of tailors, and also from his elderly siren's charms, to attend to national affairs.

On the day after Pitt's death Prinney arrived at Lord St. Vincent's with word to be transmitted to Addington that the King intended to send for Grenville.

The Whigs were in at last.

Grenville sent for Charles Fox and Fox sent for the Prince, with whom he discussed the three points of Whiggery and omitted any reference to the reason of the breach between them.

The Ministry of All the Talents belied its ambitious name, and Fox, the eloquent, soon followed his great rival into the silence of the grave. Above no man's tomb has a friend written a sadder epitaph than was written for Fox:

'Genius is an indefinite term – I never think a man really an able man, unless I see that he has attained the

object of his pursuits, whatever that may be. I try
Charles Fox by that test. He has had three favourite
pursuits – gaming, politics, women. He addicted himself
to play and thought himself a skilful player, but lost an
immense fortune almost before he was of age – Power
was his grand object, yet he has never been able to keep
possession of it, scarcely for a twelvemonth – He was
desirous of shining as a man of gallantry, and he married
a whore.'

3
'THE DELICATE INVESTIGATION'

THE Princess of Wales' chief preoccupation was her little daughter. She was in Charlotte's nursery as often as possible when the Prince was out of town, and she could visit Carlton House without the fear of meeting him. When the nurse was away, the Princess loved to put her baby to bed.

'I was upstairs when my dear little Charlott was un-dress'd and stay'd till she was in bed and the dear little Angle was remarcable well. I am much obliged to you for your great attention to her and hope you will not return at eight o'clock if it is not convenient to yourself as I am quite alone with my Lady's so I can go upstairs if anything should be the matter and then I will lett you know hope to have the pleasure of seeing you much better to-morrow.

I am,

CAROLINE.'

So the Princess wrote to Charlotte's nurse. If she had been allowed she would have nursed the child herself and done everything for her. But it was not to be per-mitted. The Princess Charlotte of Wales must be sur-rounded with all the authorised pomp of her high birth.

Miss Hayman, the child's sub-governess, was quite charmed with the Princess of Wales, who would stop to chat about dress, the latest book, or society gossip, in the most friendly fashion, and whose devotion to her baby would have moved a much harder heart.

The Prince, of course, heard of it; his spies infested the palace as well as the household of the Princess. Miss Hayman was dismissed abruptly because of her friendly relations with the Princess. Caroline, indignant, took her into her own household, and made her keeper of her private purse.

As Charlotte grew older, more and more difficulties were put in the way of her intercourse with her mother. She was a pretty, lively child, very fond of romps and games, and enchanted with her mother's gift for romping on her hands and knees upon the carpet. The King was devoted to his grand-daughter and liked her to be with her mother, but during his attacks of illness Caroline hardly saw her child at all.

Fresh causes of dispute with her husband arose over Charlotte's education. Caroline was content to leave that in the hands of the King. He had a theory that the little girl ought to be educated on the lines laid down for a boy. Her father appeared anxious to deprive the child of any education at all.

The King appointed Lady de Clifford as governess and arranged for Charlotte to have a household at Windsor. The Prince asserted himself and, with great sensibility and many tears, talked of the natural rights and affection of a father. Charlotte was carried back to Carlton House.

The King gave up the contest. The Princess of Wales was helpless and knew that she must acquiesce. As the

King loosened the reins of government and let more and more domestic matters slide from his hands, the Queen and the Prince gathered them up. The Princess, they determined, should see her child as seldom as was possible without rousing the King's wrath.

Deprived of her baby's company, the Princess set about finding friends and occupations. Her passion for children led her to adopt them, to arrange for their education, and to set them up in life. She had, at one time, nine little protégés for whom she had made herself responsible and in whom she took a personal interest. *She* did not mind if they were ill or if their noses wanted wiping; in fact, the more they needed care the more she gave them. Nothing could be more generous or harmless, but, of course, an interest in strange, grubby infants of the *poor* was a terrible eccentricity in a Royal Princess.

She made friends in her household, and even those attached to the Prince's interest could find nothing worse to say of her than:

'She is certainly not discreet in her confidences, but she is, on the other hand, certainly all nature.'

She gave formal parties which she detested, and intimate parties which she loved. She had a passion for the opera and the playhouse, and generally had a party in her box. London rejoiced to see her, but, in that respect, she showed unusual tact; the Prince resented her popularity; she would be seen very little abroad.

Her position was difficult. Many who would have visited her from feelings of friendliness were kept away through self-interest. Caroline was quite willing that her friends should visit Carlton House, but the Prince made it very clear that those who visited her could be no friends

COUNTESS OF JERSEY

To face page 144

of his. There was no depth of pettiness to which his spite could not probe. He intimated that he would not go to any place where he might meet his wife. He made a public statement that he never intended, either publicly or privately, to meet his wife again. People with axes to grind could not afford to show her kindness.

The Princess moved from Charlton to Montagu House, Blackheath, and, as she saw less and less of her daughter, began to play at domestic life. For the first time her indiscretions sometimes verged on eccentricities which raised even friendly eyebrows.

'How easy it would be to smuggle babies into this house,' she said pensively.

Her ladies looked at each other in alarm.

'I have nine children,' she announced gravely, and the ladies were even more concerned. How could they explain to strangers that she meant 'adopted' children, and that she did not even have them in the house.

She liked her ladies, but she found that no other society than theirs entailed extreme dullness, and amusement was for her as absolute a necessity as food. She encouraged visits from anyone whom she found interesting; her visitors included Members of Parliament, men of letters, musicians, and other people whom her ladies considered very odd indeed. But many of the fashionable world came too. She kept company as good as, and more intelligent than, that kept by the Prince. People came because they liked her, because she was herself good company, and they were nearly all very brilliant talkers and willing to dispense with the ceremony which galled the Princess. Some of her parties were extremely amusing; she made her guests play blind man's buff regardless of their dignity; the great William Pitt, who repelled most people, under her instructions had been made to kiss the Queen of Prussia's bust as a forfeit.

She was often silly, sometimes vulgar, in her conversation, and, as she could not speak English properly, she frequently said things which sounded terrible and which she certainly did not mean. Her ladies did not know which way to look.

'There is nothing really wrong in what she says,' they whispered to each other, 'but it is odd to say such things in general company.' Even Lady Charlotte Lindsay, the most brilliant of them, was not always sure whether the Princess spoke in earnest or in jest. Her humour was impish, disconcerting. She rejoiced in mystification; she had a horror of dullification – to use her own word. 'He is the dullest person God ever did born,' was a frequent and hopeless disqualification in her eyes.

Her disregard of the conventions was alarming. She visited the houses of poor people and fondled their babies; she wandered about the streets and into public gardens dressed in remarkably short skirts, untidy shoes, and a hideous bonnet completely out of fashion. At the seaside she spent half the day in a rowing-boat with an old lady and two sailors and enjoyed picnic luncheons. It was deplorable. It was carrying eccentricity to the verge of impropriety. The Duchess of York behaved in the most peculiar manner with her little dogs, but she never did things as odd as that.

'I know you tink me funny and make fun of de way I talk,' Caroline laughed good-humouredly. It amused her to exaggerate the trouble that she had in speaking English; she mocked herself with her 'tink' and 'dis' and 'dat.' When she took the trouble she could speak English quite well, but when she was at ease or excited, her pronunciation was very quaint indeed. Her spelling was execrable; her two Lady Charlottes and Lady Anne Hamilton had to supervise her letters very carefully.

Of all her indiscretions the most alarming was her habit of talking disrespectfully of the Prince and the Queen, regardless of her company.

'Dat old béguine,' she said contemptuously. 'Old Snuffy! She hates me as she hated my moder. And my beloved, my *cara sposa*, my better half, he is her true son. If he were dead I could enjoy myself and have my little Charlotte. The Princesses are no better. I like English-men very well, but I cannot say the same of English-women. It is impossible to open one's heart, they are so cold.'

'I am sorry my countrywomen are so disagreable to your Royal Highness,' said Mrs. Vernon primly.

'They certainly are. They have no friendliness,' insisted the Princess. 'Except, of course, my friends.' She smiled sweetly, but Mrs. Vernon was not to be mollified.

Caroline laughed. 'Now I will tell you a good story to put you in a good humour. Somebody had lent the lives of the Cæsars to a man who was famous for speaking well of every one and when he returned the book asked him what he thought of Nero? He answered: "Why, I must say he was a *wag*." '

Mrs. Vernon was compelled to laugh.

'I heard a good one of my better half,' Caroline went on with great good humour. 'The great Wilkes once dined in company with the Prince who made a little free with him, and among oder tings pressed him to sing. He would not, but the Prince insisted, and Wilkes sang "God Save the King." "How long," says the Prince, "has dat been a favourite song with you?" "Why, ever since I have had de honour of your Royal Highness' acquaintance." '

The ladies laughed uneasily. It was not wise to laugh with his wife at the foibles of the Prince of Wales.

Lord Glenbervie came in with beaming face. 'A Gazette Extraordinary was published this morning,' he announced, 'which contained only this paragraph.'

The Princess took it and read it aloud:

'Downing Street, October 2nd.

Preliminaries of peace between His Majesty and the French Republic were signed last night at Lord Hawkesbury's office in Downing Street by the Right Honourable Lord Hawkesbury, one of His Majesty's principal secretaries of State, on the part of His Majesty, and by Monsieur Otto on the part of the French Government.'

'Is every one surprised?' the Princess asked.

'I suppose no State secret was ever so well kept. It was not suspected by any news-writer, nor by the public in general. Stocks have risen to-day. 3 per cent. Consols from 59 to 68, and Omnium from 5 to 18.'

'If it were not for Charlotte I would go abroad,' said Caroline.

All the world of fashion set out once more on Continental tours. Paris was a magnet as it had been before the Bastille fell. Madame Tallien ruled where once Marie Antoinette had been queen; sensibility had taken the place of courtesy. The travellers wrote home amusing tales of society in Paris where simplicity was now the mode. Ladies held receptions in Greek garments, lying on Greek couches in graceful attitudes and draped rather than dressed. If they desired a guest to sing they fell on their knees before her and pleaded, with tears running down their cheeks. Women were determined to be interesting, and achieved their object by posings, faintings, nerve crises, and the like. There had been a most amusing *Bal des victimes*, to which only those were admitted who had lost parents or brothers or sisters by the guillotine; the hair was shaved from the nape of the neck as if preparatory to execution; they greeted each other with a nod as of heads falling into the basket; they wore red ribbons tied round their necks to show the place where – oh! most realistic and amusing. It was not at all modish to be seen in clothes which weighed more than nine ounces. Paris was a long way behind London, though, in some ways. The roads were execrable; it was nothing to be turned over in one's coach. The city smelt dreadful, too; the Parisians were very curious about the new water-closets with which London houses were fitted, and about gas lighting for the streets.

The Princess of Wales read her friends' letters and longed to be free to travel as she wished. She was not free. Her parties grew duller and duller as more and more of the fashionable world rushed to the Continent. She wanted new distractions, new friends; she grew more restless and even less discreet.

She heard that Sir John and Lady Douglas had taken a house upon Blackheath, and that Sir Sidney Smith, the hero of Acre, was living with them. She thought they must be interesting and wanted to make their acquaintance, especially as she heard they had a pretty little child. She chose the most unconventional way of doing so.

Lady Douglas told the story later, twisting it so that it sounded even odder than it was:

'In the month of December when the ground was covered with snow, as I was sitting in my parlour, I saw to my surprise the Princess of Wales, elegantly dressed in a lilac satin pelisse, primrose-coloured half-boots, and a small lilac satin travelling cap faced with sable, and a lady passing up and down before the house. I stood at the window and, as she stared so much, curtsied. To my astonishment she returned my curtsey by a familiar nod, and stopped. Old Lady Stuart who was in the room said, "You should go out. Her Royal Highness wants to come in out of the snow." Upon this I went out, and she came and said, "I believe you are Lady Douglas, and that you have a very beautiful child. I should like to see it." '

If Lady Douglas had heard anything at all of the Princess she must have heard of her passion for children. She pretended to be surprised. 'My little girl is in town. I am sorry I cannot present her. I am only here to pass an hour or two upon the Heath.'

The Princess, however, wanted to go in and, accompanied by Miss Hayman, passed an hour laughing with Lady Stuart, who was a very amusing and singular old lady.

Caroline was delighted with her new acquaintances, and a few days later sent to invite Lady Douglas to dine at Montagu House.

Miss Hayman ventured to remonstrate, pointing out that Lady Douglas bore a bad reputation, was of low origin, and not in any respect a fitting person for the

Princess to know. Caroline was angry. She had taken for Lady Douglas one of those violent friendships which Lord Malmesbury had long ago deplored; but even stronger than her feeling for the mother was her affection for the Douglas children, to the second of whom she stood godmother, giving the little girl her own name.

The Princess made frequent visits to Lady Douglas, and was lavish with compliments: 'You are so pretty. I love you better than any woman I ever knew.' Lord Malmesbury would have called it a 'missish friendship.'

Her ladies were used to this kind of thing, and thought little of it, except that Lady Douglas was quite unworthy of such enthusiasm.

'Your Royal Highness must look at Lady Douglas' eyes,' Caroline cried to the Duke of Kent. 'Now she has disguised herself in a hat you cannot see how handsome she is.'

The ladies-in-waiting exchanged eloquent glances.

The Princess drew Lady Douglas aside. '*Ma chère*, I want to ask a great favour of you which I hope you will grant me.'

'I am sure your Royal Highness could not make any request unworthy of you, and I shall have great pleasure in doing anything to oblige you.'

'What I have to ask is for you to come and spend a fortnight with me in waiting, and bring your little girl and maid.'

Sir John consented to the arrangement after a show of reluctance, and Lady Douglas, amid raised eyebrows, attended the Princess at the play and the opera and when she went out to dine.

Caroline enjoyed her company, and quizzed her with

great friendliness. 'I have a plan for you. Prince William of Gloucester likes you and I have written to tell him a fair lady is in my tower but that I have left it to his own heart to find out who it is. If he is a gallant prince I think he will fly and see.'

Lady Douglas pursed her mouth primly: 'Good God! How could your Royal Highness do so? I really like Sir John better than anybody and am quite satisfied and happy. I waited nine years for him and never would marry any other person.'

The Princess was delighted with her jest. 'Nonsense. Nonsense, my dear friend.'

Prince William heard about the jest and was displeased. The Duke of Gloucester rode over to Blackheath and remonstrated, pointing out how peculiar was the position of the Princess of Wales and how much more careful she should be than other people.

Caroline took their solemnity in good part. 'Lady Douglas is so handsome, so good-natured looking, and she has made me one of the most delightful children in the world. Her little girl is the prettiest little thing.'

'*Made me!* What a terrible phrase,' thought the Duke.

After Gloucester had gone, Lady Douglas went upstairs to take her leave. 'My husband desires me to return,' she explained.

The Princess was in bed. 'Sit down, ma chère. You see I have the most complaisant husband in the world. I have no one to control *me*. I see whom I like. I go where I like. I spend what I please and His Royal Highness pays for it all. Other English husbands plague their wives, but he never plagues me at all. I am better off than my sister, who was heartily beaten every day.'

Lady Douglas took it all seriously.

At Caroline Sidney Douglas' christening, the Princess was in great spirits. She sat, as she was fond of doing, on the carpet instead of on a chair and played with the baby.

It pleased her to be humorous about the baby *she* was going to have.

'You will see how well I manage it,' she said, mysteriously nodding her head.

Lady Douglas, of course, took her seriously, or for her own purposes pretended to do so, and expressed great alarm. 'What will you do if the Prince of Wales suspects and seizes your person.'

'I will never suffer anyone to touch my person,' Caroline laughed. 'You know nothing about these things. If you had read *Les Aventures du Chevalier de Grammont*, you would know better what famous tricks princesses and their ladies played then.'

Lady Douglas took her departure, and the Princess did not see her for six months. Caroline had other interests; she was busy making arrangements to adopt a little boy named Willie Austin. Also she had belatedly decided that perhaps Lady Douglas was not a fit person for her to know. She determined to let their intimacy drop. Lady Douglas returned to Blackheath, and finding the Princess very distant in her manner was furious. She called at Montagu House, and Caroline's kind heart would not allow her to refuse to receive her former friend.

Lady Douglas was shown into a room where the Princess was packing a small black box, and an infant was sleeping on a sofa with a piece of scarlet cloth over it.

The Princess seemed a little confused. She wanted to

be distant and found it difficult. Of course her good nature made her greeting warmer than she had meant it to be. She remembered her former jest, too, and could not resist the temptation to continue it.

'Here is the little boy,' she said, leading her visitor to the sofa. 'I had him two days after I saw you last; is it not a nice child?'

Lady Douglas was scandalised. Mrs. Fitzgerald came into the room and looked angry. She had her own, very unfavourable, opinion of Lady Douglas, and refused to leave the room with a message from the Princess. With a pursed mouth she rang the bell for a page. She knew her mistress too well, liked her too well, had too strongly developed a sense of discretion to leave her alone to talk dangerous rubbish to a malicious, credulous fool like Lady Douglas.

The Princess insisted on doing everything for the child. Lady Douglas was horrified when she saw her put on his napkins. The drawing-room at Montagu House looked like a common nursery.

The Princess was happy, every one else alarmed and uncomfortable.

'I tried to feed him,' Caroline's jesting voice went on, 'but it did not do. Now we bring him up by hand with all kinds of nourishing things.'

Lady Douglas went away with a fine story for her husband.

They received no more invitations to Montagu House, and in revenge began a campaign of slander against the Princess.

For several years Caroline refused to take any notice; then, at last, when she realised how seriously her reputation was being attacked by the persistent malice of the Douglases, she consulted the Duke of Kent. Kent, poor simpleton, was useless as a champion; he questioned Douglas, and ended by believing the fantastic tale.

The Duke of Sussex heard the story and carried it to the Prince of Wales.

The Prince, delighted, sent for Sir John and Lady Douglas, listened to their tale, and encouraged them to add as many disgusting details as they could invent.

Caroline's servants were bribed to corroborate Lady Douglas' narrative and to add anything damaging which they could think of for themselves. As they had been placed in her household as spies, in the first place, they were, naturally, only too anxious to oblige the Prince. Not only were they willing to state that Willie Austin was the child of the Princess, but they were quite prepared to prove her guilty of familiarity with almost any man who had been with her alone – Captain Manby, the painter Lawrence, among others. The Prince had, at last, the evidence he wanted to rid him of his wife; he had, indeed, in his enthusiasm, collected too much, allowed the colours to be laid on too thick in that picture of depravity which, oddly enough, the ladies-in-waiting had not noticed. No one of intelligence and decency believed the slander. The Princess' ladies were staunch and incredulous when questioned, though much given to scandalising among themselves.

The Prince laid his evidence before the King and asked for an inquiry into the conduct of the Princess of Wales.

'The Delicate Investigation' they called it, and, though secret, the whole town whispered of nothing else. 'The Princess' business,' wrote a gossip, 'is like a cover'd volcano. Every one wishes to talk, but it is generally understood that it is a dangerous subject of conversation.'

It was, for those who wished to stand well with the Prince. He was determined to divorce his wife, and quite unscrupulous in the use of tools.

The King, hitherto Caroline's friend, remained oddly passive. His health was, in fact, much worse, but his apparent acquiescence did his daughter-in-law great harm.

The inquiry lasted for months. The Princess was isolated.

The specific charges were not proved – were emphatically disproved in fact. The Prince was not powerful enough to effect so gross a miscarriage of justice. But he was powerful enough to influence the committee to leave over his wife's head a vague charge of general levity of behaviour which was damaging. The publicity of the affair, in spite of its nominal secrecy, the revelation of her silly, indiscreet jests and indiscriminate friendships, did the Princess almost as much harm as a verdict of 'Guilty' would have done. She passed definitely under a cloud of vague suspicion which made the cautious shun her company.

The King, after an odd and unkind wavering, received her publicly once more, and she was allowed to see Charlotte after a year's separation. She was given apartments in Kensington Palace as a proof that she was restored to Royal favour.

It was useless. The Queen's coldness was a condemnation, and the Prince's hatred pursued her and thenceforward never ceased pursuing her until her death.

She stood in his way; he had no decency and no mercy.

BOOK IV

The 'Delicate Investigation' had destroyed any lingering
hope of a reconciliation between Caroline and her
husband. It had freed her from certain petty persecutions
in her own household, proved to her husband that he
would never be able to discard her without the lifetime
of the King, but it had increased his hatred to mania and
it did not teach her to be more discreet. Her inclinations
thwarted in every direction, her natural affections thrust
back at her unwanted with many stabs of cruelty and
disdain, she still kept up a courageous fight with misery
and boredom.

Since she was deprived of all the rights of her position,
she would strip herself of its conforming restrictions. Her
amusements were harmless, if a little rackety and
childish. She liked amusing people, and the humour she
most enjoyed was of the brightest kind. She naturally
preferred men's society to women's, but in witty women
she took a generous delight. She flung herself whole-
heartedly into friendship and held out an entreating hand
to woman after woman who turned her head away.

She was deeply attached to Lord North's ugly but
good-humoured daughters, Lady Sheffield, Lady Glenbervie, and Lady Charlotte Lindsay, whose company she
constantly demanded. Lady Sheffield was not very

I

CAROLINE AND HER FRIENDS

'The Delicate Investigation' had destroyed any lingering hope of a reconciliation between Caroline and her husband. It had freed her from certain petty persecutions in her own household, proved to her husband that he would never be able to discard her during the lifetime of the King, but it had increased his hatred to mania and it did not teach her to be more discreet. Her inclinations thwarted in every direction, her natural affections thrust back at her unwanted with many stabs of cruelty and disdain, she still kept up a courageous fight with misery and boredom.

Since she was deprived of all the rights of her position she would strip herself of its annoying restrictions. Her amusements were harmless, if a little rackety and childish. She liked amusing people, and the humour she most enjoyed was of the broadest kind. She naturally preferred men's society to women's, but in witty women she took a generous delight. She flung herself whole-heartedly into friendship and held out an entreating hand to woman after woman who turned her head away.

She was deeply attached to Lord North's ugly but good-humoured daughters, Lady Sheffield, Lady Glenbervie, and Lady Charlotte Lindsay, whose company she constantly demanded. Lady Sheffield was not very responsive, but the other sisters were the kindest of all the women whom the Princess knew. They were always loyal to her but they deplored her behaviour, talked scandal among themselves, and avoided her intimacy as far as they could.

Caroline turned to Lady Charlotte Campbell, a humourless beauty, whose unmalicious indiscretion did more harm to her Royal mistress than her bitterest enemy could have contrived.

The men whom she chose as friends were, on the whole, more responsive, though many of them avoided her when friendship became impolitic. Sir Walter Scott was one of her fair-weather friends, but Lord Byron was her friend in all weathers. He hated the Prince for his persecution of his wife, and put his hatred into verse on a suitable occasion:

WINDSOR POETICS

[Lines composed on the occasion of His Royal Highness being seen standing between the coffins of Henry viii and Charles i in the royal vault at Windsor.]

'Famed for contemptuous breach of sacred ties
    By headless Charles see heartless Henry lies.
Between them stands another sceptred thing.
    It moves, it reigns – in all but name, a king;
Charles to his people, Henry to his wife,
    – In him the double tyrant starts to life.
Justice and death have mixed their dust in vain,
    Each royal vampire wakes to life again.
Ah! what can tombs avail, since these disgorge
    The blood and dust of both to mould – a George.'

The Princess had a taste for good company and was not squeamish; wit and gaiety were the necessary passports to her table.

Between 1806 and 1810 there were brilliant gatherings at Kensington and Blackheath. They were the most peaceful years she spent in England, and in spite of the griefs which gnawed at her heart she often contrived to enjoy herself very well. She went to Court occasionally; the Royal Dukes and Princess Sophia of Gloucester constantly visited her; the King was kind. She could find humour in the fact that the Prince of Wales turned his back on her and that the Queen received her with a chill which might have frozen a woman with less spirit. She was outwardly philosophical, though the slights did not fail to wound.

'If I had always lived with my cousins, the royal family, and if they were kind to me, I should like them and care for them. But I cannot say, treating me as they do, that I feel the affection for them I should otherwise feel, except for my dear old uncle, and he, poor dear, is lost to me now,' she remarked during the King's last illness.

The King, who, bitterest of irony, had wrecked his reign through blindly following his mother's 'George, be a King,' was not master in his palace. Queen Charlotte and his daughters disobeyed his orders to show kindness to the Princess of Wales. They would not visit her, but the King himself kept his own counsel, slipped away from his attendants and rode to Kensington and Blackheath when he felt inclined. Queen Charlotte pursed her lips when he returned gleefully from his expeditions. Uncle and niece were fond of each other and sorry for each other; their enemy was the same, and they were both in

the grip of remorseless circumstances and could see no
hope of freedom.

There was a pathetic occasion when one of these visits
looked extraordinarily like an attempt to escape on the
King's part. The Princess told a tale of it which made
her hearers open their eyes and ask if the King were more
insane than she.

His Majesty's attendants decided that he had recovered
from his last attack of illness and might go riding, though
not out of his riding house. With a chuckle he gave them
all the slip, rode madly through the Park to the astonishment of the beholders, under the windows of the public
offices whose windows rapidly filled with curious faces,
out at Storey's Gate, and over Westminster Bridge. Behind him clattered his equerries, grooms, and life-
guardsmen in a state of great uneasiness, anxious to catch
the fugitive or at least learn where he was going.

The King shook them all off, and arrived at Blackheath
looking so wild that any physician might have been
pardoned for saying he was insane. His appearance
terrified Lady Sheffield, who was in waiting, and alarmed
the Princess, who was made of sterner stuff.

On the heels of the King thundered the Duke of
Cumberland. The old man shrank from his son, and with
a hunted look begged the Princess to see him alone. Soothingly she led him into another room and shut the door.

The Duke of Cumberland and Lady Sheffield waited.
Behind the closed door they heard nothing but the drone
of voices, certainly no screams nor sounds of a struggle,
yet when the Duke had taken his father away the Princess
had a strange and horrible tale to tell. She was agitated
and dishevelled, though that was not unusual.

'He threw me on a sofa and would have ravished me if, the couch happening to be without a back, I had not contrived to get over it on the other side.'

Lady Sheffield did not know whether to believe the story or not. Mr. Canning, to whom she repeated it, laughed and said it was a joke.

It was impossible to know whether the King was mad or not; it was a matter of politics. The King's sanity ebbed and flowed according to the state of the political parties. He was sane when it suited his Ministers, yet gossips sniggered that 'his words give his sanity the lie. Why! as he drove in his state coach to prorogue the Parliament he said to his attendants: "I shall begin my speech to-day, My Lords and Peacocks." ' Canning said *that* was a joke.

'If the King was not mad, then the Princess must be,' remarked Lady Sheffield, but Canning continued laughing: 'The Princess is sane enough, though sometimes a little free in her behaviour and a little scandalous in mind. She saw harm where none was meant.'

Canning's gay wit and common sense blew away the miasma of sex which clung like a veil to the unfortunate Princess. Most people could not look at her without being conscious of it. She was constantly conscious of it herself. The most harmless gesture seemed wrongly interpreted. Her indiscreet, vulgar, practical jokes were taken seriously; her undoubted public familiarities were taken as an index to her private behaviour. Every word and act could be twisted to give colour to the scandalous rumours which were never silent. Canning was often bored with her, but he saw very clearly that the vapourings of thwarted sex and motherhood were very far from being an indication of guilt.

The Princess had been accustomed to lax morals and loose speech in Germany; she was too much of a foreigner still to comprehend that in England nowadays only whisperings were permitted. She would have been more at home in the Court of George II than in that of George III.

Her parties at Blackheath were popular with many people who would not cross the threshold of Buckingham House. The talk was often brilliant, but often savoured rather of Covent Garden than of Queen Charlotte's family life. Yet the actual behaviour of the Princess was decorous enough, though she chafed at etiquette and ignored it when she could. Her parties were amusing, and she was a good hostess, though Beau Luttrell said she had bad dinners and worse wine. Since she had no favours to bestow, her visitors must have gone either to see each other or to see her.

There was a party at Kensington in March 1810, which Lord Glenbervie attended. The company, besides the Glenbervies, included George Canning, John William Ward, afterwards the mad Lord Dudley, Payne Knight, Lord Gower, Lord Archibald Hamilton, Lord Henry Fitzgerald, who was accepted as the reigning 'favourite,' Beau Luttrell, Lady Charlotte Lindsay, and Miss Hayman.

Canning was out of spirits; it appeared as if his favour or the confidence in him of the Princess was on the wane.

Caroline was very talkative. She started the subject of reviews and sermons.

'I am *engouée* with the wit and agreableness of Sydney Smith. Have you read his latest sermons, Mr. Canning?'

'Only his late visitation sermon.'

'What do you think of it?'

'I think it execrable.'

'Ah, Mr. Canning is one of the props and they say undertakers of the *Quarterly Review*, where Sydney Smith's sermons were lately very severely handled,' the Princess said to the company. 'They do not like new stars. Now I do, and have a system of seeing all remarkable persons.'

Mr. Canning said drily: 'So I am aware, Madam.'

The Princess laughed good-naturedly and chuckled as she remarked: 'Ah! Mr. Canning has a sort of humour. Lady Glenbervie wrote to him for me to ask for Henry Salt's address. Listen. I will tell you his answer. I was so amused I remember the exact words: "My dear Madam, Mr. Salt lodges at the Rasi's (I do not know the name nor the number) somewhere in Abyssinia. Ever, dear Madam, Yours, Canning." Is not that amusing? You mock me, I tink, Mr. Canning.'

'On my honour no, Madam. It was the exact truth.'

A servant brought a note to Her Royal Highness. She opened it impatiently and read it with a frown.

'I won't go. I won't go. It is from Madam Haeckel to say my moder desires me to go to-morrow to meet the Queen. I am going to be very naughty. I am determined not to go.'

'It is important, your Royal Highness,' Lady Glenbervie began in distress.

Caroline turned on her with flashing eyes. 'The Queen did not invite me to the Court on Tuesday. It is of a piece with the treatment I have from the first received. I asked my moder why I had not been invited. She did not know. But the Princess Sophia said: "Yes. It was a pity; the omission was a mistake." But the Queen said noding. She is a devil, that woman. When I meet her at my moder's she kisses me because dat is the etiquette, and den she turns her back and speaks to me no more.'

Canning said softly: 'Perhaps she has heard of the Grenville election.' Lady Glenbervie cast him a warning look and broke in hastily: 'Princess Sophia ascribes it to the malice of the Duke of Cumberland. She says he is a perpetual meddler and mischief-maker, and the dread of them all when he comes to Windsor.'

The Princess laughed mirthlessly. 'It is more likely my husband. He interferes in everything that concerns me. He forbade me to receive Lady Oxford, who is very beautiful and amusing.'

Lady Charlotte Lindsay said hastily: 'Oh! but, Madam, it is not fitting.' The Princess interrupted: 'She is a good woman. When she takes a new lover in the absence of the former she does not attempt to hide it from him, but on the contrary writes to inform him of it. Now that I call being a good woman.'

The company stared. Ward remarked ironically: 'That is certainly being good. But the lady, I think, has also a husband. Does she inform him?'

The Princess looked surprised. 'Indeed, yes. She has a certain graceful openness in avowing her love and practice of pleasure that exceeds anything I ever met with. Lord Oxford finds her candour so amiable that he quite forgives her. She is a very kind mother to all her children.'

Ward grinned. 'They call them the "Harleian Miscellany."'

The company roared with laughter. The Princess

wiped the tears of mirth from her cheeks. 'It is so unusual to see such attachment between husband and wife, and it certainly is not the fashion for a wife to practise chastity.'

'Oh! Madam,' choired the ladies.

The Princess shook her head at them. 'If the Prince should die I am determined to go to see her. I shall not care then what people may say.'

Luttrell said plaintively: 'I have been in the country. What is the latest in the scandalous chronicle?'

Ward bowed to him ironically. 'I wish you joy of the progress vice and immorality have made since your absence from town.'

'I am mortified to find that this should have happened without my having contributed to it,' Luttrell answered smiling.

Ward chuckled. 'There are the Pagets. Don't you think they have made a very bold stride?'

'Well. I confess fairly to you I am very glad of it,' said the Princess seriously.

Luttrell looked interested. 'I have not heard of this.'

Ward leaned forward confidentially. 'Lady Charlotte Cadogan has been divorced from Mr. Wellesley for criminal conversation with Lord Paget, but as he is at present a married man he cannot marry her. But Lady Paget, if she can procure a divorce from him in Scotland, is engaged to marry the Duke of Argyll. Proof of any new act of adultery with Lady Charlotte would not answer Lord Paget's object of marrying her, because, by the law of that country, the two guilty parties cannot marry together. So the plan between the four is that Lord Paget shall, by connivance, be detected by Lady

Paget and witnesses appointed for that purpose, in bed with some woman hired for the occasion.'

'How shocking!' said Lady Cha.

'These silly laws,' the Princess broke in impatiently. 'Why cannot they marry together without all this fuss? There are other tales in the scandalous chronicle. Lady Salisbury is said to have had a child by a Mr. Hales of Hertfordshire.'

Ward chuckled again. 'Someone said to her friend, Lady Essex, that he wondered Lady Salisbury could have liked so plain and vulgar a man. Lady Essex said it was all a mistake; she never liked him. It was a mere surprise. They had been hunting. The chase was long, and Hales being accidentally up with Lady Salisbury when it was over, they returned home together in a hack chaise. So you see it was all a surprise.'

Luttrell supplied his quota of scandal. 'Lady Antrim had an amusing tale of an Irish lady of quality who had long been married without having any children. She happened one day in the course of a walk to stroll near the cottage of one of her husband's tenants where his wife was surrounded by a group of fine handsome children. The lady of quality called her, and asked to what she attributed this great fertility. "Oh, my lady," said the woman, "now by my faith it is all the potatoes." "Indeed, do you think so? Then pray send me home some bushels of your potatoes immediately." "Ay, indeed that I will," said the woman; "but pray, my lady, had I not better send John with them."'

The Princess laughed. 'And did she?'

Luttrell said gravely: 'I will ask Lady Antrim.'

'I cannot blame any woman who loves children, and

must get them how she can,' the Princess cried emphatically.

There was an embarrassed pause. Each pair of eyes sought another pair of eyes with a significant leer. The Princess, lost in thought, was unaware of the silence. Lady Glenbervie, kind soul, broke in hurriedly:

'Lady Antrim is, I think, a disagreable woman.'

Lord Glenbervie's head was nodding, Lady Cha was delicately struggling with a yawn. The Princess looked at them kindly. 'When I am interested I could talk all night, but all the same perhaps we have sat too long.'

Lady Glenbervie whispered to her husband. 'Does not the conversation go more towards a portrait of her Royal mind than a volume of painting by another person could do?'

The Glenbervies believed many of the tales that were told of her Royal Highness; all the ladies of the household were sad gossips and collected significant scraps of news for each other, putting them together with lowered voices and in distant corners. The Princess, with impish humour, herself supplied many of the scraps. She would leave off her stays, draw attention to the fact, and watch them cast suspicious appraising glances at her swelling figure. Lady Glenbervie and Lady Cha Lindsay, her sister, talked their Royal mistress over in family counsels, and shook their heads; but they did not talk her over outside the family, and Lord Glenbervie's journal was not intended for publication. He was more credulous than his wife. She and Lady Cha were kind and clever and had abundant humour; they did not believe the worst of the stories the Princess hinted about herself. But they all, except Canning, were sometimes filled with doubts. Caroline's unguarded tongue, wrestling with a foreign language which she had learned late in life, gave colour to the rumours which flew from tongue to tongue. Once more, now, she set her company exchanging sly glances as she picked up little Willie who was playing with an orange in the room to which they withdrew.

'My Willikin,' she murmured affectionately, 'it is a long time since I brought you to bed.'

The child understood her. 'I will go to bed immediately,' he answered, and ran out of the room. The rest of the company was astonished and disconcerted. Lord Glenbervie noted the words for his journal, with the cautious addition: 'This is a secret that must be at least a century old before it ought to be whispered.'

Canning saw the sly exchange of glances and frowned.

'Poor fool,' he thought. 'How her tongue betrays her. If only I might correct her speech, and tell her she should say: "It is a long time since I took you to bed, Willie." These silly mistakes start so many scandalous whispers, and that, though amply disproved, is a tale which will never die. Poor fool. She is a worse enemy to herself than the Prince can be.'

Canning took his leave, and the Princess retired to the garden with Lord Henry Fitzgerald.

There was no need any longer to confine comment to sly glances. In groups, in corners, side by side on sofas, the whispering began.

'They say the quarrel with the Duke of Cumberland originated from the good advice he gave her about this child. "Treat him with every kindness in private if you will," the Duke advised, "but do not treat him as if fit to be brought up with your daughter. It will cause scandal and furnish a pretext for malicious conversation." '

'Lady Townshend gave the same advice and has never been forgiven.'

'Her infatuation for Lord Henry cools, I think.'

'There are indications that Sir Harry Vane Tempest is intended for the vacant throne.'

'One would think so since his wife, that vulgar Lady Antrim, is so much disliked by the Princess. What is he like?'

'He is handsome and profligate, but *blasé*, coarse in his manners, a jockey, and a hard drinker, with a violent temper and no understanding.'

'A change for the worse. Lord Henry is gentle, well bred, decent in conversation with women, and eager for the company of clever and agreable people.'

'In the hopeless ambition, perhaps, of passing for one himself,' sneered Ward.

'The Princess once told me,' put in Miss Hayman, 'that while in Brunswick she belonged to a society of *Illuminés*, and used to get out of her window in the night to attend their gatherings.'

'Silly woman. This affair with Lord Henry is become the universal talk and is never spoken of but with disgust. It is barefaced and disgusting.'

'He and she are continually receiving anonymous letters on the subject.'

'She must be for ever running after famous people. Now she is full of compliments for Sydney Smith.'

'Which he swallows with the smirking complacency of a man who thinks he deserves them all.'

'He has the neck of a little bull and two hands like

thick raw beefsteaks. He uses too much action for an English clergyman, and particularly has an awkward habit of clenching his right fist.'

'Miss Berry thinks no man with such a hand should pretend to action, grace, or even taste.'

'Miss Berry on taste! She never finished one short sentence in her life, and accounts by that defect of nature or habit for the dry, dull sterility of her notes and letters.'

'I never understood that infatuation of Lord Orford's.'

'*His* affectations were ridiculous.'

'Yet his company was much sought after by the wits – George Selwyn and his friend, old Queensberry.'

'I never saw George Selwyn. Was he so great a wit?'

'I think his reputation made him father of all the wit there was. They said he kept a Foundling Hospital for wit '

'Old Q. is dying.'

'Did you hear of Erskine's jest? When Opie the painter's death was first mentioned he said: "If O.P. is dead, old Q. will probably go next." '

The Princess of Wales came into the room looking a little confused, Lord Henry following, an open book in his hand.

'Lord Henry has been reading to me,' the Princess said quickly. 'Did I hear old Queensberry is dying? I have a weakness for him and so I believe he has for me.'

'Your Royal Highness never minds how rude people are to you,' Ward remarked ironically.

'I hate ceremony, and never think of taking things ill or being affronted by inattentions,' the Princess said with dignity. 'The Duke is an old man, and cannot be expected to seek my company.'

'I wonder if half the tales they tell of him are true,' murmured Lady Charlotte.

'Impossible! The man has become a legend. In any case, manners were freer in his youth. He was Gentleman of the Bedchamber to the King, and *he* would not have suffered such a monster as report makes the Duke to attend him.'

'The Queen . . .' began Lady Cha.

Lady Glenbervie hastily broke in: 'The late Lady Palmerston liked his society, and she was a good-natured woman.'

'She loved to draw agreable society to her house and, to attract gay young men, was a great protectress of the class of demi-rips.'

'I detested that woman,' said Ward bitterly. 'She was so fawning and mean. There was no sort of *bassesse* she was not guilty of in order to get that monster Ashburton to marry her ugly daughter.'

Lady Glenbervie stiffened. Perhaps the 'ugly daughter' went home. More probably she was tired of the atmosphere of backbiting and spite. She loved scandal as much as any of them, but purely in the way of conversation. Ward's bitter malice disgusted her.

'Upon my word,' she said loudly, 'you have a very long and very sharp scythe. You have just mown down three at one stroke.'

The Princess looked at her quickly with affectionate concern. *She* did not mind sitting up all night, but such sharpness of tongue from her dear Lady Kitty meant that her companions were tired. Reluctantly she dismissed them, and sat alone with her sad thoughts.

The Princess amused herself with the fashionable

pastime of writing short 'portraits' of the men and women with whom she was acquainted. It was an embarrassing amusement, imported, like so many others, from France, where Saint Simon had perfected it, and Madame du Deffand had adapted it to her English friends. The Princess wrote, of course, in French, and showed the portraits to her friends. Of Lady Glenbervie, to whom she was greatly attached, the portrait was most flattering: '*Femme essentielle, sensée, spirituelle, amusante, bonne, vraie, sincère, mais discrète et sure. Beaucoup de culture et de connoisances et avec cela ayant grand soin de ne jamais attacquer les autres.*'

It was not surprising that Lady Kitty was pleased with this and found others of the portraits extraordinarily good. They were in lively, concise, epigrammatic style, with a great tinge, in most of them, from her partiality and prejudices, but she seized with great discernment the leading features and particularities of the originals and those contradictory and contrasting qualities and tendencies which often may be observed in the same individual. She was indulgent to her friends, and almost any agreable person could win and keep her friendship as long as he, or more often she, refrained from offering advice. She admitted quite frankly that she hated advice, and always felt a coolness towards those who insisted on giving it, with the sole exception of Lord Malmesbury on her bridal journey.

Miss Hayman found herself treated with the greatest reserve for two or three years because she once presumed to caution her mistress against some glaring impropriety. Lady Townshend, a less agreable woman, was never forgiven for a similar offence, and on her husband's death resigned her place. The Princess drew a portrait of her in which she described her as being '*basse et flatteuse à la cour, Messalina chez elle*.'

The three North sisters only gave advice when asked for it, and remained in favour. Lady Sheffield was the first of them to tire of the difficult position, and to beg leave to resign. The Princess protested vehemently, then acquiesced, and gave herself up to the pleasure of looking forward to a fresh companion. Lady Charlotte Campbell was appointed, and the choice was universally approved.

Lady Glenbervie praised her sister's successor: 'She is noble, agreable, fashionable, poor, and *sans tache ou reproche*.'

The Princess was excited. Lady Charlotte was also very beautiful, and however much one liked them, it was impossible to call the Norths *that*. Lady Charlotte Campbell was so beautiful that no one noticed that she was rather stupid, and without a gleam of humour. She suffered from excessive sensibility, and was inclined to be lachrymose and ready with pious platitudes. She was much inclined to sentimental affairs of the heart, and to dwell upon things soulful on the smallest provocation. She had none of the robust good sense, and little of the unfailing good humour and tolerance of the Norths. She was full of self-pity, and considered herself unfortunate, as indeed, in many ways, she was. Her mother, that Elizabeth Gunning whose beauty had become a legend, was not always wise, and she died when her youngest daughter was seventeen. Charlotte's childhood had been embittered by the scandal which set her half-sister, Lady Derby, outside the social pale. Her own marriage with her kinsman, Colonel John Campbell, had been chiefly occupied in child-bearing. He left her a widow at thirty-four with nine children and no money. She indulged herself in sentimental melancholy but, being beautiful, was forgiven.

With the example of Lady Derby ever before her as a warning, she felt that she could not be too careful in everything that concerned herself. She did not want to be lady-in-waiting to the Princess of Wales, whose position was so invidious; the prospect was distasteful to the spoilt beauty. But, as Lady Glenbervie said, she was poor and she needed money. The salary was five hundred guineas a year, taxed down by the property tax to four hundred and fifty; it would be extremely useful. She wrote to all her friends for opinions of the Princess, and kept the letters that reached her in reply. . . .

'1810.

. . . You ask me for news of the Princess. Her Royal Highness appears gay and well in health. I have dined frequently lately at Kensington, and the society has been most agreable and "select" as the papers say. But when I tell you that these parties were made up of the Lindsay and the Berry *par excellence* of all the Berries in the world, Lady Oxford, who is lovely indeed to look upon, my Lord Byron, sometimes Sydney Smith, from whom issues perpetual and dazzling sparks of the most brilliant wit, the grave Lord Henry, and though last, not least, your humble servant, you can believe these parties must be super-excellent, reflecting on the superior qualities of each individual who has composed them. It is wrong in me to have omitted our royal hostess herself; for to "us" much of the gaiety and spirit of these entertainments is due.

LADY CHARLOTTE CAMPBELL

To face page 176

"We" are most irresistibly good-natured and droll in despite of ourselves. . . .'

'Monk' Lewis said much the same. '. . . She is extremely good-humoured and obliging, and seems very much attached to the persons in whose favour she conceives a prepossession. She is by no means *exigeante*; at the same time no little attention is lost upon her. She seems grateful for the slightest indication of good-will. (Probably, poor soul, the treatments she has at times received since her arrival in this country have made such doubly acceptable to her.) And she is generous, indeed I may say profuse, in her manner of returning them.'

Lady Charlotte thought that men might, perhaps, be prejudiced and uncritical. She read with more consideration the opinion of a woman whom she liked and respected:

'. . . I believe the Princess to be exceedingly amiable, a true and zealous friend to all those whom she once takes *en amitié*; and is, moreover, an extremely agreable companion, full of natural talent, and combines in a surprising manner the dignity of her position with an unaffected and natural ease very rarely seen in a Princess. It is indeed only fair to add that she makes it a point to draw about her all the clever and agreable persons she can; and that, particularly in a *Royalty*, is no small merit. There are no courtiers or parasites in the society at Kensington. . . . You ask me to tell you something of the individuals who form the Princess of Wales' household. . . . Of Lady Charlotte Lindsay's wit and proverbial good humour and kindness of heart you must be well acquainted; her sister also, though less brilliant, is fully as amiable. Miss Garth is a very estimable character, simple minded, and very downright in all she says, and little suited to a Court, except from her high principles and admirable caution. . . . Miss Hayman is shrewd and sensible. She has strong sense and good judgment; she plays well on the piano-forte, and understands the science of music, and has very agreable manners though not polished ones. . . .'

Lady Charlotte folded the letters; she was considerably reassured, though not wholly. There must not be a shadow of disrepute on the company with which *she* mixed. She asked almost every one whom she met what they thought or had heard of the Princess of Wales.

Mr. Ward, whose malicious tongue was seldom without its barb, said: 'She is a lively, good-natured, amusing woman.'

Walter Scott wrote: 'She is an enchanting Princess who dwells in an enchanted palace, and I cannot help thinking that her Prince must labour under some malignant spell when he denies himself her society.'

Even Mary Berry, so hard to please, was conquered by her: 'Her conversation is certainly uncommonly lively, odd, and clever. What a pity it is she has not a grain of *common* sense.'

Lady Charlotte put aside any remaining scruples and made application to the Prince of Wales for her appoint-ment as lady-in-waiting to the Princess of Wales. The Prince, seeing no opportunity of putting his creatures in *that* position, raised no objection. Lady Charlotte set out for Blackheath.

The Princess fell in love with her with all her ardent tempestuous heart. This was the friend of friends for whom, all her life, she had been looking. Her ladies hitherto had had husbands, or had not had husbands, or were unsympathetic or censorious. They had not been beautiful or unfortunate and had not had a bevy of small children at their heels. Lady Charlotte Campbell, as she revealed herself in her diary and letters, was not worthy of the affection the Princess lavished on her; she was always ready to ridicule and not very loyal though her intention was not malicious. She was, intermittently, sorry for the Princess, but she did not like her. What the quality was that attracted Caroline to Lady Charlotte is not clear, but it was as irresistible as a magnet, and lasted. The Princess was a proud woman; never, even in her worst hours, did she wear her heart on her sleeve. If there was any humour to be extracted from a situation she extracted it; if pride could serve her, pride was always at her call. Her fortitude was amazing; she left tears to the Prince. Only to Lady Charlotte Campbell did she unbend and pour out her heart.

The Princess said confidentially: 'I, you know, was the victim of mammon. The Prince of Wales' debts must be paid, and poor little I's person was the pretence. Parliament would vote supplies for the heir - apparent's *marriage*; the King would help his little help. A Protestant Princess must be found – they fixed upon the Prince's cousin. To tell you God's truth I always hated it; but to oblige my Father, anything. But the first moment I saw my *futur* and Lady Jersey together I knew how it all was, and I said to myself, "Oh, very well." I took my *partie* – and so it would have been, if – but oh! mine God,' she burst out passionately. 'I could be the slave of a man I love; but one whom I love not, and who did not love me, impossible – *c'est autre chose*.'

'Well, Madam, it is the most surprising thing in the

world, that the Prince was not desperately in love with
your Royal Highness.'

'Not at all,' she replied. 'In the first place, very few
husbands love their wives; and I confess the moment one
is obliged to marry any person it is enough to render them
hateful. Had I come over here as a Princess, with my
fader, on a visit, as Mr. Pitt once wanted my fader to
have done, things might have been very different. But
what is done cannot be undone.'

'Did you leave Brunswick with regret, Madam?' Lady
Charlotte asked.

'Not at all; I was sick, tired of it; but I was sorry to
leave my fader. I loved my fader dearly, better nor any
oder person.' The tears streamed down her face. She
mastered her emotion. 'I will tell you; there is no affection more powerful than that we feel for a good Fader;
but dere were some unlucky tings in our Court which
made my position difficult. My fader was most entirely
attached to a lady for thirty years, who in fact was his
mistress; she was the beautifullest creature and the
cleverest; but though my Fader continued to pay my
moder all possible respect, my poor moder could not
suffer this attachment; and de consequence was I did
not know what to do between them. When I was
civil to the one, I was scolded by the other, and was
very tired of being shuttlecock between them. To tell
you God's truth, I have had as many vexations as most
people.'

Presently she went on: 'My life has been an eventful
one from my earliest years. At one period I was to have
been married to the uncle of the Queen of Prussia; he
turned all the women's heads except mine; at another, to

this Queen's brother, a most agreable man, not at all ugly, and very pleasant in his manners. I liked him as a friend, but nothing more.'

She was silent for a time, and then burst out passionately: 'Judge what it was to have a drunken husband on one's wedding day, and one who passed the greatest part of his bridal night under the grate, where he fell and where I left him. If anybody say to me at dis moment – Will you pass your life over again or be killed? I would choose death. For you know a little sooner or later we must all die; but to live a life of wretchedness twice over – Oh, mine Gott, no. Oh! how happy I was to leave Carlton House. Everybody blamed me, but I never repented of dis step. Oh, mine Gott, what I have suffered. Luckily I had a spirit, or I never should have outlived it. And then, when I needed my fader most he was killed. My moder loves me, but she cannot help.'

The Princess wept a little, and then made a valiant effort to throw off her depression. 'Have you seen this game, *ma chère?*' she asked with a sly laugh.

From a box she took a lump of wax, and with clever, practised fingers fashioned it into a figure which bore an unmistakable likeness to the Prince of Wales. She added large horns, then took three pins out of her garments, and stuck them through and through the wax figure, which she then put to roast at the fire.

Lady Charlotte could not help laughing.

'She always does this when there are no strangers present,' whispered one of the ladies. 'Do you really think that she has a superstitious belief that destroying this effigy of her husband will bring about the destruction of himself?'

'Two hundred years ago I should have been burnt as a witch,' said the Princess with a laugh.

Lady Charlotte did not know whether to regard it as a joke, a silly piece of spite or a genuine belief in superstition. The Princess did not enlighten her.

The sad part of Caroline's affection for her new friend was that Lady Charlotte did not like her at all. All Caroline's faults, all her absurdities of dress and speech and behaviour were noted in letters or diary without kindness or understanding.

The time was near when, more than ever before, Caroline would have need of her friends. Superior sense, perhaps, made her despise the friendship of her own people. Her mother she had always scorned, and with her brother she had very little patience, though she had an affection for him and encouraged her little Charlotte's devotion to her 'Black Brunswicker' uncle, who gave her real affection, and had from her a love which her other uncles could not win. All Caroline's love had been given to her father, and when he was killed at Jena she wept bitterly indeed.

The widowed Duchess of Brunswick came to England, but found herself in a very difficult situation. The King had once been fond of her, but the Queen hated her, and took care that brother and sister should never have a moment alone together. The Prince of Wales invited her to Carlton House, with a great flourish, setting a trap for the foolish old woman into which she very nearly fell.

'Don't you see he is wanting such a public confession that you also condemn me? If you go he will say all his accusations are true and you acknowledge it.'

The Duchess was obstinate. 'I do not see it so. Quite otherwise. I shall be able to make him see differently.'

The Princess wrung her hands. Her mother was immovable. Caroline wrote a letter of three pages when she reached home. The Duchess wept a little: 'If you think there is a doubt upon the subject, I shall not go to Carlton House,' she answered.

'Was there ever such an idea entered a mother's head?' Caroline sighed. 'It was so evidently a trap. Already she has eaten humble pie to the Queen. Yet she only did so from cowardice; she is grown old and is soon terrified. I believe she love me for all dat. I must go to her dullification, but I would rather be at home. She has de dullest old fograms dat God ever did born.'

The dinner-parties which the Duchess gave were very dull indeed, yet her daughter dined with her dutifully twice a week. Only, if she dined with the Duchess one day, she did not expect her mother to visit her next morning. If she insisted on doing so, she must expect to be coldly received. The Princess liked to lounge all the morning by a fire in the room off her bedchamber, which was intimate and comfortable, and in which she breakfasted and often took her intimates to sup.

The Duchess was put in the drawing-room, where there was no fire and where Lady Glenbervie had to entertain her until her reluctant daughter appeared. The lady-in-waiting thought the Duchess wanted to say something privately to her daughter, and wished to withdraw. The Princess recalled her and began to fidget, walking up and down between the window and the fire. The Duchess went away at last looking troubled. The Princess was not troubled at all. 'I saw Ward outside,' she told her lady, 'and was afraid he would come in. If he had come in I should have told her he was my Italian master.'

Lady Glenbervie looked bewildered. 'Why this mystification?' she wondered.

The Princess continued to fidget: 'My mother herself taught me deception when I was very young,' she said at last, 'and to tell you God's truth I find it amusing. Princes and princesses are forced to deceive. Think of my cousins, the Princesses Sophia and Elizabeth, and even the King's darling, Amelia. They have to practise deception. Princess Elizabeth had a child by Mr. Carpenter, son to the General Carpenter who drowned himself. I had the history from Miss Hayman, who had it from the midwife. A gentleman came and offered her £500 as a reward of her discretion, and some time afterwards a sedan chair arrived at her house with a lady in a long thick veil. She was put to bed with the veil on, but fell into a sound sleep. The woman could not refrain from lifting it. The lady was in a short time brought to bed and carried away as she had come. The curious midwife went to St. James' the next King's Birthday. Nobody resembled her *accouchée* until the Queen and Princess Elizabeth appeared; then she was sure without a possibility of doubt or hesitation that she was the person.'

Lady Charlotte clasped her hands. 'Can such things be? It is like so many stories one has heard, but can all this be really true?'

The Princess was emphatic. 'It is a maxim with the Princesses that as the King will never allow them to marry, they may indulge themselves if they manage matters with prudence and decorum. Yet it is very strange: when the Princess Sophia was with child she was so ignorant and silly that she did not know till the last moment.'

Lady Charlotte looked astounded. 'Does your Royal Highness think it possible that she did not perceive something particular had passed, and that she could think it a matter as indifferent and as unlikely to have consequences as blowing her nose?'

The Princess nodded. 'It would appear so. The Duke of Kent tells me that the father is not Garth, but the Duke of Cumberland.'

'How horrid,' cried Lady Charlotte, genuinely shocked. 'Is it true that the Princess Amelia is privately married to General Fitzroy?'

'Not married, but engaged, the Duke of Kent thinks, and that the Prince of Wales has promised to permit the marriage when he comes to be King. Her amours with Fitzroy have long been notorious to the courtiers.'

'The news from Windsor says that she is very ill.'

'My poor uncle,' cried the Princess. 'If she dies his heart will be broken. He loves her more than anything in the world.'

Lady Charlotte wondered. She was shocked at the Princess' appetite for scandal; she, herself, only listened, of course, because she was obliged. Could all these disgusting stories of the Princesses be true? Did the Duke of Kent really discuss them with his sister-in-law? Or did the Princess of Wales invent them? And if her tongue could be so dangerous how could her heart be so kind? Lady Charlotte noted the conversation for her diary, and added a few sententious sentences of the highest moral tone. Lady Glenbervie repeated the scandal to her husband, and he entered it in his journal with an equally shocked commentary.

In the evening the Princess of Wales gave a fête for the Persian Ambassador. The House was sitting late, so that very few Members of Parliament were present; otherwise the company was large and the best in London, Lady Charlotte noted with satisfaction.

The Persian Ambassador, a tall, stout man with good teeth, a black beard, and a high turban of fur, showed particular attention to the ladies, especially when handsome and short, a circumstance which, he explained, he thought a material ingredient in beauty. The ladies returned his kindness with much interest, and whispered with surprise when he drank wine and used his knife and fork with as much dexterity as they did. The Princess received him graciously. She was at her best, richly dressed and, the occasion being formal, she was dignified and conscious of her rank. Supported by the Princess Sophia of Gloucester and the Duc de Berry, she stood surrounded by a circle in an ante-room to receive her guests. When she had greeted every one she retired to the dining-room, and with the Princess Sophia seated herself on a sofa opposite the middle pier between the two chimneys. She bade the servants place another sofa against the pier for the Persian Ambassador and his interpreter. At the end of the room was a harpsichord, on which Naldi accompanied Madame Catalini, who sang some popular music both alone and in duets with him.

While the Catalini was singing the Persian cried out: 'Fine fellow. Fine fellow,' and the rest of the company applauded with 'Brava. Brava.'

The Princess, to whose qualities as a hostess even Lady

Charlotte Campbell paid tribute, saw that the Ambassador was uncomfortable on his sofa in the totally unnatural position, for him, of sitting with his legs hanging down, and when the singing was over she strolled about the room, and begged her guest to do the same. Monsieur and Madame des Hayes danced the Minuet de la Cour, and the Princess Sophia led in a country dance. The Duke of Kent's band played in the hall.

The Princess was happy. It was one of the rare occasions on which she was not conscious of sadness, of deep humiliations, and of petty slights. All that summer she entertained and was entertained a great deal.

'I never saw any person, not royal or royal, who understood so well to perform the honours at their own table as the Princess,' said Lady Charlotte Campbell grudgingly. 'She does it admirably, and makes more of her guests than anyone else ever did.'

Her graciousness carried her through the detested formal gatherings with credit. The Prince, waiting for tales of her disreputable company, waited in vain. To her beloved Lady Charlotte she might sometimes confess how bored she had been. . . . 'Last night I gathered together, my dear, a room full of people, and when I did look round at them, I said to myself, à quoi bon this dull assembly of tiresome people? And it so happened that they were all ugly, and I longed to get them out of my sight, yet I could not send them away, having made them come. De fact is I know not what to do. I am tired, or rather sad, because I have no grand intérêt to busy myself with. A princess, and no princess. A married woman, and no husband, or worse than none. Never was there a poor devil in such a plight as I am.'

She liked small parties composed of her intimates, who were uncommonly well chosen from among the wits and brilliant intellects of the time. She liked to be natural and easy and childish. They played a gay and silly game of cards called 'Ninycumtwit' or some such name, and romped in 'Blind Man's Buff,' as Napoleon loved to do. When a man was boring, they made him pay forfeit. Thomas Campbell had to dance a Highland reel for reading dull verses, and Rogers was shaken out of breath by the quickest and most strenuous of country dances.

When the Princess was tired of dancing and conversation she indulged in 'escapades' which shocked the censorious Lady Charlotte. She would insist on going, with her ladies, into Kensington Gardens, and thence into the public roads, *walking*, and sometimes even calling at empty houses in Bayswater and asking if they were to let, and inspecting them if they were. The Prince of Wales, of course, heard of these terrible affairs and criminal expeditions. No honest woman with a properly developed sense of decorum could ever have dreamed of having amusements like these. Marie Antoinette had played at an exaggerated simplicity, and look what tales they told of her!

Caroline went often to the opera, which she loved, and where the people of London loved to see her. When she could slip in disguised she enjoyed nothing better than a masquerade, but then so did the Duchess of York, about whom no one talked scandal.

At home, at Blackheath and Kensington, there were music parties at which she sometimes sang herself; 'squalled,' Lady Charlotte said. The Prince of Wales also sang to his friends and beat time to the music on his rather fleshy thigh.

Of the professional musicians who were often in attendance on the Princess, Lady Charlotte particularly disliked the Sapios, father and son, whom she nicknamed the Old Orang-Outang and the Young Orang-Outang, and cordially hated. The Princess delighted in their music, but Lady Charlotte detested it and, after talking loudly to her neighbours in order to try and drown the dreadful noise, went to bed and wrote acidly: 'The horrible din of their music hardly ever stopped the whole evening except when it was interrupted by the disgusting nonsense of praise that passed between the parties. Interest and cunning excuse it from the low and servile, but really, to hear her let herself down so as to sing praises to the Fiddler's son . . . it is more than human patience can bear to witness such folly. The perpetual silly nonsense of the old buffoon, amounting often to impudence, crowns the whole.'

Perhaps Lady Charlotte was right in her estimate of their musical gifts, yet Sapio had been music master to the Queen of France, and they were much sought after.

Lady Charlotte seldom wrote of the Princess without a sneer or a malicious barb. Yet she must have dissembled her dislike cleverly, for Caroline wrote constantly: 'If I could be of any use to you, you know how glad I should be. I had a party last night and much lamented your absence.' To her friend she could be indiscreet without fear: 'My better half, or my worse, which you choose, has been ill, I hear, but nothing to make me hope or fear. Pray burn this piece of high treason. I am in a state of rage, being just returned from a visit to the Queen, who received me

in a most cavalier manner. Luckily I restrained myself
while in her august presence, but I could have abused her
gloriously, so angry did I feel at the old béguine. She
never asked me to sit down, and when I asked after my
poor dear uncle and said I should like to see him, she
made me for answer: "The King is quite well, but he will
not see you." I have let out all the ebullition of my wrath
to you, *chère* Lady Charlotte. Do not repeat it though,
for the more said, the less easy is it to mend matters. Only
sometimes it is necessary to open the safety valve, to let
some of one's feelings escape or else I should be suffocated.
I am pretty well and try to fight with the blue devils,
which, alas, often get the better of me.'

The trusted friend copied the letters into her diary and,
later, published them for all the world to read.

'The blue devils' were routed with parties. Lord Byron
was a welcome guest, and was very lively and, as the
Princess thought, odd, but he kept the company in a
roar of laughter the whole dinner-time. He was 'very
couleur de rose,' Caroline said, and had him beside her at
supper. She quizzed him on his moodiness, and said
there were two Lord Byrons, one who visited people he
liked, and the other who went to see people who did not
please him.

'When I invite you I ask the agreable Lord, not the
disagreable one.' He was immensely entertained, and
certainly appeared at his best with her. His detestation
of her husband did not lessen her liking for him. He
brought her news of her child, not always happy news. He
had seen Charlotte in the Prince's box at the opera, and
the Prince rolling into it dead drunk while the girl wept
and tried to hide her tears from the watching house.

Caroline approved Byron's indignant lines:

'Weep, daughter of a royal line,
    A sire's disgrace, a realm's decay;
Ah, happy if each tear of thine
    Could wash a father's fault away.

Weep, for thy tears are Virtue's tears –
    Auspicious to these suffering isles:
And be each drop in future years
    Repaid thee by thy people's smiles.'

Under Caroline's amused and sympathetic eyes his
affaire with Lady Oxford flowed and ebbed. She would
not tell anyone else, of course, but Lady Charlotte must
hear the ludicrous side of the affair: '. . . Lady Oxford,
poor soul, is more in love this time than she has ever been
before. She was with me the other evening, and Lord
Byron was so cross to her that she was crying in the
outer room. Only imagine if anyone but myself had
discovered the fair Niobe in tears! What a good story it
would have made about the town next day.'

Lady Charlotte saw no need to keep such deplorable
absurdities secret.

'If I do not amuse myself, if I cannot be at ease with
my friends, I cannot bear it,' thought the Princess. 'It is
perhaps not wise to confide in anyone, but Lady Charlotte is as good as she is beautiful. She will not betray
my confidence. At last I have the happiness to have a
friend. That, at least, my husband cannot take from me.'
So she wrote all that was in her heart to Lady Charlotte.

Reluctantly, the Princess set out for one of those duty

dinners at her mother's which she found so tiresome. It was as dull as usual, yet she was always to remember it, for it marked the end of a comparatively happy interlude in her unhappy life. While the King was there to protect her the Prince must curb his malice and desire to hurt. But the King would not always be there. As they sat at dinner a messenger came from Windsor with the news that Princess Amelia was dead.

The Duchess of Brunswick wept and the Princess Sophia of Gloucester could scarcely speak without tears. 'Do you believe, Caroline, that people go anywhere else after death before going to Heaven?' she whispered. Caroline took her hand. 'My dear, all I know is that God has been so good to me here that He will not make things worse for me after I die. This satisfies and I think no further about those sort of subjects.'

Princess Sophia looked at her curiously.

Caroline said: 'Amelia was the best of them. Oh my poor, poor uncle. How will this new grief affect him?'

It was a question all England was asking, and the answer was not long in coming. The old, blind King had loved his youngest daughter more than anything in the world. During the many months of her illness he sat by her bedside weeping or sunk in melancholy silence, so that any heart with humanity in it ached to see him. When she was dead he seemed calmer, as if glad that her sufferings were ended at last. With trembling hands he sat playing chords of his beloved Handel on the organ. Then he sent for his child's papers and directed the disposal of them. When he had done he said he should now endeavour to dismiss the subject from his mind, or only think of his daughter's death as of an event which had happened years ago. He went back to his organ, struck a few notes, then his white head was bowed into his hands.

Sir Henry Halford and Dr. Baillie were sent for. The King raised his head and smiled at them wanly; then he said with dignity: 'I have a great reliance on you both, not only as skilful physicians, but as men of sense and integrity. I feel that I am going to be ill in the former way, and I request of you two, that you will not be induced on any account to represent me as fully recovered till you are satisfied that I am perfectly so. By permitting me to go abroad on the last occasion before that was the case, the physicians were the cause of my doing a great many absurd and foolish things. I am afraid that I have a great deal of fever.' Pathetically he held out his hand.

Harder hearts than Caroline's wept for him. Thereafter, day by day, there were bulletins from Windsor; the King had more fever or he had less. He had had a little sleep or a sleepless night. Bodily, he grew a little better. On the anniversary of his accession, the Queen assembled all her children, but two, at Windsor. The King, looking haggard and old and pathetically helpless from his blindness, came into the drawing-room leaning on the Queen. He seemed excited and flurried as he always did before his attacks of illness, but he went round the room speaking to all who were present.

It was the last time his people saw him. They heard of him from time to time; sometimes he was better, sometimes very odd indeed. He was constantly talking, laughing, sometimes singing. He had strange hallucinations; his poor Amelia was not dead but living in Hanover and possessed of the gift of everlasting health and youth. He had long conversations with his little Octavius, on

whom he doted, and who died when he was five years old.
The King formed a plan of his marriage, supposing him
to be seventeen. He fancied that he had the power of
raising persons who were dead, and making them seventeen, and that his having an interview with the Almighty
gave him this power. He had long talks with God. He
could only be persuaded to dress in white, and wore a
towel, bedgown, and drawers, no stockings, and only
garters. All his ideas were on purity. He would only
drink water and milk, and would not eat. Sometimes he
thought himself in Heaven, and that it was the Day of
Judgment, and he was pleading for all the wicked. He
often thought that he was dead and that he had left a
loving and united family behind him.

'I must have a new suit of clothes,' he said anxiously,
'and I will have them black in memory of George III; he
was a good man. I hope the Queen and all his family are
doing well, for he loved them very much when he was with
them.'

The physicians were examined by the Privy Council,
by a secret committee. The question of the Regency
became an interminable debate. Perceval was no Pitt,
but he remained firmly opposed to appointing the
Prince of Wales to fill the office as long as there appeared
any hope that the King might recover. The King was
sane enough to take an interest in the question, but
perhaps he had lost the desire to recover fully and take up
the burden of his life again. 'How is the Prince of Wales
behaving?' he asked Perceval, and was pleased when the
Minister informed him 'Well.'

He had lucid intervals, but they did not grow
longer.

On February 6th, 1811, the Prince of Wales took the oaths. The Regency had begun.

The King stayed at Windsor. His people forgot him as the years passed. His wife shrank from him and refused to be with him; his daughters saw him rarely, and his sons not at all. He was totally blind and almost deaf, worn and stooping, his white hair hanging on his shoulders, his silver beard flowing over his chest, and entirely neglected by those he loved. Aimlessly he wandered from room to room, seeking something, but what it was he could not tell. In his happier moments he sang hymns in a quavering, mournful voice, accompanying himself on the harpsichord.

When he had ceased he fell on his knees and prayed for Her Majesty, for his family, and for the nation, concluding with a touching petition that it might please God to avert his heavy calamity from him, but if not to give him resignation to submit.

Then he shed a few bitter tears and went back to his Handel.

The Prince Regent sat in his seat.

2

THE PRINCE REGENT DISCARDS HIS FRIENDS

THE Prince Regent, fickle by nature, changeable by compulsion, whirled like a weathercock in the path of variable winds. He had been a Whig when the King was a Tory; now that he sat in the King's seat he threw over the Whigs. He had courted popularity by seeking low company; from being too familiar he suddenly found himself too exalted to consort with lesser men. Fox was dead; Sherry, discarded, was drinking his wits away. The riff-raff crowds of the Pavilion thinned and vanished; only his boon companions remained.

The Prince Regent occupied himself with the Crown which dangled tantalisingly before his eyes, with trying to tame his rebellious daughter, and with employing every shaft which malice could devise to wound his wife. None of these occupations, of course, interfered with his serious attention to clothes.

There had been some coolness between him and Mr. Brummell, but it was natural that he should summon the latter when he wished to impress Europe. His attire must be worthy of him at this moment when all eyes were upon him.

Though Tom Moore sang:

' "Let's see," said the R – g – t, like Titus perplex'd
With the duties of empire, "Whom shall I dress next?"
He looks in the glass, but perfection is there –
Wig, whiskers, and chin tufts all right to a hair . . .'

the Prince was not absolutely satisfied.

Mr. Brummell had progressed a long way from the point at which he had burst as the supreme Dandy upon the astonished town. He had perfected his philosophy of clothes and of behaviour. He had begun with dress, but he soon relinquished that as unworthy or untenable as an empire of which to be sole ruler. 'He scorned to share his fame with his tailor and was, moreover, seriously disgusted at seeing a well-fancied waistcoat, almost unique, before the expiration of its "honey-moon" adorning the person of a natty apprentice. He grew tired of giving names to cloaks, hats, and pantaloons, and yearned for a higher pedestal than a tailor's shop-board. His coats and carriages were copied by others almost as soon as they were exhibited by him and, as it was his ambition to be inimitable, he found it much better to share these outward expressions, and trust alone to the nameless grace of polished ease which he possessed in a superlative degree.'

He despised the Prince and found him pinchbeck. He had better gifts, great powers of entertainment, a keen and lively turn for satire, and could talk down his superiors, whether in birth or talent, with an imposing confidence. He saw the advantages of being formidable, and observed with derision how those whose malignity he pampered with ridicule of others, vainly thought to purchase exemption for themselves by subservience to him. He had sounded the gullibility of the world, knew the exact value of pretence, and raised himself by his own gifts into the place he wanted, where he could dictate, unrivalled, to a subservient world.

He was not malicious, but he used malice as a weapon. He could condemn or commend by a witty word. He was sparing of both praise and censure, but he had a gift for causing an unconscious subject to reveal his own absurdities under his bland banter. He could tumble down pretensions by a lifted eyebrow, make a reputation with a gesture.

'In the art of "cutting" he was supreme; he knew the "when," the "where," the "how." Without affecting shortsightedness he could assume that calm but wandering gaze which veers, as if unconsciously, round the proscribed subject, neither fixing, nor to be fixed, not occupied, nor abstracted.' It was a gift which the Prince coveted extremely; his 'cuts,' in spite of constant practice, were clumsy.

Mr. Brummell's idol was originality; he wished to astonish even if he did not amuse, and would rather commit a folly than be commonplace. He was led by this sometimes to approach the verge of rudeness and vulgarity, but he had tact and a happy hardihood which carried him through difficulties. Indeed he knew that what would, in the current condition of his reputation damn another, would pass with the world in him.

His position was unique and unassailable, or so it seemed.

He could foist anyone upon society, but if, exceptionally, a young man had failed to secure the position he had claimed for him, Mr. Brummell made no second effort, but with a shrug dismissed him: 'Really I did my best for

the young man. I once gave him my arm from White's to
Watier's.'

He polished his philosophy, and the maxims were
learnt by heart by eager pupils:

Do not require your dress so much to fit as to adorn
you. Nature is not to be copied but exalted by art.
Apelles blamed Protogenes for being *too* natural.

Always remember that you dress to fascinate others,
not yourself.

Keep your mind free from all violent affectations at the
hour of the toilet. A philosophical serenity is perfectly
necessary to success. Helvetius says, justly, that our
errors arise from our passions.

To *win* the affection of your mistress, appear negligent
in your costume; to *preserve* it, assiduous. The first is a
sign of the *passion* of love; the second of its *respect*.

There may be more pathos in the fall of a collar or the
curl of a lock than the shallow think for. Should one be
so apt to compassionate the misfortunes of Charles I if
his pictures had portrayed him in a bob wig and a pig-
tail? Vandyck was a greater sophist than Hume.'

Mr. Brummell's charming insolence won him friends
and foes; he thought no foe could touch him; he thought
he could pick or discard the friends he chose. He thought
he could discard the Prince.

It had been possible to offend the Prince of Wales with
comparative impunity; it was not possible to offend the
Regent and not feel his power.

Mr. Brummell helped him with the Regency Gala, by
which he celebrated his father's madness and his own

assumption of power. The Gala created a sensation; it was the most magnificent affair since the Field of the Cloth of Gold, but over the arrangements appeared a coolness between Beau Brummell and the Prince.

The breach widened.

The fashionable world was shaken to its foundations by the report that Brummell and the Prince had quarrelled, and, in modish circles, the event caused as much excitement as the news of a victory over the French. For days nothing else was talked about and every one had some theory, reasonable or preposterous, as to the cause of the rupture. The wildest rumours flew from mouth to mouth: There had been a dinner-party at Carlton House at which the Beau had issued the command: 'Wales, ring the bell'; he had insulted Lady Hertford, and spoken disrespectfully of Mrs. Fitzherbert; no, it was the other way about. Why had they quarrelled? Nobody knew.

The Princess of Wales invited a party, as she usually did when there was any particular news of the Prince to be discussed.

'What is this about a quarrel between Mr. Brummell and the Regent? What has happened?' she asked the company.

'Mr. Brummell spoke sympathetically of Mrs. Fitzherbert when His Royal Highness was bestowing his smiles in another direction,' hazarded Lady Glenbervie.

Ward sneered: 'If the Prince was annoyed, Brummell was a match for him. His Royal Highness heard the Beau call him "Big Ben," after the fat porter at Carlton House, and made it worse by calling Mrs. Fitzherbert "Benina."'

'My husband does not like to tink he is growing fat.'

Lady Glenbervie murmured 'Growing!' in amazement. Ward said in a loud aside: 'When he lets loose his belly it now reaches to his knees.'

'His physicians say his corsets do him harm,' remarked the Princess.

'But you have not heard the end of the story,' Ward went on. 'Lord Alvanley, Sir Henry Mildmay, Henry Pierrepoint, and Beau Brummell had next night a great run of luck at hazard, and decided to celebrate their good fortune by giving a "Dandies' " Ball at the Argyll Rooms. The others wanted to invite the Prince, but Brummell vetoed it.'

'So would I, by God!' put in the Princess.

'Alvanley thought the invitation should be sent,' Ward continued, 'since if the Prince were on bad terms with Brummell he would be certain to refuse it. But Brummell said "No." The Prince heard of it, and without an invitation took a Royal privilege and announced his intention of being present.'

'Dat Brummell would be a match for him, I tink.'

'He was. The four hosts waited at the door to receive him; and when the Prince arrived he shook hands with Alvanley, Pierrepoint, and Mildmay, but looking Brummell full in the face passed on without giving him any sign of recognition. Brummell, quite unconcerned, turned to his neighbour (while the Prince was still within hearing) and asked, quite loudly: "Alvanley, who's your fat friend?"'

The Princess laughed delightedly. 'My God, if only I could take such a neat revenge.'

Ward shook his head. 'He will never forgive it.'

'I think Mr. Brummell is a bold man. He says he will

himself cut the Prince and bring the old King into fashion,' Lady Glenbervie remarked.

The Princess sighed. 'Ah! if the old King had his wits again it might be possible. But the Prince Regent is too powerful. He robs me of my friends, yet he throws away his own. He abandons them all the time: Mrs. Fitzherbert, Lady Jersey, Sheridan, Mr. Fox, the Jockey, Hanger, Lade. He has no conscience.'

'The Duke and Duchess of York are much attached to Mr. Brummell,' Lady Glenbervie remarked.

'Ah! de Duchess. She only loves her little dogs. Mr. Brummell is a character. I like his wit. I heard him once when he had a cold; he said that a rascally landlord had put him in a room with a damp stranger. He was very amusing. All the same it is not well to quarrel with the Prince. He is a bad enemy.'

3

CHARLOTTE

THE Prince Regent set spies once more about his wife.
As long as there had been a chance that the King might
recover no one had dared again attack her openly; but
as soon as his case became hopeless, and she could rely
no more on his protection, the insidious campaign
began. The Prince laid a bet that the Princess would
be the first person of the Royal family to go again into
public.

He, who had none, under-estimated her affections. She
grieved for her uncle. 'Everybody thinks he is going to
die,' she said sadly. 'Though he is not able to befriend
me yet I shall feel more desolate still when he is gone and
there will be no restrictions on the tyranny of the Regent.
I am not a coward, dear Lady Charlotte, and tink I could
bear most suffering, yet I felt my heart smite me the other
day when I had a curious letter, sent me by an anonymous person, written well and full of fearful predictions
as to my future fate. I cannot suppose why it was sent me
since the writer asked for no money nor appeared to wish
me evil, but rather to lament my fate. Have you heard
these rumours?'

'Yes, Madam,' Lady Charlotte began, for once genuinely affected.

'Oh! well, you need not tell me. Among other things it

contained, the writer said: The Prince had said that
never should I be crowned. When I was Queen I should
not be suffered to remain at Kensington, for that would
be too near the other Court, and meaning, I suppose, that
two Kings of Brentford could not reign peaceably together. He said also that very likely I should be sent to
Holyrood House and play the part of a second Mary
Queen of Scots. What think you, dear Lady Charlotte, of
this strange intelligence?'

'Madam, they would not dare.'

'I tink they would. Everybody except me is longing for
the change and hoping they know not what from the
poor old King's death. Ah, well! we must wait like others.
Old Q. is dead at last. I had a weakness for him. General
Wemyss is to have a lawsuit with Lord Wemyss about the
succession which he thinks he has a right to. The Duke's
disposal of his money is very confused, and there are so
many revocations after he had left the legacies, nobody
knows who has got anything. Lord Yarmouth gets the
chief part, or rather his *chère moitié*.'

'I hear Mrs. Fitzherbert has been to Carlton House.'

'What will Lady Hertford say to that?'

'It is extraordinary. The Prince visits or writes to her
every day, writes even when they are both in London,
employing the greater part of every morning on the
letters. What can be the topics of correspondence? She
is near fifty, and has been a grandmother more than
twelve or fourteen years. The Prince is not much younger.
How much, I wonder, did the Duke leave? Lord Hertford is said to have a revenue of above £70,000.'

'It is a liaison of vanity on her part, and I think the
Prince's affair with Lady Hertford is only sentimental.

He must always have a woman to advise him. He does not trust men.'

The Princess may have been right, but the Prince's heart, or attention, could only hold one woman at a time. The star of Lady Hertford was in the ascendant; Mrs. Fitzherbert's totally eclipsed.

The Prince had determined to set about ridding himself of both his wives. He knew how to deal with Mrs. Fitzherbert, but the Princess Caroline appeared just as formidable an obstacle as she had always been. He employed his toadies to set in circulation the most outrageous rumours concerning her. It was not long before they reached her attendants' ears.

'Of so degrading and dishonouring a nature that I am almost ashamed to hint at them,' murmured Lord Glenbervie to his wife. 'An intrigue with one of the meanest and lowest description possible.'

'Who?' Lady Glenbervie inquired.

'One Raymond, a second-hand player at the Lyceum.'

Lady Kitty raised her eyebrows.

'Sir Henry Englefield wishes us to warn the Princess that the Friths have been set to spy upon her. They are all day on the watch, and carry everything immediately to Bloomfield, the Prince's equerry. Bloomfield is a canting, methodistical hypocrite, always talking religion and morality, but living, though a married man, in barefaced adultery with Lady Downshire.'

'The Princess is in a great fidget,' his wife remarked.

The Princess was certainly restless. 'I am tormented by the advice of different friends,' she lamented. 'Some commend my plans and some abuse me and tell me I am ill advised and the time ill chosen to bring forward my wrongs. My dear Canning has the gout, and is depressed. Mr. Perceval, I tink, does not like me. Perhaps it is not a good time. Everybody is so busy about the war just now, and the Government is very strong, so that perhaps it would be well to *retirer mon épingle du jeu* till the questions of the Catholics, East India Charter, and other tings are decided. I shall consult wiser heads than mine.'

She remained lost in thought for a moment, and then went on: 'I will wait. People cannot attend to minor things. The King may die, or there may be a Peace, or a destruction of the "Beast," as Lewis calls Buonaparte, which might be all in my favour, as making more money going; and I should gain praise from the public by enduring my present state patiently a few months longer perhaps, and at present it would be considered quite a *Party Question*, not concerning me individually.'

Never had the Princess better displayed her acumen. She was, indeed, fast becoming *the* party question.

A very odd situation had arisen. The Prince Regent who, in his youth, had been so ardent a Whig, refused to put the Whigs in power. Mrs. Fitzherbert advised him to keep his promises to them; Lady Hertford advised him to support the Tories.

None of the Whigs had entertained the slightest suspicion of the Prince's devotion to Whig principles. His perfidy filled the party with consternation and amazement. Mr. Creevey, an amiable man, could not contain himself: 'The folly and villainy of this Prinney is certainly beyond anything,' he wrote. 'He actually dined with Perceval, he whose wife Perceval set up against him in open battle.'

The Prince kept the Tories in power. The Whigs, enraged and disgusted, remained in opposition and, since their hatred of the Regent was personal, chose to take the injuries of the Princess of Wales as their chief party weapon.

The Princess herself waited and, while waiting, began to write a novel whose scene was laid in Greece.

The Prince's other wife made one dignified protest against Lady Hertford's insults and Bloomfield's insolence, which were being encouraged by the Prince: 'Whatever may be thought of me by some individuals, it is well known your Royal Highness four-and-twenty years ago placed me in a situation so nearly connected with your own that I have a claim upon you for protection. I feel I owe it to myself not to be insulted under your roof with impunity. The influence you are now under, and the conduct of one of your servants, I am sorry to say, has the appearance of your sanction and support and renders my situation in your house, situated as I am, impossible any longer to submit to.'

Bloomfield sniggered; the proud Isabella sneered. The Prince did not answer, but set about buying pictures and designing new uniforms and giving the great Gala which was to rival if not exceed the Field of the Cloth of Gold. He considered his situation not unlike that of Bluff King Hal, and wished that the times would have permitted that Caroline's head might have fallen where Anne Boleyn's had done under the axe on Tower Hill. But the times did not permit. The People had become a force with which even popular monarchs had to reckon, and all the popularity was on Caroline's side. He cursed her heartily, and drank himself fuddled, and Lady Hertford

went on with the preparations for the Regency Gala and
the entertainment of the exiled King of France.

The magnificence of the Gala almost won him favour
with the fickle London mob – but not quite. Both the
Regent's wives stayed at home. Mrs. Fitzherbert had
expected to be present. She visited the Regent in advance
to know her place.

'Madame, you have none,' he answered coldly.

She was as cold as he, but she wrote one last protest:
'You, Sir, are not aware, in your anxiety to fill your table
with persons only of the highest rank, that by excluding
her who now addresses you, merely for want of those titles
that others possess, you are excluding the person who is
not unjustly suspected by the world of possessing in silence
unassumed and unsustained a rank given her by yourself
above that of any other person present. Having never
forfeited my title to your Royal Highness' public as well
as private consideration by any act of my life, to what
could this etiquette be for the first time imputed? No
one, my dear Sir, has proved themselves thro' life less
solicitous than myself. But I cannot be indifferent to the
fair honourable appearance of consideration from you,
which I have hitherto possessed, and which I feel I
deserve, and for which reason I can never submit
to appear in your house in any place or situation but
in that where you yourself first placed me many years
ago.'

When they next met, the Prince cut her. Mrs. Fitzherbert, in future, serenely cut him.

She had lost her uneasy happiness, but nothing could
rob her of her calm pride.

Caroline was proud, but not calm. There was no

PRINCESS CHARLOTTE OF WALES

To face page 208

question, for her, of attending the Gala, but she did expect that the visiting French Royalties would at least come to pay their court to her. She invited them all to a breakfast: 'Louis xviii, Madame d'Angoulême, all the French princes, and about thirty French people,' she enumerated them. 'My moder and the Princess Sophia of Gloucester and some old fograms male and female to enliven the party.'

She hid her mortification bravely when the Princes began to send excuses: 'Louis xviii could only offer me the gout in one knee and one toe, and Madame d'Angoulême a swelled face.'

She cried a little in her own room as she saw her fair-weather friends deserting her because their cowardice did not allow them to offend the Prince. Her parties still made a brave show, but her acquaintances were un-doubtedly falling away. The Prince could not isolate her, but he could cause her bitter hurt. Once she burst out bitterly to Lady Charlotte:

'They left me as time servers and I never can ask them back again. I am too proud for that.'

She put a brave face on things, but her temper was altering. She one day seized a poker, and broke a bust of the Duke of Cumberland, whom she hated for his evil influence over her husband.

The Prince grinned when he heard of the incident, but his grin changed to a scowl. Breaking up busts did not indicate the meekness of resignation and defeat. He might detach the more weak-minded of her friends but he could not detach the Opposition leaders. It was impossible to take any effective steps against her. Perceval was her friend as well as the Whigs. He brooded sullenly while those around him discussed Wellington and the victories in the West of Spain.

'Damn the West. Damn the East. Damn Wellington,' the Prince broke in furiously. 'The question is, *how* am I to rid myself of this damned Princess of Wales?'

None of his sycophants could offer suggestions, but they could think of methods by which he could annoy. Perhaps it was Isabella Hertford (only a woman could have thought of such a weapon) who suggested that the surest way of annoying the obnoxious Princess was through her child.

The Prince was enchanted. His hatred for his wife had grown to monstrous proportions owing to her apparent immunity to his malice. What could one do with a woman who said : 'As for me, no changes will make any difference in my lot, so I remain indifferent to them all. The world is decidedly cutting me, right and left, since my poor uncle's relapse. *Mais que voulez-vous*, 'tis the way of the world.' The Prince Regent could see nothing great-hearted in that.

She had not thought of Charlotte when she said no change could affect her. He would part her from her child again, and see if that would make her humble and come begging for terms.

He opened the new campaign at once. He forbade the Princess of Wales to see her daughter more than once a fortnight, or ever alone. Mother and daughter bitterly resented the new tyranny. They had never been allowed to see much of each other since Charlotte's infancy. The King had reluctantly taken the little Princess from both parents and insisted on her being brought up as the child of the State, but the King had allowed them to meet as often as seemed convenient; sometimes he had even let them have a little holiday together by the sea. When the King was ill the privileges were withheld; when he was better he restored them again.

He would never be better. 'Once a fortnight, for an hour, and never alone,' decreed the Prince Regent.

Mother and daughter alike were up in arms. To the Prince's astonishment his daughter was the better fighter.

Charlotte was an attractive child with fine features, a beautiful white skin, hair of shining gold, and remarkably pretty legs and feet. She did not spell very well, and would rather run and fetch a chair than make someone else do it, which was, of course, very undignified and unroyal. She was generous, impulsive, and vehement, and as warm-hearted as her mother, with an equal taste for fun. But she had the Regent's slight stammer and his gift for mimicry.

The Regent did not love his child, and she disliked him and hated the Queen. 'The Great Mahomet,' Caroline called her husband. 'The Merry Wife of Windsor,' Charlotte grimaced about the Queen. They laughed and caught hands and were very gay and unconcerned.

Charlotte was attached to Lady de Clifford, whose grandchildren were her chief playmates. She liked the boys best, for the old King's ideas for her education had given her boyish tastes. The little girls were rolled down hillocks into beds of nettles, and their tears staunched with gifts of dolls, but young George Keppel, a year or two her junior, was her partner in all kinds of pranks. She climbed railings and could saddle a horse. She inveigled George into the kitchen to cook Lady de Clifford's dinner, an appalling mixture which enraged the lady.

'A pretty Queen you'll make,' jeered George.

Charlotte smuggled him 'grub' into school, and peered wistfully through the railings at the horde of Westminster boys. 'If only I could go to school,' she sighed.

George said scornfully, 'You wouldn't like it. Lend me some money, Charlotte.'

She gave him all she had, but when she reached home thought it necessary to write him a quaint, elder-sisterly letter of advice:

'DEAR GEORGE,

Your grandmamma de Clifford allows me £10 a month. But though I spend it I take care never to go farther than my sum will allow. Now, dear George, if you do the same you will never want for money; say you have a guinea, well then, never go beyond it, and in time you will save up. That is the way everybody does, and so never gets into debt. If you will call at Warwick House my porter, Mr. Moore, will give you half a guinea. If you use that well and give me an exact account how you spend it, I will give you something more. I wish you was here. Write to me often and believe that no one loves you better than I do nor will be more happy to help you in all troubles than I. We have very fine weather, and your mamma is here and is pretty well. Gramma de Clifford sends her love to you, and I remain, Dear George, Your very sincere and affectionate

CHARLOTTE.'

Dear little lonely girl! The worst accusation ever made against her was that she was a hoyden. She was an excellent mimic and was perilously funny in her imitations

of Old Snuffy and her over-plump papa. When good
Bishop Fisher was more boring than usual, Charlotte
thrust out her lower lip and mimicked him so boldly
that George Keppel choked. When the Bishop's admoni-
tions were too heavy, Charlotte sent him long letters and
expressed the hope that he would have to pay because
they were over-weight.

'Pray don't call me your Royal Highness. My name is
Charlotte,' she said to the Bishop's daughter, and inveigled that sprig of propriety into playing leap-frog in
the drawing-room of Carlton House.

'There are only two things I do not like at all,' cried the
breathless Charlotte. 'One is apple-tart and the other is
my grandmother.'

She escaped from her grandmother's company to a
horse as often as she could. She was passionately fond
of riding, a taste she shared with her grandfather and
which he had sedulously encouraged. She was always
wild with excitement when she found herself in the
saddle.

Lady Glenbervie remarked to Lady de Clifford:
'Princess Charlotte is buckish about horses, and full of
exclamations very like swearing. She is a hoyden. She
sat after dinner with her legs stretched out and showed her
drawers.'

Lady de Clifford was shocked and glanced across the
room at her charge.

'My dear Princess Charlotte, you show your drawers.
They are much too long.'

Charlotte giggled. 'The Duchess of Bedford's are much
longer and they are bordered with Brussels lace.'

Lady de Clifford sighed: the child was a hoyden; it was

impossible to implant in her a sense of decorum which would satisfy the Queen.

All Europe had its eyes on the little Princess; she would be a great match for some impecunious princeling.

Charlotte had had more than one battle with her papa before she was fourteen. There was, for instance, the battle of Dr. Nott. Dr. Nott was her instructor, and she was fond of him. Some household intrigue, of which she knew nothing, caused his dismissal; Charlotte blamed Bishop Fisher and Mrs. Udney, but most of all the Queen. She protested by letter, and by excited, heated speech. No result. Charlotte sat down to write her *Will*:

'. . . Nothing to Mrs. Udney for reasons. I have done my Will, and trust that after I am dead a great deal may be done for Mr. Nott. I hope the King will make him a Bishop.'

The Prince of Wales read this document with displeasure, and called it 'High Treason' without a smile. Caroline laughed till the tears rolled down her cheeks.

'They do not love my daughter very much,' she said. 'But I do not say anything to make her grumble; it is best she should be satisfied with what is. She sees little of the Sultan, and he does not take the way to win her heart. She does not look well.'

Charlotte was often very unhappy, but, in spite of her impulsiveness, she had a great deal of discretion. 'It would not be wise to tell mama how unhappy I am,' she thought. 'She cannot do anything, and she may make bad worse.' Nevertheless she often wrote her mother long letters, sometimes daily letters of twenty pages, and more in times of stress.

There was no one whom she could trust, and, after her early childhood, no one except her mother – whom she knew to be foolish – of whom she could be fond. She was gay and lively, and the Queen kept her in such conditions that a girl far less spirited would have been driven to revolt. Her loneliness and unhappiness made her think a great deal and write long letters which were smuggled to her friends and to her mother when she could find a chance. She was romantic and craved happiness. She wrote friendly, indiscreet little notes to handsome young men, generally royal illegitimates, like Captain Hesse and the Fitzclarences, with whom she would have liked to be more friendly still. The Queen and her father raised shocked hands to Heaven and saw depravity in these harmless little notes.

The girl began to think seriously of her position. She was her father's only child, and likely to remain so. She was heiress to the Crown of England, though she had been told that her uncles said: 'Do you think we shall let that girl reign?' If they dishonoured her mother they would disinherit her. If her mother could be divorced her father would marry again and perhaps might have a son. Charlotte considered her situation gravely. She wanted to be Queen of England. Though sometimes she despised her mother, all her sympathies were on her side.

As she drove through the streets the people greeted her with loud and prolonged cheers. Not all the pomp with which he was surrounded could raise a hat when the Prince Regent drove abroad. The people adored

Charlotte. Her heart swelled with a warm, generous impulse towards them.

She observed and her eyes brightened. The Prince's unpopularity was so great that it was her mother's best protection. *The mob* was for her. Popularity, since the French Revolution, mattered tremendously, whatever it may have done before. And her father knew it. She and her mother could not always be kept apart. Mr. Perceval had promised. Mother and daughter believed in him.

'The Book' which contained the whole statements of the Douglas investigation, and which had been suppressed, was republished and sold openly. The affairs of the Princess of Wales were constantly under discussion in Parliament, were a never-ending source of scandal in the press. The mob read the evidence with fury; its feelings were wholly on Caroline's side. Dressing an effigy, labelled Lady Douglas, in white, with a parasol in its hand on which was written, in letters so large that all might read, the words 'Conspiracy and Perjury,' while on the figure's back was the inscription, 'Diabolical Perjury,' they carried it through the town preceded by a bell-ringer and exhibited it in front of Carlton House, where a vast concourse of people howled execrations on the perjurers.

In Parliament, amid derisive jeers, Lord Castlereagh stated suavely that 'the Government had not prosecuted Sir John and Lady Douglas for perjury because unwilling to place many indelicate accusations before the world.'

Princess Charlotte publicly turned her back upon her papa.

Thomas Creevey remarked ironically, 'Prinney tells Moira that no Prince was ever so idolised by the people of this country as himself.'

In May, 1812, Spencer Perceval was murdered. Caroline wept: 'I have lost my best friend. I do not know where to look for another.'

The Tories came back triumphant from the polls in 1812. Lord Liverpool had succeeded Perceval as Prime Minister, but Liverpool was the Prince's toady, and disinclined to be the friend of the Princess of Wales. Canning was her friend, but Canning remained, an ominous, brooding figure, on the outskirts of the party. Castlereagh at the Foreign Office did not concern himself with the Princess; the successes of the Peninsula campaign convinced England at last that Buonaparte was doomed. The Tories would attain to popularity on the tide of victory.

The deserted Whigs saw no hope of realising their long-deferred ambitions. They hated Prinney for his treachery, and the extreme wing of them, 'The Mountain,' caught up the sharpest weapon with which they could goad him and avenge themselves. Henry Brougham found the weapon and saw how to use it. The wrongs of the Princess of Wales should be used to serve 'the Mountain's' turn.

Brougham offered his legal services to the Princess.

Caroline was to fight for her right to see Charlotte.

Brougham stepped into the breach left by Perceval, but the Princess did not trust him as she had trusted Perceval. He seemed too volatile.

Charlotte broke down. She found the Prince was intercepting her letters and trying to intrigue her dear old easy-going Lady de Clifford out of her place, to install a new, severer governess and to forbid his daughter to see her mother at all.

The Princess of Wales went to Windsor, but was not

admitted to her daughter. She saw the Queen, who referred her to the Prince of Wales.

Caroline wrote to Brougham and Charlotte prepared to fight her father in earnest.

She was seventeen, and believed that she would be legally of age in another year. She considered one wild plan of escape after another. Lady de Clifford found her position intolerable and was induced, at last, to resign. The Princess refused to accept another governess. Father and daughter had stormy interviews. There were even more stormy interviews with the Queen. The Princess Charlotte played her trump card: 'Mr. Brougham will appeal to the people.'

With hatred and jealousy of his daughter in his heart, the Prince Regent yielded. Charlotte should leave her prison at Windsor, have Warwick House for her home, and two ladies as companions instead of a governess, should even be allowed, within limits, to choose them herself.

Warwick House was an old, moderate-sized building, miserably out of repair. Its situation was at the extremity of a narrow lane with a small courtyard and gates at which two sentinels were placed. The interior was very meagre. Charlotte's bedroom at the top of the staircase had bay windows which looked on a small garden with a wall and a road which divided it from the gardens of Carlton House to which there was a communicating door. It was her own house, but she was under her father's eye; all her comings and goings could be noted.

Nevertheless, she was pleased with her victory, and at once plunged into a new fight. She was seventeen; she must be publicly presented.

'Presented by the Duchess of York,' said the Regent to the Queen.

'Either by my mother or no one,' said Charlotte, and snapped her pretty white teeth.

The presentation was postponed. Charlotte was angry. A drawn battle was no fun at all.

Caroline took up her part. She began to write her husband long letters of protest which he returned un-opened with insulting covering letters from Lord Liverpool.

The letters appeared in the press. The people were wildly indignant. The affair became a Parliamentary one. The whole disgraceful matter of the Delicate Investigation was reopened, but this time in public. The Queen and the Prince Regent were hooted when they appeared in the streets; the Princess of Wales and Princess Charlotte were cheered to the skies. 'Never desert your mother,' the people cried to the young Princess. Every scrap of sentiment in the heart of the sentimental British public was enlisted on the side of the persecuted Princess.

A flood of addresses to Her Highness were voted, the City of London, of course, at the head.

The Lord Mayor and Aldermen were received at Kensington. The Prince Regent, purple with rage, went out of town that day.

When her Royal Highness appeared at the opera, every person in the house stood up and cheered. The Prince Regent stopped away from town. He had planned a fête at Vauxhall, and intended to be present; when the Princess wrote for tickets, Prinney himself was obliged to stay away. There was comedy in the situation,

and the Princess of Wales drew such fun as she could from
it, but her humour was flagging, her heart breaking, her
temper souring under the strain.

'The Regent is dangerously ill,' she wrote to Lady
Charlotte Campbell. 'Still, I am not sanguine enough to
flatter myself that the period to all my troubles and misfortunes is yet come. Yet one must hope for the best.'

'If only he would die,' she whispered to herself. 'If
only they would shut him up and let the old King out.'

The Whigs were equally hopeful that the Prince might
die. 'Prinney in a bad way. They have positively ordered
him to give up his stays as the wearing them any longer
would be too great a sacrifice to ornament, indeed might
end his life,' wrote Creevey.

Their hopes were not fulfilled. The Prince recovered,
and resumed his stays.

The Peace had come. Louis xviii had gone back to
France, Napoleon was on Elba, the exiles and the curious
followed the King of France to Paris. A passionate desire
was growing in Caroline's heart to give up the fight and
go abroad, go back to her own country which had been
ravaged by the war and taken from her family, go south
to Italy where the sun shone and hearts were driven by
blood, not made of stone. She longed desperately for
music and laughter, for sun and vivid colour, for everything as different as possible from the cruel persecutions
and the cruel circumstances which were breaking her at
last.

Charlotte was nearly of age and the nation's charge.
Her child did not need her; she could not help her child.

She thought bitterly of the friends who had deserted
her from cowardice or from self-interest. She snatched

enjoyment out of such pleasures as remained. Lord Byron, a topic of scandalous gossip even more exciting than herself, came gaily to bid her farewell, in high spirits, like a bird in the air, having just got rid of his chains. He must go abroad, he had told her, 'but where, how, and with whom?'

Caroline longed to go too; she was as stormy and passionate as the poet whom she so much admired.

Byron was going, but the Emperor of Russia was coming in a fortnight. For the last time Caroline thought Fortune's face might be turned her way. Alexander was almost the only person in the world who might be able to do something with the Prince Regent. Since Buonaparte had abdicated, the Czar had been behaving as if he were responsible for rearranging Europe and setting damaged kingdoms on their feet.

Charlotte was also looking forward to the Czar's arrival. There would be splendid entertainments at which, now she was nearly of age, it would be right for her to appear, and at which she would be able to savour the homage and popularity of which she had had so small a meal.

Her father had also intimated that it was time that she should marry. She was not reluctant; at least marriage would mean liberty and an establishment of her own. The Prince of Orange had been selected. She was not enthusiastic about him, but, after all, she did not know any other prince who would do. So she consented, ignorant that the Prince, as heir, would be obliged to make his home in Holland.

Her mother opened her eyes to the plot to exile her from her own country. The battle between father and daughter was renewed with increased bitterness, for they were open rivals now. Charlotte could, and would, fight this issue without her mother's active help. Between mother and daughter a little rift appeared. Charlotte saw that her mother's championship injured her, that without it she stood a better chance of fair treatment from her grandmother, if not from her father. The girl was dismayed and distressed as the realisation grew on her that, through unhappy circumstances, her mother was the greatest enemy to her own hopes.

Charlotte was loyal, affectionate, and generous, but she was impulsive and sometimes as tactless as Caroline herself. 'If only my mother would be quiet and let me manage this affair for myself,' she sighed aloud.

Eager gossip carried the wish to Blackheath. That hurt Caroline more than anything had hurt her; with bitterness of heart she watched the breach between her daughter and herself widen. 'I have not seen Princess Charlotte for nearly five months,' she wrote. 'Her unnatural father assured her that she should never have an establishment in this country. I expect Mr. Whitbread every moment about this interesting subject. It will make a great rumpus in the Houses, both of Lords and Commons, which I trust will accelerate his departure to the skies.'

Princess Charlotte had as much faith in herself as she had in Parliament. She did not like anything that she heard about the Prince of Orange. He was a very thin, ill-looking young man in a plain suit, and he was lodged at his tailor's. All Charlotte's youthful fancy was for a well-looking young man in fine clothes who had spirit enough to insist on being lodged royally at the Prince Regent's expense.

At an informal dinner at Carlton House, Charlotte was formally presented to the Prince of Orange though she had seen him before and had told her mother that he was so ugly she had to turn her head away in disgust when he spoke to her.

She was anxious to please her father, however, since the marriage seemed inevitable, and was civil to the young man, indeed, liked him better than she had at first. She was dressed in a sad-coloured costume of violet and black, and looked very well. In fact, except that her figure was rather too full and already showed signs of becoming unshapely, she was a very pretty and charming young woman.

The Regent was delighted with her docility, and paced up and down the room with the young couple.

'Will it not do?' the Regent suddenly asked his daughter.

Charlotte bit her lip with a momentary hesitation. 'Oh,' she said, 'I do not say that. I like his manner very well, as much as I have seen it.'

The Regent, taking that for consent, caught her hand in delight and placed it in that of the young man. He left them together, the pale, sickly, spindle-shanked youth and the lively, romantic young girl.

The boy was tongue-tied. Charlotte, already repenting her acquiescence, burst into hysterical tears.

The Prince of Orange looked very frightened when the Regent came hurrying back.

'What! Is he going away?' he asked facetiously.

Charlotte could not answer. With a scowl the Regent led the boy away.

Charlotte threw herself into Miss Knight's arms. 'He

told me I should have to live in Holland,' she sobbed. 'I won't. I won't. I won't.'

She sent for the marriage contract, and eyed its provisions with fury and disgust. She said firmly that she would stay in England or there would be no marriage. In vain the Prince Regent sent emissaries to coax and threaten; his daughter was as determined as he was, and knew that she had *her* people on her side. The Prince tried trickery. He said : 'As she had received presents and made promises she could be compelled to marry the Prince of Orange.'

Charlotte was troubled, but, reassured by Brougham, countered by an artless request: 'If this is so,' she wrote to her father, 'and I am ignorant of law, I beg that this opinion may be given me in writing so that there can be no mistake when I consult Mr. Brougham, who is advising me.'

The Prince Regent cursed Brougham, cursed Parliament, cursed the country, but chiefly he cursed his daughter and his wife. He calmed himself with an effort, and sent his brothers to see if they could do anything with this obstinate young woman. Charlotte regarded them as amiable old fools who were as jealous of her as her father, though with less bitterness. She was heiress of England, Brougham assured her, in spite of the jealous Dukes, who protested publicly that 'she laboured under a great mistake, for she seemed to consider herself as heir-apparent, whereas she could hardly be regarded as a presumptive heir.'

Defied by his daughter, the Regent revenged himself by a fresh affront to the Princess of Wales. The Queen, acting on his orders, refused to receive her daughter-in-law at the drawing-rooms or at any of the festivities arranged for the Allied Sovereigns in London.

Caroline protested, then acquiesced, and sent the resulting correspondence to the House of Commons. The Allied Sovereigns were entertained by public debates upon this domestic scandal in the household of their host.

The Princess of Wales consoled herself with the thought that, since the Emperor Alexander had visited Josephine at Malmaison, he would certainly call on Caroline at Kensington.

The Prince Regent proceeded with preparations for his daughter's wedding. He sent her a list of wedding guests which omitted her mother's name. Charlotte returned it after scratching out the name of the bridegroom.

The girl was tired and unhappy, though at intervals she found considerable enjoyment in her father's excursions and alarums. She might have capitulated if she had not been more fortunate than her mother in the matter of friends. Her adored Miss Mercer and Miss Cornelia Knight, with discretion, aided and abetted her in her resistance, and presently they hatched a plot.

They hatched it, very suitably, at a house in Piccadilly which had once belonged to 'Old Q.' London was full of great and fashionable personages come to celebrate the Peace. The Czar of all the Russias had brought his sister, the Grand Duchess Catherine of Oldenburg, and an impecunious but handsome young *aide*, Prince Leopold of Coburg. The Grand Duchess had a little political scheme of her own in hand which included the Prince of Orange, and she was not entirely indifferent to the romantic heart of youth. Princess Charlotte's friend, Miss Mercer, was

for ever whispering in the ear of the Grand Duchess, and
attending the great dinners which the Grand Duchess
gave. The Prince of Orange was invited to one of them
on a night when he was afterwards to waltz at a ball at
Carlton House with his betrothed, the Princess Charlotte
of Wales. The Grand Duchess plied him with champagne
and his glass was refilled and refilled and refilled. He
could not refuse, of course, and his head was evidently not
very strong.

The ball at Carlton House was the only State function
to which Charlotte had been invited, although the Prince
of Orange went everywhere and was fêted as her betrothed. The girl's anger was at boiling point; her own
indignities, added to the insults heaped upon her mother,
were more than her pride could brook. The Prince of
Orange should have been her champion; he only added
to her humiliation. This was his first public appearance
with her; by his behaviour on this occasion should the
engagement stand or fall.

As the room gradually filled – the great crimson room
in which State receptions were held – her attention was
caught by a singularly handsome young man who was
paying court to a young lady whom she knew. She
watched him; she noticed his tall, soldier-like figure, and
quiet dignified manner, and observed how strange it was
that the young lady did not seem much gratified at his
attentions. She did not learn his name nor was he presented to her – Prince Leopold of Coburg was not of
sufficient importance – but the thought of him lingered in
her mind long enough for her to wish that the Prince of
Orange might have been like him. There was another
young man, Prince Augustus of Prussia, who was pre-

sented to her, and to whom she took a fancy, thinking he would do very well as a husband.

The Prince of Orange, very tipsy, came to dance with her. White with anger Charlotte turned her back.

The public insult on such an occasion was too much. Charlotte wept in Miss Mercer's apartments and hither came the Duchess of Oldenburg, most innocently accompanied by Prince Leopold of Coburg. The young man was presented. Charlotte fell, tempestuously, in love. Leopold responded with discretion. The Grand Duchess smiled.

If Charlotte had been determined to break off her engagement to the Prince of Orange merely because she disliked and despised him, she was doubly determined when she fell in love with a handsome and agreable young man who, though of very little importance, was still eligible as a husband for the heiress of England.

She received the Prince of Orange in the presence of her mother's lady-in-waiting, Lady Charlotte Lindsay, and told him positively that she would not marry him unless there were inserted in the marriage contract a clause giving her the option of remaining in England, as she would not leave her mother under existing circumstances.

The Duchess of Oldenburg said approvingly : 'That is right. Be firm. Though I would not marry him at all.'

'I won't,' Charlotte assured her with bright eyes.

Her father, as Brougham had told her, was jealous of her to a point which was perilously near insanity; the nearer she approached to her legal majority and the more intensely the people applauded her the more intense his feeling had grown. He would gladly have seen her dead.

He commanded her to Carlton House. She sent a
pretty apology that she was too unwell to go; it was true
she had hurt her knee.

In a raging temper he stormed over to Warwick House.
'You will be confined to your rooms here for five days,'
he informed his pale but determined daughter. 'I dismiss
here and now these women who have encouraged your
undutiful behaviour. All your household is dismissed.
And you, Charlotte, shall go to Cranbourne Lodge, and
receive neither visits nor letters until you come to a better
mind. You are mistaken; you have not attained your
legal majority. You are under my absolute authority.
You shall see no one, no one, I say, but the Queen.'

Charlotte swayed and put her hand to her heart. 'I am
ill, Papa, may I go to my room?'

'Go,' he commanded harshly.

The girl limped slowly up the stairs.

When her father had left the house, she snatched up a
bonnet and shawl, crept down the back staircase out into
the street, and hailed a hackney coach to take her to her
mother, who had a house in Connaught Place and had
been staying there. The Princess of Wales had gone to
Blackheath. A messenger was sent after her.

Charlotte waited, pacing up and down the room with
quick breath and nervous fingers twisting and lacing.
'Why is she not here?' she thought. 'Oh God! when most
I need her, why is she not here? I am afraid of him. Her
house is the only place to which he will not dare to come.'

The Princess of Wales came at last, alarmed by her
daughter's rashness, and Charlotte felt bitterly that her
mother was failing her as in her heart she had known she
would do.

Brougham, hastily summoned, appeared at Connaught Place and, in his turn, sent for the Duke of Sussex, the only one of her uncles in whom Charlotte had any faith.

Her flight was discovered, and emissaries arrived from Carlton House: the Duke of York, Lord Chancellor Eldon, Lord Ellenborough, William Adam, and John Leach. Charlotte would not see them. She cried for her dear Miss Mercer, and Miss Mercer joined the Princess and her mother in an upstairs room, while downstairs the great men argued and tried to negotiate with the rebel upstairs.

At three o'clock in the morning she consented to see Brougham. His face was grave and troubled, and his eyes dark with sympathy, but he would not uphold her rebellion.

'Your Royal Highness,' he said quietly, 'you must go to Carlton House. You cannot legally refuse to go to your father.'

Wide-eyed the girl stared at him as if she were stunned.

'I will not. I will not,' she faltered through white lips. Brougham, who was not remarkable for tenderness of heart, felt as if he had pronounced sentence of death on a prisoner.

'Look, madam,' he said pleadingly. 'In a few hours all the streets and the Park, now empty, will be crowded with tens of thousands. The Cochrane case comes on to-day. The passions of the mob are already stirred. I have only to take you to this window and show you to the multitude and tell them your grievances, and they will rise on your behalf. The commotion will be excessive. Carlton House will be attacked, perhaps pulled down. The soldiers will be ordered out. Blood will be shed. And if your Royal Highness were to live to a hundred years, it would never be forgotten that your running away from your father's house was the cause of the mischief; and you may depend upon it, such is the English people's horror of bloodshed, you never would get over it.'

'*My* people,' came almost inaudibly through Charlotte's white lips. She wiped her eyes and turned to find her bonnet and shawl.

'I will go,' she said. 'Where is my uncle? I heard the Duke of York was here. You are right, Mr. Brougham, I must go to Carlton House. Let them send for one of my father's coaches.'

She sat down weakly, and once more put her hand to her side. Caroline was weeping. Her daughter turned her head away. She could draw no comfort from her mother, and the thought of carrying on, unaided, the fight with her father, appalled her. She sprang to her feet again.

'I will not marry the Prince of Orange, Mr. Brougham. There, at least, the law is on my side. Will you please draw up a declaration that I am so resolved, that any announcement of the marriage will be against my will, and without my consent, and that if any such announcement is made this declaration will be published. Parliament and the country can protect me so far.'

In silence the declaration was drawn up and signed by Charlotte and her mother, by the Duke of Sussex, Lady Charlotte Lindsay, Miss Mercer, and Brougham himself.

'Please send a copy to my father,' the Princess said as she went down the stairs.

In the dawn the Duke of York led her up the steps of Carlton House. She was sent to Cranbourne Lodge immediately, and treated as a prisoner, watched implacably by day and night. For a year and a half this imprisonment lasted, until she fell ill, and was taken to Weymouth for the sake of her health, when the supervision was slightly relaxed. The Duke of Kent saw her, and with whispered confidences arranged a secret correspondence with the handsome young man who was to rescue her when the right moment came. Leopold was distinguishing himself; he had won honours in war; he was winning praise for his diplomatic skill at Vienna. Charlotte hid his letters above her fast-beating heart.

Her mother could not help her child, and she could not help herself. Caroline was tired of being a political pawn, and there was no end to the Prince Regent's malice.

'I tell you what,' she said to Lady Charlotte Campbell, 'they only want to make a cat's paw of me.'

It infuriated her to be told what to do, what not to do, what to wear, to whom to write, and what to say. Mr. Whitbread even had the insolence to advise her to cover up her neck. It was intolerable that the Princess of Wales should be spoken to like this.

There was a gala performance at the opera at which the Prince Regent and all the foreign princes were to be present. The Princess went to this and entered while 'God Save the King' was being played. As the music ceased the whole pit turned and applauded her.

'Acknowledge it,' her chamberlain advised, 'otherwise you will be hissed.'

'No. No,' she protested. 'Punch's wife is nobody when Punch is present. I know my business better than to take the morsel out of my husband's mouth. I am not to seem to know that the applause is meant for me till they call my name.'

As she spoke the Prince rose and bowed profoundly to the house. 'You see,' Caroline remarked with humorous mouth, 'he can believe it was for him.'

It was not. When the performance was over the mob surrounded the livid Prince, shouting threateningly, 'Where's your wife?'

He drove away in a hurry, and Caroline, still smiling, stepped into her coach while the people applauded her loudly, surrounding the coach, opening the door, and begging for a handshake.

'Shall we burn Carlton House?' someone cried, and the cry was repeated from a hundred mouths.

Caroline raised her hand with dignity, demanding silence.

'No, my good people,' she said. 'Be quite quiet. Let me pass and go home to your beds.'

The crowd good-humouredly let her pass. 'Long live the innocent. God save the Princess.'

'They have shut up Buonaparte. Now I can get out of my cage,' she said. 'I will leave England. I do not know who plagues me most, my friends or my enemies. Now Brougham and Whitbread say I must not take the extra money Parliament has voted me. It is my dower; it is my right. They say it is an insidious and unhandsome offer meant to injure me. It is all the *Party*.'

'My dear,' she said to Lady Charlotte, 'it is not *in* me to suspect evil till I see it plainly. If de Princess refuse de money they will say: "What de devil does de woman want? We cannot make her husband like her or make de Queen receive her, but we can set de seal upon all our public doings of last year by settling upon her a sufficient sum to enable her to hold her rank of Princess of Wales." I will therefore accept. I will. I will do it myself. And

I will tell Lord Liverpool to tell my husband dat I will go to Brunswick.'

The Prince raised no objection to *that*. On the eve of her departure he gave the toast to his cronies: 'To the Princess of Wales' damnation, and may she never return to England.'

Her political friends protested strongly; they said she was putting herself in the wrong, that the Prince Regent would take advantage of her absence from the country to secure a divorce, that she would forfeit the affection of the people if she left England now, since they distrusted all foreigners and those who lived among foreigners. The Princess would not listen; her only desire, now, was to leave the land where she had spent so many miserable years. She had another motive, too; it had been whispered in her hearing that life would be made much more bearable for Princess Charlotte once her mother was out of the way.

'It is pitiable,' that mother said to herself, 'to see a child rendered on all occasions a source of dispute between her parents. When I am gone they will set her at liberty once more.'

She hurried her preparations and left London for Worthing. Her child was allowed to say farewell to her. She found Charlotte pale and thin, but more resigned to her confinement than she had expected. She did not know that Leopold's letters were beckoning the girl to a starry future.

'I will come back when you are Queen,' Caroline said affectionately. 'I do not wish to be Queen of England myself, the Queen's mother is enough for me. The second Prince of Orange is arrived in London, Charlotte. He is of the same age as you; if you took him as a husband you would not be obliged to leave England.'

'I will marry at my own choice,' the girl said firmly. 'Someone devoted to myself, and not to the Royal family, for I mean to be free.'

'But, my dear,' Caroline protested, 'whoever you marry will be King, and you will give him power over you.'

'Pho. Pho. Never,' laughed Charlotte. 'He will only be my first subject. Never my King.'

'Dat's de spirit, Charlotte,' cried her delighted mother. Charlotte looked at her wistfully. Should she tell her that she was in love? Perhaps it would be wiser not to. Her mother's lively tongue might give the secret away and spoil it all. The girl's eyes filled with tears. She was being deserted.

'Listen, my child. Have you heard the latest quiz on the Emperor?:

> "Je lègue aux enfers mon génie;
> Mes exploits aux aventuriers;
> A mes partisans infamie;
> Le grand livre à mes créanciers;
> Aux François l'horreur de mes crimes;
> Mon exemple à tous les tyrans;
> La France à ses Rois légitimes;
> Et l'hôpital à mes pagrens." '

Charlotte smiled faintly. She admired the Emperor.

The Princess of Wales sailed from Worthing gaily on the *Jason* frigate, on an August morning in 1814. With her went Lady Charlotte Lindsay and Lady Elizabeth

Forbes as ladies of the bedchamber; Sir William Gell, and Antony St. Leger, her chamberlain; Keppel Craven, her equerry; Dr. Holland, her physician; Captain Hesse, who was too fond of the Princess Charlotte for his own peace of mind; John Jacob Siccard, her steady old steward; and that tiresome young man, Willy Austin, about whose birth and parentage there had been so much pother.

At Brunswick the Princess of Wales was met by her brother, and the operatic journey really began.

Charlotte returned to Cranbourne feeling very miserable indeed. She was only allowed to have a few books and a few lessons and a very occasional visit, under strict guard, to the opera or the play. Her health and spirits gave way; she grew ailing, thin, and nervous. She started if a door opened suddenly or a hasty step were heard. If people whispered in her hearing she turned pale and looked terrified in case some punishment was being devised. Her uncles did not concern themselves with her; only the Duke of Sussex ventured to protest, and so earned the undying enmity of the Prince Regent. The doctors shook their heads over the Princess, and recommended sea air. The Prince Regent forbade it. A whisper reached the Press, and a pertinent question in the *Morning Chronicle* induced her father to send her hastily to Weymouth.

She had been there with her poor old grandfather, and the associations were too sad for the change to do her a great deal of good. Still, the sea air brought back some colour to her cheeks. Her letters were intercepted so that she had no news of the things she really wanted to know. Where was her mother? And when was Prince Leopold coming back? There was no one to ask, since she could trust no one.

An unguarded moment of the Regent's, or perhaps a desire to trap her, permitted a visit from Miss Mercer.

'Don't lock your heart, dear Charlotte,' her friend entreated. Confide in someone. Isn't Mrs. Campbell kind?'

Charlotte smiled ironically. 'My dear Margaret, till I choose for *myself*, the people that are about me, I never will speak but of matters of fact, for I cannot and will not submit to have people chosen for me, not even angels from Heaven.'

'It shows a sad, obstinate spirit,' said Princess Augusta when told this by Mrs. Campbell, who had been listening at the door.

There was no hope of rescue from her family or friends. 'When will he come?' she whispered to her pillow.

Suddenly the Prince Regent realised the futility of this imprisonment. The mob, Parliament, would soon intervene. He had heard whispers of her liking for Prince Leopold of Coburg. He did not wholly dislike the young man, though he called him sneeringly: 'The Marquis Peu à Peu.'

Since Charlotte would not have Orange, Leopold would do as well as any other princeling who had no power to interfere with *him*.

He sent the Duke of York to ask her whom she would consider.

York asked with apparent sympathy: 'Tell me, my dear, have you seen among the foreign princes any whom you would like to have for a husband.'

Charlotte answered demurely: 'No one so much prepossessed me as Prince Leopold of Coburg. I have heard much of his bravery in the field, and I must say he is personally agreable to me.'

The Prince Regent invited Prince Leopold to come to London.

Charlotte only asked her betrothed one question. 'You will befriend and support my mother?' Leopold promised. Charlotte gave him her hand.

On May 2nd, 1816, the great crimson drawing-room at Carlton House was bedecked for the wedding. Before a crimson-covered altar the Princess stood in gossamer draperies, and a long train of silver brocade, her fair, curly head surmounted by a wreath of large diamonds and roses.

Charlotte's voice was clear and unhesitating, and her eyes were bright as stars. But she laughed under her bridal veil when Leopold solemnly promised to endow her with all his worldly goods.

In the drawing-room after the wedding she stood apart from the Royal circle in a window with her back to the light. She was deadly pale and did not look well. She was thinking of her mother, and her loving heart forgot its own happiness.

The Prince Regent turned his back on several ladies whom he knew to be friends and partisans of the Princess of Wales. Charlotte spoke to them with marked graciousness.

The Tower guns thundered out the news to London that the beloved Princess was married to the man she had chosen.

The Regent kissed her and gave her a hug, the first spontaneous one of his life, because he was quit of her.

The Queen kissed her with less chill than usual, and

expressed uneasiness that the newly married couple should be going alone to Oatlands.

'Let Mrs. Campbell go bodkin with them; it is improper they should drive without a chaperone.'

The Prince Regent was gratified to observe that happiness achieved what coercion had failed to do. Charlotte had no desire but to live in the country at Clairmont as quiet as a mouse with her husband. She adored him; even his lack of humour, which left her to enjoy her jokes alone, did not dim her happiness. And Leopold was an excellent husband. Stockmar, his German physician, described him as 'always quiet, always circumspect. He will never be elated by prosperity or cast down by adversity. He sees everything in its true light. This preserves him from mistakes and mortifications.' Leopold considered himself admirably fitted to control the destinies of England and to give advice to its Queen. As it happened his advice was welcome and, on the whole, good when he gave it to the Queen of England; but the Queen he advised was not Charlotte, and by that time Leopold himself was King elsewhere. But the future was hidden; Charlotte, in spite of her protestations to her mother, was very submissive, and supremely content. As seldom as might be did she appear in public.

'I am so utterly happy that I fear it cannot last,' she said.

Both she and her husband wrote to the Princess of Wales, and read her amusing answers together. No one was cruel enough to spoil the girl's happiness with malicious tales of that theatrical progress across Europe which was disgusting and entertaining the world. Caro-

line did not write very often, though the thought of
becoming a grandmother amused and delighted her. She
was touched by her child's loyalty to her, and pointed it
out to others who were less loyal: 'They mistake if they
think Charlotte will like them better for not noticing the
Princess of Wales,' she remarked.

Charlotte was very cold indeed to those who slighted
her mother, but even her retirement and protecting wall
of happiness could not for ever keep out the tales that
were abroad. Why were her mother's English attendants
deserting her? Charlotte wrote at last to Lady Charlotte
Campbell on the matter: 'The only person now remaining
with my mother, and who I trust will take courage and
continue with her, is Dr. Holland, who, I believe, from
everything I have heard of him, is a most respectable and
respected character. I have it not in my power at present
to repay any services shown to the Princess of Wales, but
if I ever have, those who remain steadfast to her shall not
be forgotten by me, though I fear sensible people like him
never depend much on any promises from anyone, still
less from a Royal person, so I refrain from making pro-
fessions of gratitude, but I do not feel them the less
towards all those who show her kindness. I have not
heard from my mother for a long time. If you can give me
any intelligence of her, I should be much obliged to you to
do so. I am daily expecting to be confined, so you may
imagine I am not very comfortable. If ever you think of me,
dear Lady Charlotte, do not imagine that I *am only a princess*, but remember me, with Leopold's kind compliments, as
your sincere friend, Charlotte, Princess of Saxe-Coburg.'

Dear, sensible, generous, warm-hearted Charlotte! She
was 'not very comfortable.' She looked forward with

joy to the child who was to come, but she felt ill; she had a fixed pain in her side for which she wore a perpetual blister. She made little fuss, for she did not want to disturb Leopold; she was still prodigiously in love. Leopold was still in love, too, but he was a prudent young man, whereas Charlotte was anything but prudent. He found much in her of which he disapproved. She was impetuous, wildly generous; she had a perfectly shocking disregard of decorum and etiquette; she quizzed, she stamped, she had a loud, though exceedingly musical laugh. Her manners were so frank and natural as to be abominable from his point of view. He set to work to train her, kindly, gently, but firmly, with the perseverance of a schoolmaster.

Charlotte raged. There were scenes at Clairmont. But the scenes always ended in the same way, with Charlotte with bright eyes and flaming cheeks, her body thrust forward, her hands behind her like a rebellious schoolboy, standing before him saying: 'If you wish it I will do it.'

'When I press something on you it is from a conviction that it is for your interest and for your good, Charlotte.'

The rebellious boy in her was lost in the lover. 'I am so happy, so very happy,' she whispered in his arms.

There were disturbing symptoms in her pregnancy. She was left alone in the hands of Sir Richard Croft, the fashionable surgeon of the hour, who was jealous and forbade consultation with any other doctor, though the Germans of Prince Leopold's suite were muttering ominously of carelessness, stupidity, and inconceivable ignorance. Sir Richard Croft had a new theory based on an exiguous vegetarian diet and much bleeding. Stockmar looked on with misgiving as Charlotte was starved

MARCHIONESS OF HERTFORD

To face page 240

and bled, but his position was a very subordinate one and his sagacity was reluctant to risk reproof by interference.

Charlotte liked him, called him 'Stocky,' and romped with him along the corridors at Clairmont. He returned her liking, and did at last venture to warn Leopold that Charlotte's health was causing him alarm. Leopold was uneasy, but the English doctor would not listen and poured scorn on the little German's fears.

When her time came her state was alarming. The child of Charlotte's love and England's hopes was still-born. Still Croft seemed unconcerned.

Prince Leopold hovered in the background like an uneasy ghost.

The heiress of England, attended only by her old nurse, tossed and groaned. They plied her with wine.

At last Stockmar was admitted. She seized his hand, and pressed it.

'They have made me tipsy,' she moaned.

Leopold had been persuaded to go to bed. Stockmar sent for him and turned to pass into the next room.

'Stocky. Stocky,' Charlotte called.

He ran back. The death rattle was already in her throat. She tossed herself from side to side, drew up her legs, and turned upon her face. Leopold knelt by her bedside and kissed her cold hands. 'Dear, beautiful hands,' he whispered, 'which always seemed to be looking out for mine.' Stockmar touched him on the shoulder. Leopold rose. 'Now I am quite desolate,' he groaned, and stumbled into Stocky's arms.

The Princess of Wales was on her fantastic travels and was not officially informed of her daughter's death, but left to learn it as she might; the Prince Regent was

sunning himself in Lady Hertford's house. The Queen
was at Bath with her daughters. They had none of them
concerned themselves very much with Charlotte, though
the Queen had offered to remain and been refused. They
came back to London now, the Prince posting frantically
through the night, for once moved by genuine emotion;
the old Queen was stricken behind her grim quietude, the
Prince Regent dissolved in noisy and emotional grief.

The bells were tolling for the nation's darling. Charlotte was dead – Charlotte the dear, delightful, her
country's hope. From a dust-heap had sprung a flower;
she had all the passion of her father and her mother, but
in her it turned towards a passion for the generous, the
fine, the welfare, according to her lights, of those who
would one day call themselves her people. She might
have been another Elizabeth, but an Elizabeth not only
masterful but good, generous, true.

England had never been so stirred to tears as when
Charlotte's death deprived the people of hope, darkened
their prospects, and left them to the mercy of that elderly
Silenus, her father, and his brothers, hung round the neck
of England like millstones round the neck of a drowning
man.

London was dazed with grief. In the streets people
were sobbing and their tears were not of sensibility, but
of sorrow. And, as evening drew on, the evening which
was to have been one of rejoicing, the city shrouded itself
in fog and the bells of St. Paul's beat out a slow message
of despair. The message was echoed from Southwark,
from Lambeth, from churches far and near: 'Charlotte is
dead, is dead, is dead.'

Foreigners looked on in amazement; such genuine,

such extravagant grief was remarkable. 'It is impossible to find in the history of nations or families an event which has evoked such heartfelt mourning,' wrote the Russian Ambassadress to her brother. 'One met in the streets people of every class in tears; the churches were full at all hours; the shops shut for a fortnight (an eloquent testimony from a shopkeeping community); and every one from the highest to the lowest is in a state of despair which it is impossible to describe. That charming Princess Charlotte, so richly endowed with happiness, beauty, and splendid hopes, is cut off from the love of a whole people.'

Prince Leopold was in a distressing state. The Prince Regent had himself bled.

The bells of all England took up the lament and wailed for a nation's woe.

The mob was nearly frantic with dismay and rage. A victim must be found for the Londoners' fury; they fixed on the Queen. The hatred of London fell on her; the City whispered, and believed, the rumour that the Queen had suborned the nurse or doctor out of hatred to the Regent's wife. A dense mob surrounded her carriage, horrible yells and threats were raised; wild heads were thrust through the windows, snarling: 'What have you done with the Princess Charlotte?' Rough hands tried to disarm her footmen; she would not have been safe if the High Constable of Westminster had not been by her side. The mob believed that she had poisoned Charlotte; willingly would the people have torn her limb from limb.

Even Queen Charlotte's iron nerve was shaken. She, who had been impervious to emotion, was destroyed by emotion at the end.

Caroline learned the news, and fainted. But she did

not, even now, wear her heart on her sleeve. Those who expected extravagant expressions of grief were disappointed.

'I have lost one most warmly attached friend, and the only one I have had in England. But she is only gone before,' she said, and erected a pathetic monument in her Italian garden.

The exiled Byron voiced the nation's sorrow:

'Of sackcloth was thy wedding garment made,
   Thy bridal fruit is ashes; in the dust
The fair-haired daughter of the Isles is laid,
   The love of millions. How we did entrust
Futurity to her.'

In England, sorrow was long in healing. The Prince Regent recovered, but it broke the Queen. Leopold was despairing. The unfortunate Croft shot himself; and the Royal Dukes, at Parliament's request, went seeking brides to ensure the succession.

The Duke of Sussex declined the request – unlike his brother he had no taste for bigamy – but Kent reluctantly parted from his Madame Laurent, Clarence less reluctantly from his Mrs. Jordan, to keep the succession from the hated Cumberland. The Clubs had a merry epidemic of betting as to which of them would first produce the necessary heir. Kent won it, in the end, though Princess Alexandrina Victoria was very newly arrived when her father died.

The Prince Regent snarled at this indecent haste to replace his daughter. He would supply the heir for himself. 'God damn his soul if he didn't rid himself of that damned Princess of Wales.'

The spies he sent after her came hurrying back with reports which brightened his eyes.

BOOK V

The Princess of Wales kept carnival in Brunswick; there were theatres on gala nights, suppers, balls, and masquerades. All Europe was a little mad after the closing of the Peace. "The Beast" had trampled upon a continent, toppled over thrones and dynasties, carrying devastation and famine in his train; his situation reduced to the island of Elba. Europe breathed again, and little states lifted up their heads. The Duchy of Brunswick had fared as badly as the other little states; now its Duke was restored to it, and his sister, shockingly ill-used in that barbarian England, came back to her home. Brunswick gave itself up to an orgy of rejoicing until the Princess Caroline's suite collapsed from sheer fatigue. She herself was tireless and crammed with mirth. When Brunswick was exhausted she must explore fresh fields.

The Napoleonic Empire had expired like the crackling of fireworks, but the firework smell remained in the air. In the reaction from fear nothing could be too fantastic. The fantastic microbe attacked the Princess Caroline very violently indeed; her humour overflowed into a perpetual caricature. Her husband's household had always amused her; she would have an amusing household of her own. She put the gentlemen of her suite into a costume of her

THE PANTOMIME PRINCESS

The Princess of Wales kept carnival in Brunswick; there were theatres on gala nights, suppers, balls, and masquerades. All Europe was a little mad after the signing of the Peace. 'The Beast' had trampled upon a continent, toppled over thrones and dynasties, carrying devastation and famine in his train; his kingdom reduced to the island of Elba, Europe breathed again, and little states lifted up their heads. The Duchy of Brunswick had fared as badly as the other little states; now its Duke was restored to it, and his sister, so shockingly ill-used in that barbarian England, came back to her home. Brunswick gave itself up to an orgy of rejoicing until the Princess Caroline's suite collapsed from sheer fatigue. She herself was tireless and consumed with unrest. When Brunswick was exhausted she must explore fresh fields.

The Napoleonic Empire had expired like the crackling of fireworks, but the firework spirit remained in the air. In the reaction from fear nothing could be too fantastic. The fantastic microbe attacked the Princess Caroline very violently indeed; her humour overflowed into a perpetual caricature. Her husband's household had always amused her; she would have an amusing household of her own. She put the gentlemen of her suite into a costume of her own invention – low black coats, richly embroidered, with gold button-holes and lined with crimson silk, waistcoats embroidered with gold, and hats with high feathers. The gentlemen submitted, protesting, and carried themselves with an embarrassed, apologetic air.

The ladies were less docile; but Caroline threw herself with enthusiasm into new and, judged by English standards of propriety, quite inadequate attire. Mrs. Jordan had appeared at Drury Lane in the Empire fashion, and the audience in the stalls had thrown handkerchiefs on the stage with requests that she would kindly appear properly clothed. On the Continent the fashion was carried to extraordinary lengths. In Hanover, a lady laid a bet that she would walk through the streets clad only in a chemise without attracting attention, and had won the bet. Caroline was immensely amused, and would not have minded winning such a bet herself. Away went corsets and petticoats, and as Venus she appeared at a masquerade, very scantily attired indeed. She saw no harm in it. She turned night into day, and thought nothing of rousing her attendants and guests from their beds for an impromptu midnight ball.

Her English ladies were shocked at her behaviour, which appeared to them very Continental and so to be deplored; Queen Charlotte would not like it. Caroline was tired of trying in vain to please Queen Charlotte. She was wild with delight at regaining her liberty, and a constant whirl of pleasure of the more fantastic kind did a great deal towards numbing the pain at her heart.

At Geneva she saw Byron, and in her company, perhaps, he created an immortal phrase:

'On with the dance, let joy be unconfined
No sleep till morn, when Youth and Pleasure meet,
To chase the glowing hours with flying feet.'

At Geneva, too, she found a merry companion in Napoleon's feather-headed Empress, Marie Louise.

Geneva was amusing, but she tired of it. Only in constant movement could she keep sadness at bay.

In October she reached Milan. Lady Elizabeth Forbes, exhausted by this constant travelling, begged permission to go home. Lady Charlotte Lindsay had already left to be with her sick sister, Lady Glenbervie, at Spa. Colonel St. Leger had returned to England on business; Craven and Gell were anxious to go, and only partially because of private affairs. They did not like this pantomime procession across Europe. They were not quite sure that the Princess of Wales, poor soul, had not had her brain turned by her troubles. They wrote letters to their friends in England which made her behaviour sound very peculiar indeed.

She let them go without comment, though she was hurt by their defection. She consoled herself with the thought that their long faces had spoilt her pleasure, and set about filling their places with Italians. Since she was going to travel through Italy, she needed a courier. The Marquis Ghisberi recommended an ex-soldier of good birth named Bartolommeo Pergami, who bore an excellent character and had such exceptionally good manners and appearance that he seemed a suitable servant even for the Princess of Wales.

At Rome the Pope received her, and at Naples she was welcomed with enthusiasm by the Neapolitan King and Queen. Naples was very gay, and King Joachim Murat and his consort both had masqueraders' minds; they had fêtes and fireworks and illuminated their gardens and borrowed her money with all the cheerfulness in the world. Joachim gave the Princess in return a pantomime carriage, shaped like a sea-shell covered with gilding and mother-of-pearl, lined with blue velvet and decorated with silver fringe. Since life in Naples was as theatrical as the background of the town behind the Bay, the carriage did not seem to Caroline too elaborate to be of use, but of course adjuncts must be suitable. So she had a boy on the box dressed like an operatic cherub, with spangles and flesh-coloured tights, and she herself wore a pink hat with seven or eight pink feathers floating in the breeze, a pink bodice cut very low, a short white skirt, pink top boots, and a wide pink sash which lent itself to draping in the way Lady Hamilton had made famous in her Attitudes.

'It is, of course, theatrical,' Caroline confessed, 'but I love the theatre, and it is all most amusing, such a delightful change after the dullness of Blackheath. If only Charlotte would write – '

They were dancing at Naples when 'The Beast' escaped from Elba.

Europe held its breath.

The Princess of Wales grew serious and, looking at Naples with more critical eyes, disgusted. In a hurry she set off for Leghorn.

'I will wait at Genoa till I see what turn political affairs will take,' she said on board the frigate. 'If Napoleon permits me I will have an establishment on the Lake of Como, and my two Lady Charlottes. I detest Naples. It

COUNT PERGAMI

To face page 250

is full of spies and slanderers. There is no society in the world except in London, though I have been very well here as a Queen of Sheba. If only a certain Great Gentleman would go from this world to the next.'

'There is the Island of Elba, Madam.'

'The Lion's Den!'

The Duke of Brunswick fell at Quatre Bras, but the Lion's power was broken for ever at Waterloo, and Europe was at peace at last. All the world was open to the wanderer. Her brother's death was but an additional grief to one who had so many. In England they ignored it, and the customary letters of condolence were not sent. 'I am alone now, except for Charlotte.'

She made her headquarters at the Villa d'Este on Lake Como. Pergami's sister, Countess Oldi, was her lady-in-waiting; Pergami himself became her chamberlain. At the Villa d'Este they led a very odd existence for the suite of a Princess of Wales. Caroline sometimes cooked her own dinner, and drifted about the lake in fantastic costumes, and allowed her manners to appear very free and gay.

'What would the English people say if they heard of it? Oh fie! Princess of Wales,' she said defiantly. 'The old *béguine*, Queen Charlotte, is on her last legs, I hear. *Mais ça ne me fait ni froid ni chaud* now. There was a time when such intelligence might have gladdened me; but now nothing in the world do I care for, save to pass the time as quickly as I can, and death may hurry as fast as he pleases. I am ready to die. *En attendant*, I am weary of Como. Let us set out for the East.'

They visited Elba and Sicily, and the Princess quarrelled with Captain Pechell, the captain of the English yacht on which she travelled, because he refused to treat her Italian chamberlain as a gentleman, having been used to regard him as a servant. 'It is,' she said heatedly, 'an insult to me.' She dismissed Pechell, and hired an Italian *polacca* and, to prevent the recurrence of so much annoyance, obtained for Pergami the title of 'Knight of Malta.'

They set sail for Tunis, and were very hospitably received by the Bey. 'I find the barbarians much less barbarous than the Christians,' she remarked, and enjoyed the pageantry, the Janissaries in attendance, the preposterous clothes she ordered to fit the surroundings. A visit to the *seraglio* greatly amused her. 'What a joy it would be to the Prince of Wales,' she remarked.

Her hosts were very much occupied with piracy, and her visit was hastily cut short by Admiral Lord Exmouth, who came to bombard the town.

They set sail for Athens, and from Athens they went to Constantinople, but were driven away by the plague. The farther the Princess travelled, the more restless she grew; the more comment her appearance caused, the more fantastic that appearance became. A game she had begun in ironical humour now could not be controlled. Her sense of the dramatic had run away with her; what she had begun in a spirit of comedy had long ago become the most ridiculous farce. All over Europe tongues were wagging. Since she could not stop she hastened the *tempo*. The fantastic, dangerous journey ended at Jerusalem, where she founded the 'Order of Saint Caroline,' with Pergami as its Grand Master and Willy Austin as a Knight of the Holy Sepulchre. The Princess chose a lilac ribbon, a red cross, and the motto, '*Honi soit qui mal y pense.*'

'Why not my Willy a Knight of the Holy Cross if my husband is made a Knight of the Saint Esprit? Which did he lack, do you think, *esprit* or *sainteté*?'

The Prince Regent suddenly saw that her desire was to make him ridiculous, and that she was succeeding extraordinarily well. The Princess had decided to be a burlesque Byronic romantic and Pergami made an extremely effective-looking hero of Byronic romance. He was six foot tall, with a magnificent head of black hair, pale complexion, and mustachios which reached from Jerusalem to London.

The pantomime procession with the Byronic air returned to Italy after a progress through Germany which afforded great entertainment to the world. The Prince Regent was right; his wife wanted to make him look ridiculous and succeeded, quite indifferent to the fact that she brought even more ridicule upon herself. She did not mind being the butt of humour as long as she knew that every jibe made her husband wince. At Baden she appeared with half a pumpkin on her head to keep it cool, which enchanted the Badeners since she appeared in their peasants' national costume at the opera in order to do honour to them.

Even her immense vitality was exhausted at last. She returned to the Villa d'Este for repose, but even in repose she gave balls, private theatricals in her little theatre, and found time to write the history of her travels.

She was at Pesaro when Charlotte died. The news stunned her. She fainted again and again. 'If my heart were not already broken,' she sobbed, 'it would be broken now.'

But her grief was not for the eyes of others. In a few

days she could face the world again with laughter on her lips. 'Since I may not be Princess of Wales, I will be Caroline, a happy, merry soul,' she cried defiantly, while the knife turned in her heart.

All her English attendants had left her now. There was no one to whom she could talk of Charlotte. She threw herself into one of her passionate attachments to pretty Victorine, Pergami's daughter. Pergami was handsome, amiable, competent, but had it not been for Victorine she might have sent him away. The Pergami family often dined at her table, one or other of its members was constantly with her, sometimes petted in public; nothing in the eyes of the English could have been more undignified and indiscreet; the very openness of the business showed how little there was of real harm. Caroline was incapable of hiding anything except the agony in her own heart.

The Prince Regent knew nothing of her heart; his hatred would have blinded him to anything which his natural intelligence might have discovered for him. He wanted to believe the worst of her; his spies, who knew it, stalked her and reported what they did not see.

'I am surrounded by spies,' she lamented. 'They dog my footsteps and follow me into the most private places.'

The censorious English of the fashionable world discussed each new rumour. Their code of manners was outraged, and they thought it was their morals. The subject of Caroline's deplorable behaviour filled every letter and every conversation. The gossips hoped the tales were true. Her friends hoped, and partly believed, that they were false.

Lady Charlotte Campbell, whose beauty was fading,

found herself as much in demand as ever; she was the constant correspondent of the Princess; she could retail the stories at first hand. She did, and, had she had the gift of humour, she would have told the truth. She would have told how the espionage amused Caroline, and how she delighted in providing the spies with news and then making them carry the letters which told how she had found them out: '*Le porteur de cette lettre est une personne qui ne dit jamais la vérité; il est un espion de la Cabal.*'

That did not strike Lady Charlotte as an amusing trick. She did not mention it and, hesitating, she told the literal truth:

'I have never been able to detect any impropriety of manner or even familiarity towards the courier; though when I was with her I lived every moment in fear of having the horrid stories confirmed. Perhaps they were on their guard before a stranger.'

Lady Charlotte's hesitating denial was almost as useful as the highly coloured confirmation which the hired spies sent. Even more useful was the servants' tittle-tattle, which self-importance made as scandalous as their wits could invent.

The Prince Regent thought that all this floating evidence, gathered together and presented to Parliament, might at last rid him of his wife. He desired Lord Chancellor Eldon to appoint a Commission and to set up a secret bureau at Milan to scour Italy for the evidence required. The Prince, of course, was outraged at any suggestion of moral turpitude and at the injustice which the existing situation inflicted upon his most wronged and moral self: 'You cannot be surprised,' he wrote to Eldon, '(much difficulty in point of delicacy being now set aside in my mind by the late melancholy event which has taken place in my family), if I therefore turn my whole thoughts to the endeavouring to extricate myself from the cruellest as well as the most unjust predicament that even the lowest individual, much more a prince, ever was placed in, by unshackling myself from such a woman.'

The Prince would not submit to exist under the degradation which lacerated his upright and honourable mind. Castlereagh, with mind as honourable and upright as his, offered assistance, and ordered his brother, the British Ambassador at Vienna, to preside over the bureau of spies. The police at Milan enjoyed the edifying spectacle of a British Ambassador steaming open letters and bribing servants to hide behind doors, pick locks, and apply their eyes to keyholes.

The Commission spent £30,000 on collecting their evidence, and one of the witnesses they bought voiced the sentiments of the rest: 'What would you have me do?' he exclaimed when a loyal servant remonstrated. 'I am desperate. I have no work. I will say what they told me to say.'

The evidence was sent to England and was put into a Green Bag. The embarrassed Cabinet decided that it did not amount to a row of pins. Eldon was deputed to tell the Regent, as tactfully as he could, to let the matter drop, that the Princess' tongue could not be bridled and that he was not in a position to throw any stones.

Caroline, though bitterly amused, was also startled by the Milan Commission. She was tired of wandering; she decided to go home. The Whigs, in her absence, might forget her. Mr. Whitbread had killed himself, but Mr. Brougham was still there, professing his readiness to act

the part of a friend. She wrote to him and begged him to
meet her at Marseilles. The pantomime travels were
over; dressed in mourning, she journeyed under an
assumed name. The old King was dying at last, her
correspondents told her; the Prince Regent had sworn she
should never be crowned, and a rumour of a Bill of
Attainder against her was in the air. Her follies slipped
from her; she would fight *that* until her last breath. Her
courage, the sense which was natural to her, her dignity,
and her detestation of the man to whom she was chained,
all demanded it. 'If only the *country* would protect me,'
she thought.

Mr. Brougham would not journey to Marseilles. He
was not sure. He, too, was a humorist, but the position
was difficult. He had never pretended to regard the
Princess as anything but a party tool. He seemed to be
playing every one false, but, in fact, he did not know his
own mind. He was tempted to accept the Government's
bribe and desert his client. Certainly he would not go to
Marseilles. He thought so long a journey unwise in view
of the critical state of the King. The Opposition was not
quite sure what use it could make of Caroline; it wanted
her near but not, just yet, at home.. Brougham would
meet her at Calais and trim his sails according to the
direction of the wind.

The Princess did not suspect treachery. She, too, was
alarmed about the state of her dear old King. She decided
to go to Calais and await Brougham there.

Her intention embarrassed the French Government.
Louis xviii was very anxious to stand well with George iv.
He bore the Princess no enmity, but there seemed very
small chance of Caroline being allowed to take her place

as George IV's Queen. So, on the whole, there was no need to be civil to her. He sent an intimation that she could not be presented and that 'he would see her arrival in Paris with great pain.'

Caroline's lip curled. 'The present King of France,' she remarked thoughtfully, 'when he was in a distressed situation, was well received at my father's court at Brunswick; a palace and every comfort was offered him. Such great personages have the talent to forget. I think my father's daughter should have been at least received kindly, without pomp and parade, but in a friendly way. That is all I should have expected as I travel incognito. I shall return to Italy and await Mr. Brougham's instructions there.' At Leghorn she heard that George III was dead.

2

IN LONDON THEY TALKED OF HER

THE friends of the Princess of Wales in England gave her no encouragement. They talked her over and answered questions as best they could.

Lady Caroline Lamb's dinner-parties were often amusing. She found some queer pleasure in collecting a strange assortment of artists and *literati* and fashionable people who were very uncomfortable in each other's company. Lady Caro's malicious, fever-bright eyes darted from one to another of her guests and enjoyed their obvious discomfort.

Lady Caro was as interested as every one else in the progresses of the Princess of Wales. She invited Lady Charlotte Campbell (or rather Lady Charlotte Bury, since she had re-married) to one of her strange parties, in order to question her about the Princess of Wales.

Lady Charlotte sat next to Sir Thomas Lawrence and turned a chilly shoulder on him since he had proved himself only a fair-weather friend of the Princess. His manners, however, were so courtly that presently Lady Charlotte's coldness thawed.

'I have been so long out of England. Tell me who some of these people are.'

'Opposite is Mrs. Mee, the miniature-painter.'

'She seems a modest, pleasing person, soft and sweet like the miniatures she paints.'

'That eccentric little person is the artist, William Blake.'

'I spoke to him. He told me Lady Caroline had been very kind to him. I agreed with him. Mr. Blake seems to me singularly unworldly, full of beautiful imagination and genius, but of course I know not how far the execution of his designs is equal to the conceptions of his mental vision.'

The great Sir Thomas sneered: 'Mr. Blake is one of those persons who follow art for its own sake, and derive their happiness from its pursuit.'

'I said he was unworldly. Lady Caro enjoys collecting types.'

Lawrence lowered his voice. 'What did you think of her novel, *Glenarvon*?'

'It showed much genius but of an erratic kind.'

'Some of the poetry scattered through the volumes is very mellifluous and has been set to music by more than one composer. She might have learned to write poetry from Lord Byron.'

Lady Charlotte was alarmed. 'Hush. That name excites her.'

Mr. Ward came into the room looking more absent even than usual. He hardly spoke, but went backwards and forwards through the rooms muttering to himself. Lady Caro yawned delicately and joined him. They came to a standstill by Lady Charlotte's chair.

'How do you like my collection of *Blues* and *Pinks*? Odd, ain't they?' Lady Caro asked with mockery in her over-bright eyes. 'Tell me, have you any news of the Princess of Wales?'

'I hear it is her intention to return to England shortly.'

'She will derive little benefit now that poor Princess Charlotte is dead. What do you *really* think of her character?'

Lady Charlotte smiled; for this question, evidently, she had been invited.

'I know nothing *against* the Princess, and if I did I should not disclose it,' she said sharply. 'I know much that is in her favour.'

'Is not her dress very injudicious?'

Lady Charlotte hesitated. 'She was never very particular about dress. I remember Lord Henry Fitzgerald was much shocked when the Princess met him in *déshabille* and invited him into her carriage. "In such unfit dress, Madam," he began. The Princess laughed. "Ah, yes, my dear Lord Henry, we know you are all over shock – but never mind your dress – let us make happy while we can." '

'I met Miss Hayman to-day,' said Mr. Ward suddenly. 'She told me *she* was convinced that the Princess never had been guilty of the crimes laid to her charge. The Princess has sent for Lady Anne Hamilton to join her abroad.'

Lady Charlotte said sharply: 'I can scarcely credit it, for I know her Royal Highness has an objection to her meddling spirit.'

Ward gave her a shrewd look. 'She is a well-intentioned woman if not a very wise one.'

Charles Kirkpatrick Sharpe joined the group. 'The good King George III is really dying in earnest, I hear. A more honest soul never went to Heaven than that of His Majesty.'

'Already his successor has had plans made for his coronation which is to exceed in magnificence all spectacles of the kind ever seen.'

'Do you think the Princess will consent to be excluded from her place in the show?'

'I should say certainly not without a tussle for it.'

'Will the great Count Bergami accompany her on the throne?'

'The Count is all prepared with honours. He generally wears the insignia of the most holy order of Saint Caroline, which consists of a cross and a heart tied together with a true-lovers' knot and the English royal motto encircling the badge, "*Honi soit qui mal y pense.*" How far these words are applicable to the case I cannot say.'

Lady Charlotte, who had been laughing, suddenly checked herself. 'I am truly sorry for her. The manner in which she has been treated is shameful. She has never even heard once from Prince Leopold since her daughter's death.'

'Do you remember all his fine promises to Charlotte to defend her mother? See how they are performed.'

'There is a saying: "Put not your trust in princes."'

'The new Sultana may bear that in mind. Lady Hertford is quite out of favour and Lady Conyngham's star high.'

Lady Charlotte lowered her voice to a vicious whisper. 'That man is entirely without a heart.'

Sharpe laughed. 'My dear Lady Charlotte! Who has ever heard of a prince with a heart? You must know that I have, ever since I knew the world, been firmly persuaded that our first parents, whether black or white, with tails or without (Lord Monboddo held the tail system, and several other things which the Rabbis dispute about), were certainly created without hearts. There can be no happiness with a heart. The heart is the seat of love, friendship, and compassion; consequently of that hell – jealousy, distrust, and pity, even for devils. My notion is that our parents acquired hearts from eating that crab of an apple. Perhaps they swallowed the pips, hence black hearts, and so the mischief grew. All the same, for a great many years I have never had the bad luck to meet anyone with a heart.'

'Yet anatomists protest we have them.'

'True. They tell us they always find a sort of heart, often ossified and frequently very small. Yet I scarcely credit them. I have read or heard somewhere that in the Hunterian Museum there is preserved a lady's heart exactly resembling a roll of point lace. Doubtless its owner felt for nothing else. How has it happened that the passion for point lace, monkeys, ratafia, and the spleen has died with our grandmothers?'

'The gossips are very curious about Princess Charlotte's heart.'

'Foolish people. There is one person's heart of which I would give a great deal to have the dissecting – the Princess of Wales.' That certainly must be a curious receptacle of heterogeneous matter, very full of com- bustible qualities. I wish Her Royal Highness would come back. She is excellent fun and good company.'

'And good-hearted,' Lady Charlotte protested.

'Hush. Mr. Moore is going to sing.'

3

TRIAL OF THE QUEEN

LONDON had not been so excited since Anne Boleyn's head fell on Tower Hill. The new King wished that he could do as he pleased like the eighth Henry, but even his obtuseness suspected that his people would object. The King took the Radicals seriously, and the Radicals shouted loudly for those that were afflicted and oppressed.

If anyone had been oppressed it was the new Queen. The Radical Alderman Wood, M.P., followed the nervous, uncertain Brougham to meet the Queen in France. Brougham urged her to consent to terms and stay abroad; Wood, in the name of the City, begged her to come home. Caroline did not altogether trust Brougham; Wood, though rather a fool, appeared to be sincere. The only agreement to which she would consent included a complete recognition of her queenship, a queen's income, and the Church's prayers.

A compromise might have been reached on every point but the last. The King was superstitious. He would not have her name in the Liturgy on any account, though all the members of the Royal family were mentioned.

Lord Liverpool suggested to her advocate: 'She is included in the general petition.'

Mr. Denman replied sarcastically: 'In the prayer for all who are desolate and sore oppressed?'

'You might as easily move Carlton House as the King,' said Lord Castlereagh.

The Queen wrote to England for patterns of silks: 'Mrs. Webbe, who was formerly my mantua maker, could send me a white silk gown and a hat of the same kind made exactly of the English fashion, as I must confess the present French mode does not please me much.'

George was really ill, and the horror of having the Queen made an object of the prayers of his people haunted his imagination and disturbed his rest. 'If they don't get me a divorce I shall change my Ministers,' he threatened.

'The Opposition is most friendly to the Princess of Wales,' remarked Castlereagh drily.

The King burst into tears. 'I shall go to Hanover where I can get a divorce whenever I choose.'

'That will not do in England,' muttered the Ministers. They were thoroughly uncomfortable, but Mr. Canning was the only one of them who had the manliness to resign. Canning sympathised with the Queen.

The Ministers believed her guilty; even her friends were afraid that the tales must be partly true.

'No smoke without fire,' they whispered the proverb, but 'if my husband had used me as hers has done, I should have thought myself entitled to act as she has done. All the world is with her except the people of fashion at the West End of the town,' they added.

The people who least believed in her guilt were those who knew her best and could sift folly from crime. Keppel Craven rejoined her; Lady Anne Hamilton went to France to attend her; Lady Charlotte Lindsay, Lord and Lady Hood and Sir William Gell once more took up their duties. They had talked her over among themselves; they had declined to make part of the pantomime procession over Europe, but they did not believe her guilty, or, if they did believe, they refused to acknowledge it, and they had no intention of deserting her in her hour of need. Her old friends stood by her, but her new, political friends were inclined to sit upon a fence. Henry Brougham certainly did not believe her innocent, which accounted, perhaps, for his apparent treachery. He was her advocate, but he had recommended her to accept terms which would have been tantamount to an acknowledgment of her guilt.

'If my head is on Temple Bar,' said Caroline angrily, 'it will be his doing. My mind is made up. I shall go home.'

She dismissed her Italian attendants, including Pergami, with no great appearance of regret, although she wept a little at parting from Victorine.

Brougham watched her curiously. 'If she is mad,' he said, 'and I sometimes think it, it is on the matter of children. There was no trouble with her till they parted her from her child.'

The Government of England refused her a yacht or an escort. She crossed to Dover by the packet. The King, who had not believed that she would come, postponed the Coronation, and the people who yelled outside Carlton House, 'Come out, you slanderer and adulterer,' were not privileged to see the Royal face.

England – the people of England – was solidly for the Queen.

The garrison at Dover gave her a royal salute. Her progress to London was a triumphal procession. The mob

QUEEN CAROLINE

To face page 266

besieged the houses of Alderman Wood and Lady Anne Hamilton where she lodged until she had arranged for a lease of Brandenburgh House at Hammersmith. No Royal residence, of course, was placed at her disposal.

The King withdrew to his most private sanctum, 'The Cottage,' in Windsor Park, where Lady Conyngham administered such comfort as she could, and where he could give himself up undisturbed to eating and drinking and devising expensive paraphernalia for the Coronation, which, if the mob got out of hand, might very well never take place. George was the most hated man in England, and the fact heaped fuel on the fire of his hatred for the Queen.

Caroline herself was not happy. Though her popularity in the country was undoubted, those whose support she craved held coldly aloof. She had hoped much from Prince Leopold, but that astute young man was not moved by sentimental considerations of what his Charlotte would have wished him to do. Charlotte would never reign in England. George did, and the Duchess of Kent might very well reign in the person of her child. Leopold wanted to have a say in the destinies of England; he sided with the Royal family against the disturbing Queen.

London gave itself a holiday. The massacre of Peterloo was too recent for the authorities to view the rioting with ease. The people demanded illuminations, and broke the windows of houses where illuminations were not supplied. They broke the windows of Lady Hertford's house, which was ironical, since Lady Hertford's place in the King's affections had been usurped by Lady Conyngham, and Caroline herself had had the kindly thought of sending

proud Isabella a copy of *The Sorrows of Love*. They broke
Lord Sidmouth's windows, and the Duke of Wellington
was stoned as he drove through the streets. Feeling in the
Army and the Navy was all for the Queen, even the
Guards were growing so restive that the witty Luttrell
remarked, 'The extinguisher is taking fire.'

The clubs were very busy recording bets. Those who
had wagered fifty guineas that she would not come were
hoping to retrieve their losses by betting fifty more that
she would not face a trial.

The town spoke and thought of nothing else; on the
roads there was but one question asked of travellers:
'How goes the affair of the Queen?'

Caroline was silent. Never in her life had she talked so
little, written so few letters, given so slight an indication
of what her attitude would be. She might have confided
in Lady Charlotte Campbell, but Lady Charlotte herself
was in disgrace for the indiscretion of embarking on a
second marriage with a parson, a quite unsuitable creature to mate with Campbell blood. Lady Charlotte had
her own grievances against society, but nursed them all
abroad. Lady Glenbervie was dead, and poor Lady
Charlotte Lindsay very much occupied with her family
affairs. The Queen had no confidante. Her attendants
only knew that she would fight this battle to the death.

Her appearance did not help her. She drove through
London in a shabby old carriage looking very unlike a
heroine of romance. She was over fifty, fat and unshapely, with a ringleted black wig, black painted eyebrows, rouged cheeks, and a large hat with an immense
bow and huge, nodding ostrich feathers. Her good-
natured face looked stern, yet flaunting. There was no

faintest echo of the fair young girl with golden ringlets curling round her neck whom John Stanley once had loved.

Her friends might regret her lack of taste, but the mob was determined to applaud her and cheered itself hoarse when the sentries outside Carlton House presented arms.

The position of the King and his Government was farcical; the country could not be controlled, the King could not be crowned, because he feared his wife. George thought the ludicrous situation would compel his Ministers to get him a divorce. With a malignant chuckle he packed up all those papers which had been sent him from his spies at Milan and sent them to the House of Lords sealed up in a Green Bag.

The wits quoted Scripture: 'My transgression is sealed up in a bag,' and for a fortnight the whole of England was obscene.

There could no longer be any uncertainty about the position; those who were not for the Queen must range themselves against her. The Dukes of York and Sussex begged to be excused from attendance in the Lords; York was refused, but Sussex carried his point. Brougham and Denman were appointed the Queen's counsel. Brougham at last, since there was no middle course, ranged himself enthusiastically on her side. William Cobbett wrote her twelve-page letters of advice. Lady Anne Hamilton's hand ached with writing suitable replies; but she did not falter as she wrote page after page of remonstrance to the King.

Caroline's friends made their opinions audible. Byron wrote from Ravenna, 'Nobody here believes a word of the evidence against the Queen.'

The Green Bag was opened by a secret committee on June 28th.

On July 4th the Committee issued its report:

'By the Lords' Committee, appointed to a secret committee, to examine the papers before the House of Lords, on Tuesday the 6th of June last, in the sealed bags by His Majesty's command, and to report thereupon, as they shall see fit, and to whom have been since referred several additional papers in two sealed bags, relative to the subject matter of His Majesty's most gracious message of the 6th of June last. Ordered to report:

'That the Committee have examined, with all the attention due to so important a subject, the documents which have been laid before them, and they find that those documents contain allegations supported by the concurrent testimony of a great number of persons in various situations of life, and residing in different parts of Europe, which deeply affect the honour of the Queen, charging her with adulterous connection with a foreigner, originally in her service in a menial capacity; and attributing to Her Majesty a continued series of conduct highly unbecoming Her Majesty's rank and station and of the most licentious character.

'These charges appear to the Committee so deeply to affect not only the honour of the Queen, but also the dignity of the Crown, and the moral feelings and honour of the country, that, in their opinion, it is indispensable that they should become the subject of a solemn inquiry which, it appears to the Committee, may be best effected in the course of a legislative proceeding, the necessity of which they cannot but most deeply deplore.'

Next day Lord Liverpool moved the first reading of a

'Bill entitled an Act to deprive Her Majesty, Caroline Amelia Elizabeth, of the Titles, Prerogatives, Rights, Privileges, and Exemptions, of Queen Consort of this Realm, and to dissolve the Marriage between His Majesty and the said Caroline Amelia Elizabeth.'

The Attorney-General declared the Queen's adultery at Naples on the night of November 9th, 1814.

The trial of the Queen had opened.

Queen Caroline protested, but, of course, in vain. The King had no decency, his Government no shame. Caroline's mouth was set grimly, but she could still manage a jest upon the 'Bill of Pains and Spikalties,' as she called it.

Between the first and second reading of the Bill, England, indeed Europe, could think of nothing else. Europe had been scoured for witnesses. Metternich obliged his friend Castlereagh with a cargo of Italians who were landed at Westminster Stairs and protected from an outraged mob by large bodies of cavalry and hustled into a temporary building adjacent to the House of Lords. The House of Lords itself was enclosed by strong timber fences; Life Guards patrolled the approaches.

The exciting contents of the Green Bag provided conversation for the world.

'By all accounts her conduct has been most abandoned and beastly.'

'If the most fertile and depraved mind were to invent a tale of private and even public profligacy, it could not equal the horror.'

'It is a Court job due to the wrong-headedness of one man and the servility of his Ministers.'

'Lord Byron wrote to Murray that the Italian witnesses

are not to be believed. For half the money spent, he says, any testimony could be brought out of Italy.'

'I am so tired of the subject that I shall go and live in Cotton Garden among the witnesses, who alone, it appears, do not talk of the Queen.'

'The discussion of the business has become an intolerable nuisance,' remarked Charles Greville when all the commentators had done.

'I am tired of it, too,' said the Queen.

She was ill, with an internal complaint which kept her in continual pain. She gave herself increasing doses of magnesia which Lady Anne Hamilton viewed with great distrust. Her counsel said she must be present in the House of Lords, and she felt that she could face her enemies better if she did not feel so ill.

'Dear Lady Anne,' she said sweetly, 'I hope God will reward you for your courage in staying with me. He knows it is no small trial. Once, when I was light-hearted, I called you Joan of Arc in mockery, now you prove yourself true to the name.'

'Madam, I will stay as long as you want me.'

'You are a good soul. I feel very unwell, fatigued, *ebayé*. I wonder my head is not quite bewildered with all I have suffered, and it is not yet over.'

'This is a political matter,' said Lady Anne bitterly.

'It is that cruel man. His *rancune* is boundless against me. He will never let me have peace. Nothing has been left undone that could be done to destroy my character. And there is no one to care for me. She who would have comforted me is lost to me. But I must have courage. What shall I wear when I attend this ridiculous trial?'

Lady Anne's taste in dress was no better than the

Queen's. Those who hoped that she might have improved in looks and dignity were disappointed. Her appearance made no new friends for her.

'She looked like a Dutch doll with a round bottom. You know the kind. We used to call it "Fanny Royds," ' wrote Creevey, who was friendly towards her. 'It was weighted with lead so that it always jumped erect in whatever position it was laid. There is another toy I was reminded of – a rabbit, or a cat, whose tail you squeeze under its body and then it jumps in half a minute off the ground into the air.'

This he wrote at Brook's on the opening day of the trial. The Club was full, and those who had been present at the House of Lords were surrounded by eager crowds of the curious with questions tumbling over one another. Mr. Creevey was an ideal observer to give the news to the town.

'Sir Thomas Tyrwhitt was there in his official dress as Black Rod. He told me the Government was stark, staring mad. They wanted to prevent his receiving the Queen at the door as the Queen.'

'He did?'

'Of course. He handed her to the chair of state, and she scored the first *bon mot*. "Well, Sir Thomas," she quizzed him, "what is your master trying me for? Is it for intermarrying with a man whose first wife I knew to be alive?" '

'I heard the populace cheering her. How did she look? I could not see her face, she had a handsome white veil so thick it hid her.'

'Her face was calm enough. Her dress outlandish, black-figured gauze with a good deal of lace and

trimming, white sleeves perfectly episcopal, a few strag-
gling ringlets on her neck which I flatter myself from
their appearance were not Her Majesty's own property.
She popped all at once into the House, made a duck at
the throne, another to the Peers, and a concluding jump
into the chair that was placed for her.'

'Who attends her?'

'Lady Anne waits behind her, and though she is six
foot high leans, for effect and delicacy's sake, on brother
Archy's arm. She bears a striking resemblance to one of
Lord Derby's great red deer. Keppel Craven and Sir
William Gell likewise stood behind the Queen in full
dress.'

'She was cheered to the echo, and the streets almost
impassable.'

'Castlereagh came smiling, though awkwardly, I
thought.'

'A minute after I passed I heard an uproar with hissing
and shouting. On turning round I saw it was Wellington
on horseback. His horse made a little start, and he was
evidently annoyed.'

'Grey made as weak a speech as ever I heard. He
wanted the opinion of the judges upon the Statute of
Edward III as to a queen's treason.'

'The judges said, as one knew they would, that there
was no Statute law or law of the land touching the
Queen's case.'

'Brougham in his speech fired a body-blow into the
Duke of York on Mrs. Clark's affair, which gave great
offence. Here is Grey.'

'I'm quite sure the Bill will be knocked up sooner
or later,' Grey said decidedly. 'I'll lay you ten to one

it will disappear even in the Lords before Saturday fortnight.'

'Done. It won't do, Grey. You will not be able to show
your face again as a public man.'

'Denman is speaking as well as possible, though I am
all against his introducing jokes, which he has been doing
too much.'

'Their lordships were much tickled at some of his
stories. Denman, holding the Bill in his hand, said
gravely: "Levity of manner is one of the charges. Why!
this charge applies to all Royal people; they are all good-
tempered and playful. I remember a conversation between his present Majesty and Sam Spring, the waiter at
the Cocoa Tree, when Sam cracked his jokes and was
very familiar with the Prince, upon which the latter said:
'This is all very well between you and me, Sam, but
beware of being equally familiar with Norfolk and
Abercorn.' " All the Lords recognised the story, and
snorted out hugely, Bishops and all.'

'Derby says that there is not a pin to choose between
them, but that the Queen has always been ill used, and
that nobody but the King would get redress in such a
case against his wife.'

'I am decidedly of opinion that the very openness of
the Queen's conduct carries with it her acquittal from the
supposed crime,' said Lord Spencer solemnly.

Brook's turned to its wagering and presently left the
subject of the Queen.

On the third day of the trial the Attorney-General
opened the case for the Crown, and two days later began
to call witnesses. The excitement in the streets and at the
clubs rose to fever heat. At Brook's the Opposition met.

'The Lords rose to receive the Queen with a better grace to-day than yesterday,' Mr. Creevey told the eager questioners. 'Everything respecting her coming to the House is now as perfect as possible. She has a most superb and beautiful coach with six horses, the coachman driving in a cap like the old King's coachman, and there is a good coach of her own behind for Craven and Gell.'

'I thought that nothing could be more triumphant for the Queen than this day.'

'The truth is the Law Officers of the Crown are damnably overweighted by Brougham and Denman.'

'Yesterday's evidence certainly shook her friends.'

'Always excepting Lady Gwydyr and her family. I stood on Lord Melbourne's steps to watch the Queen pass, and Lady Gwydyr with all her family, black as sloes, with weepers and windows open, all bowed at once again and again with the awe and devotion as if they had been good Catholics and the Queen the Virgin Mary.'

'The Queen did not stay long in the House to-day.'

'No. The sight of the first witness, Teodoro Majocchi, was too much for Her Majesty. She knew he was to testify, but when she saw him she threw back her veil, placed her arms in her sides, and stood staring at him furiously for some seconds. Then she screamed something in a most frantic voice and bounced out of the House in the most unqueenlike manner,' said Lord Albemarle.

'What did she scream?' cried the eager crowd, drawing closer.

'Teodoro, *I* thought.'

HENRY BROUGHAM

To face page 276

'Some said it was *Traditore*.'[1]

'I was close to her, and I thought it was no more than a long-drawn "Oh," a sigh of disgust and indignation,' put in George Keppel.

'I suppose the man was in possession of damaging secrets?'

'He was a trusted servant and his evidence was very damaging to the Queen.'

'Not after Brougham had begun his cross-examination,' said a late comer.

'I think we have a new phrase for the squib-writers. His only answer to Brougham seemed to be "*Non mi ricordo*." '[2]

'Brougham is deadly in cross-examination. How did the evidence go?'

'It was amusing, and went like this:

BROUGHAM: "What makes you recollect this Baron d'Ompteda coming to the villa at Como?"

MAJOCCHI: "I do not know."

BROUGHAM: "Was there any affair happened in the Princess's family, anything that made a noise in the family connected with this Baron?"

MAJOCCHI: "*Non mi ricordo*."

BROUGHAM: "During the time you were in the service of Her Royal Highness do you remember any blacksmith or locksmith being examined with respect to picking of locks?"

MAJOCCHI: "*Non mi ricordo*."

BROUGHAM: "Or about making false keys?"

MAJOCCHI: "*Non mi ricordo*."

---

[1] Traitor.   [2] I do not recollect.

BROUGHAM: "Do you remember a quarrel taking place between Lieutenant Howman and this German Baron?"

MAJOCCHI: "I have heard they quarrelled."

BROUGHAM: "At about what time did you hear of this quarrel?"

MAJOCCHI: "*Non mi ricordo.*"

BROUGHAM: "About how long was it before you left her Royal Highness' service? Was it years or months?"

MAJOCCHI: "*Non mi ricordo.*"

BROUGHAM: "Do you mean you do not remember whether it was a week or two years?"

MAJOCCHI: "*Non mi ricordo.*"

And so it went on. He recollected nothing.'

'If all these Italian witnesses are as useful, the Queen's case is already won.'

'Listen to this,' cried an excited voice. 'How will it go in to-morrow's papers?'

'NON MI RICORDO'

Theodore Majocci is my name,
   And every one's aware
From Italy I came
   Against the Queen to swear.
I was sent to Colonel Brown's
   When I was abroad, O,
Who gave me many crowns
   To say, *Non mi ricordo.*
     Tol, lol, etc.

To England I was trudged,
   Nor cost me a single farden,
And was safely lodged
   In a place called Cotton Garden.
There I eat and drink
   Of the best they can afford, O,
Got plenty of the chink
   To say, *Non mi ricordo.*
       Tol, lol, etc.

To the House so large I went,
   Which put me in a stew,
To tell a tale I was bent
   Of which I nothing knew.
There was a man stood there
   My precious brains he bored, O,
To what I wouldn't swear
   I said, *Non mi ricordo.*
       Tol, lol, etc.

He asked me what I'd seen
   While sailing on the sea.
I said I saw the Queen
   On a gun with Bergami.
He asked me what I knew,
   What sailors were on board, O,
Four or twenty-two,
   I said, *Non mi ricordo.*
       Tol, lol, etc.

Fare-you-well, John Bull,
   I've got now all I can,
If a Green Bag you want full
   To fill it I'm the man.
If you should ever send
   Another queen abroad, O,
My services I'll lend
   To say, *Non mi ricordo*.
      Tol, lol, etc.

All Brook's was in a roar. In the streets the people shouted with mirth.

The Queen saw it and laughed, though her eyes were hot.

'Madam, these Italian witnesses. It is abominable,' cried the indignant Lady Anne.

'Poor souls,' said the Queen softly. 'What would you expect? These men are poor and they are offered money – an enormous amount of money considering what they usually can earn. Can you blame them? I cannot. They mean me no harm.'

'Lord Byron writes that the very mob in Ravenna cries shame against their countrymen.'

'I know. Lord Byron has *lived* among Italians, been of their families and friendships, and feuds, he knows them well. And he says for half the money spent upon these witnesses any testimony may be bought out of Italy.'

'He says, too, Madam, no one there believes a word of the evidence.'

'Why should they, Lady Anne? They know how different are Italian customs. What is so simple there appears abominable here. One sleeps for coolness on deck under an awning, and because the crew are probably scoundrels, for safety's sake a man of my suite sleeps there too. We are both dressed. It seemed to me nothing. Now, in this evidence, it sounds a dreadful sin. By God, Lady Anne, I never committed adultery but with one man, and that with the husband of Mrs. Fitzherbert.'

Brougham went on with his cross-examination of the witnesses and produced other witnesses who contradicted every accusation made by the witnesses for the Crown. Majocchi had been supposed to be the most dangerous of them. He stated that at Tunis the bedrooms of the Princess and Pergami were separated only by a small chamber and a passage. Captain Hownam was called to prove that at Tunis Pergami's bedroom was not on the same storey as Her Royal Highness's.

Majocchi stated that at Ephesus dinner was served in a vestibule for Her Royal Highness and Pergami, that she sat on a small bed with him beside her and admitted no attendants. Captain Howman proved that the Princess and all her attendants dined together under the portico of an old mosque.

The cross-examination of the Queen's late *femme de chambre*, Louise Demont, was equally disastrous for the prosecution.

'The *chienne* Demont turns out everything one could wish on her cross-examination,' said Creevey gleefully at Brook's. 'Her letters have been produced and contain every kind of panegyric on the Queen. She has admitted they are in her handwriting. It was a most infernally damaging day for the prosecution.'

'The Bishops say they won't support the divorce part of the Bill.'

'Its title ought to be "A Bill to declare the Queen a Whore and to settle her upon the King for life because from his own conduct he is not entitled to divorce." '

'Our Bruffam is magnificent.'

'I think he bullied the Lords a little too much.'

'How did His Majesty like Bruffam's "This shape, if shape it can be called, What seemed its head the likeness of a kingly crown had on." '

'He'll like less Denman's scabrous quotation from Tacitus.'

'He told the Duke of York he would go to Hanover.'

'Do you know he is intent on turning out Lord Hertford to make room for Conyngham as Lord Chamberlain? Was there ever such insanity at such a time?'

'Will the new charmer be any worse than the old?'

'God knows! She is as elderly. I heard a noise of huzza-ing as I came. It was the Navy of England marching to Brandenburgh House with an address to the Queen. There were thousands of seamen all well dressed, all sober, the best-looking, the finest men, you can imagine. Every man had a new white cockade in his hat. They had a hundred colours with sentiments upon them, such as "Protection to the Innocent." '

'When the seamen take a part the soldiers can't fail to be shaken.'

'There is not a single vessel in the river that does not hoist its colours and man its yards for her. All the watermen in the Thames are her partisans.'

'If Brougham can prove what he has stated in his

speech I for one believe she is innocent and the whole case a conspiracy,' said Creevey stoutly.

'Brougham's speech is magnificent. I never heard anything like the perfection of the peroration.'

'Erskine rushed out of the House in tears.'

'In eloquence, ability, and judicious matter it was beyond anything I ever heard,' remarked Charles Greville.

'Lady Charlotte Lindsay said it was the most strikingly beautiful piece of eloquence, and that the Queen thought so too.'

'The Bill is doomed,' cried a loud voice suddenly. 'Lay you fifty to one it is thrown out.'

'I like the Queen no better than the King,' remarked Lord Albemarle disgustedly, 'but I shall go and wait upon her, for I have become convinced of her innocence by merely hearing the evidence against her.'

'Have you seen the lampoons on the King? Adonis the Great, Sultan Sham, Abimelech, King of the Isles, are some of the kindest titles they give him. Listen to this:

> "I am but just threescore
> Gorgeous Whelp
> My wife. Ah, there's the bore
> Haunts me on sea and shore
> Gorgeous Whelp."

·There's a lot of it. Disgusting stuff. And this:

"The Acts of Adonis the Great.

"And it came to pass, in the reign of Guelpho, King of Bull, there was much murmuring throughout all the land.

"For the King's son, George, which being interpreted

in the Bullish, signifieth 'Great eater and drinker,' had done evil in the sight of the law and had committed drunkenness and debauchery in high and low places. Moreover he had dwelt with concubines and evil counsellors and had filled the land with abominations and uncleanness, and was drunk every day from the rising of the sun to the going down of the same, and his face was bloated with drink, and the tip of his nose was of a blue colour. Now King Guelpho waxed old, and his sight departed from him, and his senses fled. . . . And the people appointed George his son to reign over them. And they called him Re – gent, which in the Bullish language signifieth 'No longer Blackguard.' And he was two-score and eighteen years old when he filled the seat of his father, and he wore a wig of many curls.

"And Queen Snuffy his mother died . . . and the tobacconists mourned over all the land, and there was a fall in the price of snuff of one silver sixpence in the pound. . . ." '

People laughed at the satires and lampoons, but the country was seething with fury. The French thought England was on the verge of a revolution. The American Ambassador was startled and shocked at the nation's hatred of its king. The feeling excited beat like a pulse through the whole kingdom.

Brougham's speech not only astonished but shook the aristocracy, and on the heels of that speech came the witness of witnesses, Lady Charlotte Lindsay, who was the more passionate in her defence of the Queen because her absence from Caroline's side during her fantastic travels had now so much the appearance of disloyalty.

'It was family affairs, my sister, Lady Glenbervie's illness, my husband's urgency, that kept me from the Queen,' she had protested.

'You never heard such testimony as hers in favour of the Queen,' Creevey announced at Brook's. 'The talent, the perspicuity, the honesty of it. Upon my soul, this Queen must be innocent after all. Lady Charlotte went on with her testimony and could not be touched though she was treated infamously so as to make her burst out crying.'

'That was a ticklish point about a letter from her brother advising her to give up her place under the Queen, which letter she said she could not find.'

'It is a fact that Lindsay, who is in the greatest distress, has absolutely sold her correspondence on this subject to the Treasury. She told Brougham so under the most solemn injunction of secrecy, and he has this instant told it to me.'

'That was why March of the Treasury was not called? Was ever villainy equal to this?'

'Gell left everything even more triumphant for the Queen, and Keppel Craven, God save his soul, gave most entire and cordial testimony in her favour.'

'The Naples case is quite gone. Trieste has shared its fate. Great doubt is thrown over the scene in the carriage and Mahomet's dance.'

'The town is drunk with joy. There is no doubt now in any man's mind, except Lauderdale's, that the whole thing has been a conspiracy for money.'

'The Government is mad. All the Italian evidence is to be flung overboard. All the same the Lords, at the suit of the Ministers, are determined to pass this Bill upon the sole point of the Queen having admitted to have slept under the tent on board the *polacca* while Bergami slept there also.'

'The tent was open on all sides because of the heat, sailors passed to and fro continually and the light made it possible to see all that went on within the tent at any hour.'

'Had she slept below it would have been in the company of seven horses and two asses.'

'This charge is absurd as anyone must know who has acquaintance with Italian customs. Admittedly the nights were hot and the crew a set of Greek and other scoundrels, and that they both slept in their clothes.'

'When Bergami attended her to the bath it appears on cross-examination that she always wore a bathing costume.'

'Have you seen the Queen? Would any man in his senses want to engage in crim. con.?'

'There have been queens of fifty who have engaged in folly before now.'

'I for one am convinced of her innocence since I heard Lady Charlotte. I am going to wait on her at Brandenburgh House.'

That was the general feeling in the town among the Opposition and even among those Tories who were independent of the Court. Those Whigs who had held aloof from the Queen since her return called their coaches and went to leave their names at Brandenburgh House.

The Duke of Sussex posted up from Tunbridge Wells, and in his wake streamed the nobility. The Queen could have set up a rival court if she had wished to do so, but she had no such desire. She still showed no vindictive spirit nor desire to divide the nation. She received the Duke of Sussex kindly, but she would not see Prince Leopold.

'I had a right to expect more from Prince Leopold than other members of the family,' she said sadly. 'Out of proper respect to my daughter's memory he ought to have shown respect to her mother. If he had endeavoured to make up the loss as a son such conduct would have done him honour and been of great comfort to me. He need not act neuter. By neglecting me he took part against me. I will not see him. Write and tell him so, Lady Anne.'

Prince Leopold was ashamed of the part he had played, of his fear of the despicable King. He declared his belief in the Queen's innocence before judgment was pronounced.

'The King will never see him again. Lay you fifty to one he will not,' was cried at Brook's.

Prince Leopold attended the King's *levée*; George turned his back on him.

Prince Leopold crossed to the Duke of York saying, so that all could hear, 'The King has thought proper at last to take his line and I shall take mine.'

It was too late to please Queen Caroline; Leopold's neglect had cut her to the heart.

The King was nearly mad with rage and mortification at the way the trial was going. He did not dare to appear in public because of the people's hostility. Outside Carlton House he heard the mob muttering threateningly: 'Nero's hotel. Let us burn it down.'

A serious young Member of Parliament, Robert Peel by

name, watching the crowd surging dangerously and muttering revolutionary threats, thought it was time some plan was evolved for protecting the metropolis supposing the mob got out of hand. The Army was too uncertain; a regular police force, now, directly under the Crown? The idea was acclaimed. 'Go ahead, Bobby, we'll call them Peelers,' encouraged his admiring friends.

The Queen would have fared very much better if it had not been for her friends. Captain Flyn, for instance, of the *polacca*, was so anxious to serve her that he perjured himself repeatedly, fainted in the witness stand, and had to be carried out.

Mr. Brougham had completely convinced himself of his client's innocence by this time. He had the manliness to say so, declaring upon his honour as a gentleman that he absolutely disbelieved the charges. Mr. Denman was equally determined to serve her. His summing up was masterly, and he did not spare her calumniators. Against the Duke of Clarence, in particular, he sped some envenomed shafts. 'Come forward, thou slanderer, and let me see thy face,' he thundered, and Clarence, who had tattled scandalous tales in mess-room and drawing-room, shrank back and grew pale with alarm.

Denman's moving and admirable speech drew to its conclusion:

'I know nothing in the whole race of human affairs, nothing in the whole view of eternity, which can even remotely resemble this inquisition, but the great day when the secrets of all hearts shall be disclosed:

"He who the sword of Heav'n will bear
Should be as holy as severe."

And if your Lordships have been furnished with powers which, I might almost say, scarcely Omniscience itself possesses, to arrive at the secrets of this female, you will think that it is your duty to imitate the justice, beneficence, and wisdom of that benignant Being, who, not in a case like this where innocence is manifest, but where guilt was detected and vice revealed, said: "If no accuser can come forward to condemn thee, neither do I condemn thee; go and sin no more." '

The spell was broken. The House, which had been enthralled and moved by eloquence, dissolved into titters.

'Could anything be more unfortunate than the conclusion?' was the universal question at Brook's.

> 'Gracious Queen, we thee implore,
> Go away and sin no more;
> Or if that effort be too great,
> Go away at any rate,'

said a wag.

The club was in a roar. All the town had it in the morning. The King was delighted; he was tired of having all the squibs let off at his expense. He sent one of his jackals to a man who could be bribed. Theodore Hook, who had some reputation as a wit, was subsidised to issue a newspaper which he called *John Bull*. The first number contained a most venomous attack upon the Queen.

The town read it with varying degrees of disapproval. The King's sycophants rejoiced in its scurrility. Brook's would have none of it.

'The climax and consummation of all villainy,' cried Denman.

Mr. Creevey, who liked a good deal of scandal, said indignantly: 'It is the most infamous newspaper that was ever seen in the world. Its personal scurrility exceeds by miles everything that was ever written before. Have you read the verses about Lady T.?'

Heads close together, they bent over the sheets. A loud hurrah startled them. 'Three times three. The Bill is gone, thank God, to the devil. Their majority was brought down to nine – 108 to 99. Eleven Bishops voted for it, the villains, and only the Archbishop of York against.'

All the club *habitués* were pouring through the doors.

'Lay you ten to one the King bolts to Hanover.'

'Did you ever hear anything so disgraceful as the behaviour of the Duke of Clarence? When his name was called in the division on the third reading he leaned over the rail of the gallery as far into the House as he could and then halloed "Content" with a yell that would have become a savage.'

'The dolorous Liverpool came forward and struck. He moved that *his own Bill* be read this day six months.'

'The Queen was in the House at the time. She had a dazed look more tragical than consternation. She was evidently all shuddering and she took hold of the ban- nister pausing for a moment.' The speaker lowered his voice to one of awed pity: 'Oh! that sudden clutch with which she caught the railing; it was as if her hand had been a skinless heart. Never say again to me that any actor can feel like a principal. It was a visible manifestation of unspeakable grief, an echoing of the voice of the soul.'

So tragic an emotion in those surroundings was uncomfortable. Someone said cynically: 'Perhaps she saw the astuteness of the Ministry. By withdrawing the Bill they have prevented an acquittal in the Commons.'

'Brougham hurried her off.'

'The state of the town is beyond everything. Castlereagh was roughly handled at Covent Garden.'

'It was the two sets of Union peers and those villains of the Church that nearly destroyed for ever the character of the House of Lords. Thank God it is no worse.'

'We must have illuminations at Brook's, and an extra bottle of claret, Creevey, before we go out to see the town.'

They had the extra bottle, and another, and another. Creevey protested that he was not screwy, only nervous. The claret, indeed, seemed to illuminate his mind, for he uttered a profound and far-reaching truth which had not yet been generally observed.

'The people have learnt a great lesson from this wicked proceeding,' he said slowly. 'They have learnt how to marshal and organise themselves, and they have learnt at the same time the success of their strength. Waithman tells me that the arrangements made in every parish in and about London on this occasion are perfectly miraculous – quite new in their nature – and that they will be of eternal application in all our public affairs.'

'It is the People versus the King, and the people have won,' assented Foley. 'The People is a growing force. "Wilkes and Liberty" proved it; this has driven it home.'

A fresh incursion of members interrupted them.

'All the town is illuminated.'

'They say the river below the bridge is the most beautiful sight in the world. Every vessel is covered with colours, and at the head of the tallest mast in the river is the effigy of a bishop, twenty or thirty feet high, with his heels uppermost.'

'Nothing has been seen like it since Waterloo.'

'Where is Brougham?'

Brougham was not to be found; he must savour his triumph in secret. The virtual acquittal in the Lords might be due to the People, but the withdrawal of the Bill by Lord Liverpool was due to him and him alone. He held the trump card and the King knew it, though the House might think his threats of confusion were general in their meaning. There were three people who knew the significance of his speech and trembled: the Queen, who did not want his knowledge used; Mrs. Fitzherbert, who with trembling hand seized a pair of scissors and cut out the names of the witnesses from her marriage certificate; and the King, who was nearly distraught with fear and rage.

He sat with Brougham's speech before him:

'My lords, the Princess Caroline of Brunswick arrived in this country in the year 1795 – the niece of our Sovereign, the intended consort of his Heir Apparent, and herself a not very remote heir to the Crown of these realms. But I now go back to that period only for the purpose of passing over all the interval which elapsed between her arrival then and her departure in 1814. I rejoice that, for the present, at least, the most faithful discharge of my duty permits me to draw this veil; but I cannot do so without pausing for one instant to guard myself against a misrepresentation to which I know this

cause may not unnaturally be exposed, and to assure
your Lordships most solemnly, that if I did not think that
the cause of the Queen, as attempted to be established by
the evidence against her, not only does not require re-
criminations at present, not only imposes no duty of even
uttering one whisper, whether by way of attack or by way
of insinuation, against the conduct of her illustrious
husband – but it rather prescribes to me, for the present,
silence upon this great and painful head of the case.
I solemnly assure your Lordships that, but for this
conviction, my lips on that branch would *not* be closed;
for, in discretionally abandoning the exercise of the
power which I feel I have, in postponing for the present
the restatement of that case of which I am possessed, I
feel confident that I am waiving a right which I possess;
and abstaining from the use of materials which are
mine. I once before took leave to remind your Lordships
that an advocate, by the sacred duty which he owes to
his client, knows in the discharge of that office, but one
person in the world, *that client and none other*. To save that
client by all expedient means, to protect that client at all
hazards and cost to *all others*, and among others to himself,
is the highest and most unquestioned of his duties; and
he must not regard the alarm, the suffering, the torment,
the destruction, which he may bring upon any other. Nay,
separating even the duties of a patriot from those of an
advocate, and casting them, if need be, to the wind, he
must go on, reckless of the consequences, if his fate it
should unhappily be, to involve his country in confusion
for his client's benefit. . . .'

The King choked and turned purple, cursing like a

madman; there was no mistaking Brougham's meaning since he had the key. He was beaten. He had the gout and was unable to get off his chair without assistance. Lady Conyngham wisely said nothing, but gave him a good tug to help him to his feet. The King sent for Lord Liverpool.

Mrs. Fitzherbert, very pale and agitated, sent a warning to Uncle Errington and Brother John and hastily withdrew to France.

The Queen drew a deep breath, and signed a paper vigorously. '*Regina* still,' she said grimly, 'in spite of them.' She meant in spite of Brougham as well as of the King. If that marriage certificate had been produced, where would they all have been? The King off his throne, perhaps, and she an adulteress indeed?

The threat had been enough. Brougham must savour his triumph in solitude. 'George knew what I meant when I threatened to throw the country into confusion,' he thought. 'I had as my witnesses Errington and Mrs. Fitzherbert herself. George knew I had the trump in my hand. He will never forgive me.'

4

THE QUEEN'S TRIUMPH

THE Queen sent her thanks to the nation, but in her own house she wept.

'It is too late. She who would have rejoiced at her mother's triumph is lost to me.'

She dried her tears and smiled wanly at the faithful Lady Anne. 'She is in a much better world than the present, and we shall soon meet, I trust, for to tell you the truth I cannot expect much comfort as long as I shall live. This business is more cared for as a political affair than as the cause of a poor, forlorn woman. There is no one to care for me.'

'Many care for you, Madam.'

'Perhaps you do, poor Joan of Arc. Many call on me now who never did before. I will not quarrel with their respect, though it is shown rather late in the day when they cannot help me. *Mais n'importe.* I ought to be grateful.'

They came in a never-ending stream to call at Brandenburgh House, those without fear and reproach as well as time-servers. *John Bull* had a lampoon on the subject which succeeded in keeping some of the more timid away:

'Have you been to Brandenburgh, heigh ma'am, ho
   ma'am,
Have you been to Brandenburgh, ho?

Oh, yes, I have been, ma'am,
To visit the Queen, ma'am,
With the rest of the gallanty show, show,
With the rest of the gallanty show.

And who were your company, heigh ma'am, ho
ma'am?
And who were your company, ho?
We happened to drop in
With *gemmen* from Wapping,
And *ladies* from Blowbladder Row, Row,
And ladies from Blowbladder Row.

And who were attending her, heigh ma'am, ho
ma'am?
And who were attending her, ho?
Lord Hood for a man,
For a maid Lady Anne,
And Alderman Wood for a beau, beau,
And Alderman Wood for a beau.

And had she no counsellors, heigh ma'am, ho
ma'am?
And had she no counsellors, ho?
Yes, one Mr. Brougham
Who sneaked out of her room
Pretending the circuit to go, go,
Pretending the circuit to go.

Will she have a drawing room, heigh ma'am, ho
ma'am?
Will she have a drawing room, ho?

Oh yes, I presume
That she might find a room
If she could but find any to go, go,
If she could but find any to go.'

Her triumph was a hollow one, as she was soon aware.

The King said: 'I would rather die or lose my crown than submit to any compromise with the Queen.'

'She shall have her legal rights,' said Lord Liverpool, 'but these do not include being named in the Liturgy or being crowned or being allotted one of the Royal palaces as a residence.'

Parliament discussed the matter of the Queen's income. On February 5th, 1821, Brougham redeemed his pledge to testify publicly on his honour to his belief in the Queen's innocence. He spoke in a crowded House:

'It is necessary for me, with the seriousness and sincerity which may be permitted to a man upon the most solemn occasion to express, to assert what I now do assert in the face of this House, that if, instead of an advocate, I had been sitting as a judge at another tribunal, I should have been found among the number of those who, laying their hands upon their hearts, conscientiously pronounced Her Majesty "Not Guilty." For the truth of this assertion I desire to tender every pledge that may be most valued and most sacred. I wish to make it in every form which may be deemed most solemn and most binding, and, if I believe it not as I now advance it, I here imprecate on myself every curse which is most horrid and most penal.'

'The Arch-Fiend did it in a manner so solemn and, if I may say so, so magnificent, that it was met with the loudest and almost universal cheers,' said Mr. Creevey at Brook's.

'I was never very much for the Queen,' said Brougham at his elbow. 'I have never liked her. Yet every day my conviction is strengthened of her absolute innocence as to Bergami. His elevation, I am certain, was all owing to her attachment to Victorine. The woman is a *child-fancier*. She has an insane passion for children, and will commit any folly for them.'

Brougham was irritable; he had, by taking the part of the Queen's advocate, so roused the undying enmity of the King that he could never hope to fulfil his political ambitions. He might rub in his dislike of the King by repeating in public Lord Thanet's nickname for him, '*Le Bourgeois Gentilhomme*,' which rankled even more than Brummell's 'Fat friend,' but the fact remained that, politically, he had ruined himself for the sake of the Queen, whom he did not like. He did not even reap the full benefit of his championship, for, to his fury, he considered that she relied too much upon the advice of Alderman Wood, 'Absolute Wisdom' Wood, he called him in mockery of the Alderman's smug complacency.

The Queen relied on none of them; she had seen too clearly how they all used her for their own ends. She had only one object now – to vindicate herself, and in her own opinion that could not be done until her name was included in the Liturgy. All else might go if the King would grant her that.

He would not, and he would not have her present at his Coronation, far less have her crowned.

GEORGE IV

To face page 298

The Queen was determined to be present at the Coronation. She prepared for her last fight.

The Privy Council heard her claim to be crowned on July 4th. It was on that day that news reached London that Napoleon had died on St. Helena on May 6th.

They took the news to the King. 'Your greatest enemy is dead, sir.'

'Is she?' cried the King with brightening eyes. They dulled again when he found it was only Boney.

Mr. Brougham and Mr. Denman spoke in favour of the Queen's claim to be crowned.

The Privy Council decided, 'That as the queens-consort of this realm are not entitled of right to be crowned at any time, Her Majesty, the Queen, is not entitled as of right to be crowned at the time specified in Her Majesty's memorials.'

Lord Sidmouth notified her of the fact, with the significant addition, 'the King does not think proper to give any orders for the Coronation of your Majesty.'

She wrote to ask what she should wear at the Coronation in the Abbey.

George's friends suggested a white sheet in the middle aisle.

She signified her intention to be present. They replied: 'It was not His Majesty's pleasure to comply with her request.'

Brougham was in a quandary; he did not know whether it would be politic for her to attend or not. She made up her own mind. She would go.

The King, very nervous, was bled and went to sleep at the Speaker's House. The Guards were stationed in the

streets all night. There was no disturbance. The Queen
spent the night at a house in South Audley Street. A
considerable crowd collected outside the gates in the
early hours of the morning. Her coach was making ready
in the yard. Spectators climbed the wall and shouted to
the crowd below: 'The horses are to. Everything is quite
ready. The Queen has entered the coach.' Each statement was greeted with cheers. Soon after five the gate
was thrown open, and a shout was raised: '*The Queen.
The Queen.*'

The Queen immediately appeared in her coach of
state drawn by six bays. She looked well, and with great
dignity and composure acknowledged the plaudits of the
crowd. The soldiers everywhere presented arms with the
utmost promptitude and respect.

Her Majesty first drove to the Dean's Yard gate, but
found that the entrance for persons of rank was at Poet's
Corner. The coachman followed the line of the platform
to New Palace Yard, but there he found no thoroughfare.
He drove on and stopped opposite Westminster Hall Gate.
Lord Hood alighted, and having found an open door
returned to the coach. The Queen, her composure
shaken at last, stepped down from the coach and, leaning
on the arm of Lord Hood, walked up the steps.

Lord Hood demanded admission for the Queen.

The doorkeeper said that his instructions were to
admit no one without a peer's ticket.

Lord Hood asked, 'Did you ever hear of a Queen being
asked for a ticket before? This is your Queen.'

The doorkeeper was respectful but firm: 'My orders are
general and without any exception. I have never been
in a similar position before, and can say nothing as to

the propriety or impropriety of refusing Her Majesty admission.'

Lord Hood said sternly: 'I present to you your Queen. Do you refuse her admission?'

Caroline broke in with agitation: 'Yes, I am your Queen. I desire to be permitted to pass.'

'My orders are peremptory,' said the doorkeeper. 'Reluctant as I am, I cannot suffer Her Majesty to pass without a ticket.'

Lord Hood said: 'I have a ticket.'

'Upon producing it I will permit one person to pass,' said the doorkeeper.

Lord Hood produced a ticket for the Abbey ceremony. It was signed 'Wellington.' The doorkeeper looked at it. 'It will admit but one person.'

Lord Hood looked at his mistress. 'Your Majesty, will you enter alone?'

The Queen hesitated. It was fatal.

Lord Hood asked hastily: 'Are there no preparations for the Queen's reception?'

'None.'

'Will you enter alone, Madam?' Lord Hood asked again.

The Queen's heart failed her. She lifted her hand to knock upon the shut door. Then she shook her head.

As they turned away some persons in a doorway burst into a loud laugh of derision. Caroline looked at them contemptuously. She retraced her steps, passing through a crowd of women of fashion who totally ignored her. A crowd followed her, disappointed of the sensational scene for which they had hoped.

As she drove away there were shouts of derision mingled with cries of 'Shame. Oh, shame.'

The Coronation was the most splendid in the annals of English history. The King was not well received, but fireworks put the mob in a good humour. In the Green Park, Mr. Green ascended in a magnificent balloon prepared for the occasion. In Hyde Park there was a boat-race and fireworks after dark.

At Covent Garden *Henry IV* was played, and every expression of broad humour was much applauded.

At Drury Lane *The Spectre Bridegroom* gave unbounded delight. The preference of a 'sovereign' to a 'guinea' was cheered without interruption.

The people had a splendid day. The King appeared somewhat fatigued, but the Queen's spirit was broken; her heart had been broken long ago.

It was the unhappiest day of her unhappy life; she felt terribly, but not even yet would she acknowledge the completeness of her defeat. She sat at supper until three in the morning, though her body was racked with intolerable pain. When at last she retired, she mixed herself a tumblerful of magnesia and water, so thick that the drug was like a paste, and in it she poured a dose of laudanum in the hope that it would send her to sleep. Lady Anne begged her not to swallow the mixture but the Queen ate it with a spoon.

'I must sleep,' she said, 'I must have a little sleep.'

For a week she was too ill to go out, but then she said obstinately, 'I have promised to go to Drury Lane to see Edmund Kean in *Richard III*. I will neither disappoint the public nor the management.'

It was the last heroic effort of her courageous life. She fainted half-way through the piece, and was carried back

to her carriage and driven by her frightened attendants
to Brandenburgh House.

The doctors bled her with leeches, and gave her
enough castor oil 'to turn the stomach of a horse.'

Dr. Holland attended her. She opened her eyes and
looked at him with a smile. 'I shall die without regret,
Dr. Holland.'

'Madam, you are going on favourably.'

The Queen smiled. 'Send for Mr. Brougham. I will
make my Will.'

When Brougham came she greeted him cheerfully,
and made her Will, leaving nearly everything to her
Willikin, whose existence had played such havoc in her
life.

'Send my body to Brunswick for burial, Mr. Brougham,
and put on the coffin, "Here lies Caroline of Brunswick,
the injured Queen of England." '

Mr. Brougham was distressed. 'You will recover,
Madam.'

She smiled at him. 'I am going to die, Mr. Brougham,
but it does not signify.'

'Your Majesty's physicians are quite of a different
opinion.'

'Ah, I know better than them. I tell you I shall die,
but I don't mind it.'

Mr. Brougham went away with a lump in his throat
which he had never thought to feel. 'Her nature was
absolutely without malice or revenge,' he said. 'She
hardly knew the merit of forgiveness of injuries because
it cost her nothing, and a harsh expression, a slanderous
expression, any indication of hatred or spite never broke
from her, even when the resources of ingenuity were

exhausted in order to goad her feelings, and self-defence almost made anger and resentment a duty.'

When Mr. Brougham had gone, the Queen said to her attendants: 'I forgive all my enemies. I owe no one any ill-will, though they have killed me at the last.'

Lady Anne was in tears.

The wind tore at the windows as if it would force them from their frames. The Queen's lips moved, but no sound came, though had anyone who loved her watched beside her bed, they might have thought the lips whispered 'Charlotte.'

A boat passed down the river filled with some of those religious fanatics who had taken such peculiar interest in her fate; they were praying for her and singing hymns as they rowed by Brandenburgh House. The sound of their singing was drowned in a mighty rush of wind which blew open all the doors and windows of the Queen's room.

Filled with sudden awe the attendants turned towards the bed. Queen Caroline was dead.

London read the notice sent out from Brandenburgh House:

'Her Majesty departed this life at twenty-five minutes past ten o'clock this night.

'August 7th, 1821.'

'So the poor Queen is gone and made an honourable exit.'

'Poor thing, it is well over. No friend of hers could wish it otherwise.'

'Her memory will be respected and her sad lot never mentioned without a sigh.'

'If ever woman died of a broken heart it was the Queen.'

'It leaves an infernal lump in the throat,' said Mr. Creevey.

They took the news to the King on his way to Ireland. He did not attempt to hide his jubilation, though the decency of others made him delay his triumphal entry into Dublin for a few days.

The Government would not even show her respect in death. They would hurry the coffin out of the country without a decent interval in spite of Lady Anne Hamilton's indignation and Lady Hood's spirited protests. Lord Liverpool was the King's toady. It was too late to matter to the Queen, but malice still persisted after her death. They would not let the people pay the last tribute of respect to their favourite. The funeral procession, on its way to Harwich, was ordered to pass hurriedly through back streets.

London fought her last battle for her, since she could no longer fight for herself.

The Government thwarted the desires of the City; the City cried 'Shame,' and took measures to have its way.

The procession went westwards to Kensington Church; it was found that the roadway was blocked by waggons whose wheels had been removed.

'Through the City. Through the City,' cried the people.

The road was dug up, trenches made, and the water pipes opened. The way was impassable; the cavalcade turned back.

Lord Liverpool sent a troop of Life Guards. There was conflict between the soldiers and the crowd, and two men were shot.

'She shall not go through the Park,' shouted a growing mob in ugly mood at Hyde Park Corner. 'Through the City. Through the City.'

The populace had its way. All the side streets were blocked by an impenetrable mass of waggons and coaches extending across the whole width of the road. At every point there was hesitation and a scuffle.

'Through the City. Through the City,' yelled the mob.

The dead Queen passed down the Strand and under Temple Bar.

EPILOGUE

THE old man lay dying at Windsor. He was restless and uneasy, turning to stare first at the Titian 'Venus' on one wall and then at the Giulio Romano 'Graces' on the opposite one; but he only saw them darkly, through a mist. On the table by his bedside was a book which he did not remember to have seen before. He stretched out his hand, over which fell the exquisite lace frills of his nightgown, and picked it up. It was a Bible. He put it down hurriedly.

'I am going gradually,' he said to the Irish apothecary who came daily to bring him all the gossip of the town.

He did not really believe it. In the twilight of his brain were strange and delightful delusions mingled with the joys of a well-spent life. He saw the green turf at Newmarket, and grew excited as he won the Derby and rode 'Fleur de Lys' in the Goodwood Cup. He was quizzing Letty Lade about her gift of swearing, and admiring her as she drove a four-in-hand. He was thrashing an insolent butcher at Brighton, and being commended by his friends. He squared his shoulders against his pillows as he remembered how he led the charge of the Heavy Dragoons at Salamanca, and changed the fortune of the Allies by leading a division at Waterloo. He had always believed in and backed the Duke.

Knighton came in and, irritable at being interrupted in

his dreaming, the old man ordered his assassination. No one took any notice, and he did not mind very much.

'I was always kind-hearted,' he said. 'I remember my father said once, "George, of all the men I have ever known you are the one on whom I have the greatest dependence, and you are the most perfect gentleman." '

His attendants looked at each other in astonishment.

The Duchess of Gloucester stepped softly to the bedside. 'Leopold is here,' she said.

The old man choked. The Duchess, exceedingly alarmed, withdrew.

A courier brought news that he had won the Craven Stakes. He smiled contentedly and went back to his dreams of the green turf and the thunder of horses' hoofs. Of all the pleasures he had tasted, that, perhaps, had been the best.

'We will give an Ascot party at the Cottage,' he murmured.

The dreams cleared a little, and he remembered that he was too fat.

'I will not allow these pert maidservants to look at me when I go in and out,' he muttered.

'There are too many people in the room,' he cried irritably. 'Send them all away.'

The room cleared, and Lady Conyngham thought it wise to begin to pack.

The old man did not miss her. Someone brought him a letter and he saw that it was from his wife.

'It's a long time since I saw her writing,' he thought, and put it under his pillow. He fingered her miniature which hung about his neck.

How many women had he made love to? There was

Caroline Vernon, the first, for one did not count the poplollies of the town, and pretty Perdita, Grace Dalrymple, and a hundred others whose names had long since slipped out of his mind. But Maria his wife was the only one he had loved. The women had been mad for him. He had always been the most popular man in the kingdom, he remembered telling Creevey so long ago.

He had had a good life, though not without troubles. He scowled as a black shadow flitted into his mind. Who was it whom he had hated and who had hung like a millstone round his neck? Ah, the German woman! He had always sworn he would not marry a German *frau*. She had poisoned his life for years. But he had got rid of her in the end.

A fine pageant life had been, and he had been the greatest ornament of his time and of his House. He had enriched London and Brighton with his building; London owed him much; there was the great park which bore his name and the new street which Nash had designed for him. Never had man spent his life better than he.

He slept, and woke again in the early hours of a June morning with a scream: 'Oh God! they have deceived me. This is Death.'

The King fell back.

The populace made holiday. His funeral was a public festival. Crowds hurried to view the pageantry at Windsor, but on no single face was a sign of grief. The park was thronged with joyous parties and shouts of joy were only interrupted by the firing of the minute gun or the rumble of the carriages conveying the mourners, who were as merry as grigs. Only the new King seemed grave.

Under one tree was heard the glee of 'When Arthur first at Court began,' and under another, 'A merry King, and a merry King, and a right merry King was he.'

The streets of the town were straddled with the booths of a fair. The hawkers cried: 'The Life and Portrait of His late Majesty for a penny. All for a penny. And for another penny you can have the "Amours of the Marchioness of Conyngham." Splendid value. All for a penny.'

Praed wrote his epitaph:

> 'A noble, nasty course he ran
>   Superbly filthy and fastidious;
> He was the world's first gentleman
>   And made the appellation hideous.'

BIBLIOGRAPHY

OWING to the form in which this book is written, it is often impossible to use quotation marks in the text. The dialogue has, for the most part, been taken from the letters, memoirs, and diaries of the time; only the more colourless remarks have been invented. For every fact of any importance there is some authority.

The chief books consulted are:

The Diaries of Sylvester Douglas, Lord Glenbervie. (Ed. by Francis Bickley, pub. Constable, 1928.)

The Creevey Papers. (Ed. by Sir Herbert Maxwell, 1903.)

Diary Illustrative of the Times of George IV, by Lady Charlotte Bury.

Diaries and Letters of the First Lord Malmesbury.

Horace Walpole's *Letters and Last Journals*.

Lewis Melville's *An Injured Queen*, and *Beaux of the Regency*.

W. H. Wilkins' *Mrs. Fitzherbert and George IV*.

Robert Huish's *Memoirs of George IV*.

Shane Leslie's *George IV*.

The Devonshire House Circle, by Hugh Stokes.

J. F. Molloy's *Court Life Below Stairs*.

Sir John Stanley's *Praeterita*.

Miss Greenwood's *Hanoverian Queens of England*.

J. Barbey D'Aurevilly's *Du Dandysm et de Georges Brummell*.

Captain Jesse's *Life of Brummell*.

The Memoirs, Letters, and Diaries of: Mary Robinson, Mary Berry, Mary Frampton, Cornelia Knight, the Comtesse de Boigne, Lady Jerningham, Princess Lieven, Frances Williams Wynn, the first Lord Dudley, J. W. Croker, Thomas Raikes, Lord Albemarle, Thomas Moore.

The *Annual Register* and numerous newspapers, periodicals, lampoons, caricatures.

H. T. Lister's *Granby, A Novel*. (1826.)

INDEX